Criminal Law

by

GLORIA A. ALUISE
ATTORNEY AT LAW

KEYED TO THE NINTH EDITION OF THE KADISH CASEBOOK

Mat # 41563667

The publisher is not engaged in rendering legal or other professional advice, and this publication is not a substitute for the advice of an attorney. If you require legal or other expert advice, you should seek the services of a competent attorney or other professional.

Legalines is a trademark registered in the U.S. Patent and Trademark Office.

© 2010 Thomson Reuters
© 2014 LEG, Inc. d/b/a West Academic
    444 Cedar Street, Suite 700
    St. Paul, MN 55101
    1-877-888-1330

Printed in the United States of America

ISBN: 978-0-314-29128-8

Summary of Contents

Table of Contents

Criminal Law

KEYED TO THE NINTH EDITION OF THE KADISH CASEBOOK

Chapter I

Institutions and Processes

A. The Structure of the Criminal Justice System

1. Decentralized System

Although the various institutions, agencies, and players involved in criminal justice are interdependent, the criminal justice system is highly decentralized. The stages of arrest, indictment, conviction, and sentencing implicate distinct administrative bureaucracies with different objectives and actors (*e.g.*, police, prosecutors, judges) with different directives. Furthermore, the federal government and the states have independent authority to enact and enforce criminal laws proscribing specified conduct within their jurisdictions.

2. Effect of High Volume of Cases

The pressure of overbearing caseloads that exceed the resources of the criminal justice system has resulted in increased use of methods to speed up the process. For instance, police use their discretion in deciding whether to investigate or arrest, and obtaining confessions saves time in developing incriminating evidence. Prosecutors use their discretion in deciding whether to prosecute or to reduce the charges, and they rely heavily on plea bargaining.

B. Criminal Justice Procedures

1. Typical State Procedure

a. Offense

The criminal justice system reacts to criminal conduct. The process begins when an offense is reported to the police. Investigators gather evidence, testimonial, tangible, or otherwise, with the objective of determining who perpetrated the crime. One significant procedural issue that frequently arises at this stage involves searches and seizures.

b. Arrest

Once sufficient evidence is gathered to constitute probable cause that an identified person committed the crime, the suspect may be arrested with or without a warrant, depending on the circumstances. The arresting officer takes the suspect into custody and brings him to the police station.

c. The charge

The police ask the district attorney to make out a formal charge and an affidavit, which is a written complaint charging the accused with a specified crime or crimes. A complaint is prepared in advance when a person is arrested under a warrant because it is used to obtain the warrant.

d. Proceedings before a magistrate

After arrest, the accused is taken before the committing magistrate, a municipal court judge, for example, who advises the accused of her rights and sends her back to jail or allows her to post bond. If the charge is a misdemeanor, the accused is immediately arraigned and must plead to the charge. If the charge is a felony, the accused normally does not have to plead; instead, a date is set for a preliminary hearing.

e. Preliminary hearing

When a felony is charged, the accused is entitled to a preliminary hearing to determine whether there are sufficient grounds to bind the accused over for a trial.

1) Sufficient evidence

The committing magistrate rules on the evidence. If the critical evidence is suppressed for some reason at this point, men the accused may be set free and the charge dismissed. The accused has a chance to cross-examine the prosecution's evidence, which is an important discovery technique.

2) Decision

If the committing magistrate finds that the evidence is sufficient, the accused is committed.

3) Writ of prohibition

If the magistrate finds sufficient evidence, the accused may bring a writ of prohibition to appeal the magistrate's findings.

f. Indictment

As an alternative to a preliminary hearing, the prosecution may seek an indictment. The prosecuting attorney presents a written accusation to an investigatory body, such as a grand jury. An indictment is simply a finding made by the grand jury that there is sufficient evidence to warrant a conviction of the crime. A grand jury indictment may either precede or follow arrest. The prosecution may choose the indictment procedure when it wants to keep its information confidential, because in most states the accused does not have the opportunity to appear or to challenge the prosecution's evidence.

g. Accusatory pleading

The prosecution of the case commences once the government files either an indictment or an information. An information is simply the written charge on which the accused will be tried.

h. Arraignment

Once the pleading is filed, the accused is brought before the court and informed of the charges. The accused then pleads to the charge.

i. Motions and pleas

The accused is normally permitted to make certain motions of one of several different pleas.

1) Motions

The accused may file a demurrer, or a challenge to the legal sufficiency of the accusatory pleading, such as that the court lacks jurisdiction or that no crime is alleged. Other motions include ones to quash or set aside the indictment or information, to dismiss, to change venue to another court, to obtain discovery, or to suppress certain evidence.

2) Pleas

If the charges hold up after consideration of the motions, the accused may plead guilty, not guilty, or nolo contendere, which is the same as pleading guilty except that the conviction cannot be used in subsequent civil proceedings.

j. Discovery

Normally, both sides continue the fact-finding process to prepare for trial. The parties use the discovery process to find out as much as possible about the opposition's case.

k. Extraordinary writs

The accused may file certain extraordinary writs before trial begins. The writ of prohibition is an appeal to a higher court to terminate the judicial process, normally on the basis of a lack of proper jurisdiction in the lower court. The other writ in common use is that of habeas corpus ("bring forth the body"), which tests any restraint that is contrary to "fundamental law," *e.g.*, to the state constitution.

l. Trial

Numerous procedural issues arise during the trial process, including the following:

1) The competency of the accused to stand trial, as well as the sanity of the accused at the time of the offense.

2) The accused's right to counsel.

3) The right to trial by jury and the selection of jurors.

4) The right to a fair trial.

5) The accused's and the witnesses' privilege against self-incrimination, including the accused's right not to testify as a witness at all.

6) The right to compulsory process to obtain witnesses.

7) The right to confront accusers and cross-examine witnesses.

8) Issues relating to trial of two or more accused persons in the same trial; to more than one trial of the same accused for the same criminal act; and to the trial of the same accused for more than one crime arising from the same act.

9) Evidence questions relating to the introduction or order of evidence, the burden of proof, motions, jury instructions, etc.

10) The verdict, the sentence, and the entry of judgment by the court.

m. Sentencing

Ordinarily the judge has substantial discretion in determining the appropriate sentence. However, modern statutes sometimes set a minimum sentence as well as a maximum sentence for a particular offense.

n. Post-trial motions

Typically, the accused who has been convicted may assert several post-trial motions, including a motion to vacate because the judgment was based on erroneous facts or was obtained by fraud or deceit, and a motion for a new trial.

o. Appeal

Most states grant a first appeal from a criminal conviction as a matter of right. Other appeals may also be available.

p. Habeas corpus

The writ of habeas corpus is available at any stage of the criminal process.

2. Federal Procedure

a. Similarities to state procedure

In many respects, federal criminal procedure resembles state procedure. In fact, the Federal Rules of Evidence and Federal Rules of Criminal Procedure ("Fed. R. Crim. P.") have served as models for state procedure. A few of the significant rules are discussed below. (Remember that only federal crimes are prosecuted in the federal system.)

b. Arrest

A warrant may be issued on presentation of a complaint by the United States Attorney, identifying the crime and the accused. [Fed. R. Crim. P. 4(a)] A valid arrest may also be made without a warrant where there is probable cause.

c. Appearance before a magistrate

If the accused was arrested without a warrant, then a complaint is prepared. If a warrant was used, the complaint was previously prepared. The accused is next brought before a magistrate. This must be done without unnecessary delay. [Fed. R. Crim. P. 5(a)]

d. Preliminary examination

Preliminary examinations are also held before a magistrate. [Fed. R. Crim. P. 5(c)]

e. Grand jury indictment

If a grand jury has returned an indictment against the accused, he is not entitled to a preliminary examination, except that Fed. R. Crim. P. 5(c) provides that if a person is taken into custody before the indictment is given, he is entitled to a preliminary examination. This avoids the problem of a lengthy holding of a defendant waiting for a grand jury.

f. Arraignment

The accused is arraigned in federal district court.

g. Motions and pleas

Under Fed. R. Crim. P. 12, the motion to dismiss is used in place of all other motions discussed above under state procedure. This motion attacks all possible defects.

C. The Process for Determining Guilt

1. The Presentation of Evidence

a. Introduction

Rules governing the admissibility of evidence are fairly complex, and a complete discussion is beyond the scope of this outline. However, a fundamental rule is that evidence that is not relevant is not admissible. To be relevant, evidence must be both material and probative, meaning that the proposition to be proved affects the outcome of the case and that the evidence tends to establish the proposition. Even relevant evidence may be inadmissible if its prejudicial effect outweighs its probative value, or if the evidence is privileged information, or if it is prohibited because of the exclusionary rule.

b. Character evidence

People v. Zackowitz
172 N.E. 466 (N.Y. 1930).

Facts. Zackowitz (D) admitted killing Coppola, who had insulted D's wife by propositioning her on the street. D warned Coppola to leave the street when he learned of the insult, then accompanied his wife to their apartment, where she told D exactly what Coppola had said, D was enraged again and returned to the street, which Coppola had not left. D began fighting Coppola and shot him. D claimed he acted in self-defense. He had been drinking that night. D told the police that he had armed himself with a pistol at the apartment, but at trial he claimed he had carried the pistol in his pocket all evening. In order to show that D had a criminal inclination, the state introduced evidence that D kept three pistols and a tear-gas gun in his apartment. Under state law, a killing provoked in the fury of the fleeting moment was first degree manslaughter as opposed to first degree murder, which required a deliberate and premeditated murder. D was convicted of first degree murder and appeals, claiming the introduction of character evidence was prejudicial error.

Issue. May the state by itself make character an issue in a criminal prosecution?

Held. No. Judgment reversed and a new trial ordered.

- ♦ The basic rule is that character is not an issue in a criminal prosecution unless brought into issue by the defendant. The purpose is to avoid the danger to the innocent that would result from making character probative of crime. A defendant may not be proved guilty by proof of character.

- ♦ Here, D admitted killing the victim and the only question was his state of mind. Ownership of weapons left at home does not indicate a murderous disposition, especially in light of D's explanation that he was a collector. The likelihood that the jury would condemn such possession regardless of D's guilt of the crime charged is a sufficient ground for reversal for prejudicial error.

Dissent. The evidence was admissible to show that D may have formed a murderous intent before he left the apartment (*i.e.*, he chose a particular weapon before leaving). If possession is a separate crime, that does not render the evidence inadmissible.

2. Standard of Proof

a. Introduction

Generally, the fact finder in a civil trial may base its findings on a preponderance of the evidence. In criminal trials, however, the defendant is presumed innocent. To convict, therefore, a jury must find the defendant guilty beyond a reasonable doubt. The conviction must be based on proof beyond a reasonable doubt of every fact required to make up the crime charged. This high standard of proof reflects the serious consequences of a criminal conviction, which should not attach to a person when there is a reasonable doubt about guilt.

b. Proof beyond a reasonable doubt

In re Winship
397 U.S. 358 (1970).

Facts. After a hearing, the family court found by a preponderance of the evidence that a 12-year-old boy (D) had committed acts, which, if done by an adult, would constitute the crime of larceny. D was ordered to be placed in a training school for 18 months. The judge relied on section 744(b) of the New York Family Court Act, which provided that a determination of a juvenile's misconduct had to be based on a preponderance of the evidence. The court of appeals affirmed. D appeals.

Issue. Are juveniles, as well as adults, constitutionally entitled to proof beyond reasonable doubt when they are charged with violations of criminal laws?

Held. Yes. Judgment reversed.

♦ A lower standard of proof cannot be applied in a juvenile delinquency proceeding than the standard applied in a criminal trial.

♦ The presumption of innocence principle lies at the foundation of the administration of our criminal law. The reasonable doubt standard reduces the risk of convictions based on factual error and commands the respect and confidence of the community in applications of the criminal law.

♦ We hold that the Due Process Clause protects the accused against conviction except upon proof beyond a reasonable doubt of every fact necessary to constitute the crime with which he is charged.

Concurrence (Harlan, J.). If the standard of proof for a criminal trial were a preponderance of the evidence, there would be a smaller risk of factual errors that result in freeing guilty persons, but a far greater risk of factual errors that lead to conviction of the innocent. An erroneous verdict in a civil suit for money damages is far less serious than an erroneous verdict in a criminal trial. In a criminal case, it is far worse to convict an innocent man than to let a guilty man go free.

c. Allocating the burden of proof

Patterson v. New York
432 U.S. 197 (1977).

Facts. Patterson (D) was charged with second degree murder and at trial raised the affirmative defense of extreme emotional disturbance, which, if successful, would result in a verdict of manslaughter. Consistent with New York law, the trial court instructed the jury that D had the burden of proving his affirmative defense by a preponderance of the evidence. The jury found D guilty of murder and the appellate division affirmed. D appeals on the basis that requiring D to prove his affirmative defense is an improper shifting of the burden of persuasion from the prosecutor to the defendant and is therefore a violation of due process.

Issue. Is it unconstitutional under the Fourteenth Amendment's Due Process Clause for a state to require a criminal defendant to prove an affirmative defense that does not serve to negate any facts of the crime that the state is to prove in order to convict?

Held. No. Judgment affirmed.

- To recognize a mitigating circumstance does not thereby require the state to prove its nonexistence in each case in which the fact is put in issue, if in the state's judgment this would be too cumbersome, too expensive, and too inaccurate.

- However, the state may not shift the burden of persuasion with respect to a fact that the state deems so important that it must be either proved or presumed in order to convict a defendant of the crime.

Dissent (Powell, Brennan, Marshall, JJ.).

- The state may not shift the burden of proof to the defendant if the following two factors exist: (i) the factor at issue makes a substantial difference in punishment and stigma; (ii) the factor in question historically has been held to be of great importance in the Anglo-American legal tradition.

- To avoid this two-step test by leaving a factor out of the statutory elements of a crime is to undermine the presumption of innocence and to establish form over substance.

d. Use of presumptions

Presumptions may allow a fact finder to infer a fact not proved from a fact actually proved. This evidentiary sense of the term is distinct from the term when used, for example, in the phrase, "presumed innocent until proven guilty." The latter usage merely is a way to state that the prosecution must prove guilt. The evidentiary presumptions, however, may allow the prosecution to prove guilt without actually proving every critical fact, when permissible inferences may be drawn from the facts proved.

3. The Jury's Responsibility

a. Introduction

The jury has the responsibility of hearing all the evidence, receiving instructions from the judge about the law, and then applying the law in finding facts and making the ultimate decision of guilt or innocence.

1) Constitutional provisions

a) Article III, Section 2

"The trial of all Crimes, except in Cases of Impeachment, shall be by jury . . . ."

b) Sixth Amendment

"In all criminal prosecutions, the accused shall enjoy the right to speedy and public trial, by an impartial jury of the State and district wherein the crime shall have been committed."

2) Effect

By virtue of Article III, Section 2 and the Sixth Amendment, a defendant charged in a federal court with any serious offense (as distinguished from a "petty" offense under the common law) is entitled to trial by jury.

3) Serious vs. petty offenses

Because the Sixth Amendment guarantees a jury trial only when a serious offense is charged, it becomes necessary to distinguish between "serious" and "petty" offenses. The court looks to the nature of the offense and the maximum potential sentence.

4) Number of jurors

The number of jurors in federal criminal trials is 12, but this is by statute [Fed. R. Crim. P. 23] and is not constitutionally required. State rules allowing use of fewer than 12 jurors (in noncapital cases) have been upheld. [Williams v. Florida, 399 U.S. 78 (1970)]

b. Application to the states

Duncan v. Louisiana
391 U.S. 145 (1968).

Facts. Duncan (D), a black youth, was accused of battery on a white youth, but he claimed that all he had done was touch the white person on the elbow. Louisiana state law provided a jury trial guarantee only for capital punishment or where imprisonment at hard labor could be imposed. Battery was punishable by only up to two years in prison and a $300 fine; D's request for a jury trial was denied. D was convicted and appeals, claiming that his denial of a jury trial denied him due process of law.

Issue. May a state deny a jury trial in a criminal prosecution if the defendant would have received a jury trial had the trial been in a federal court?

Held. No. Judgment reversed.

♦ D is entitled to a jury trial. The Sixth Amendment right to a jury trial in all criminal cases was applicable to the states in all situations where, if the trial were to have been brought in federal courts, such a jury trial would have been given. This was a "fundamental right," but also was within the scope of the Bill of Rights.

Dissent (Harlan, Stewart, JJ.). The opportunity was taken by the court in this case to act as a laboratory. This Court is available to correct any experiments in criminal procedure that prove fundamentally unfair to defendants.

c. The jury's inherent prerogative to acquit

United States v. Dougherty
473 F.2d 1113 (D.C. Cir. 1972).

Facts. Dougherty and others (Ds) entered offices of Dow Chemical Co. and destroyed property in protest of the Vietnam War. Ds were charged with malicious destruction. At their trial, Ds requested an instruction that the jury could disregard the court's instructions even as to matters of law. The judge refused to give Ds' requested instruction, and Ds were convicted. Ds appeal.

Issue. Does a defendant have a right to have the jury instructed that it may acquit regardless of the law and the evidence?

Held. No. Judgment affirmed.

♦ A jury has the prerogative to bring in a general verdict of not guilty in a criminal case, regardless of the law and the evidence. The court may not reverse such an action. The prerogative is allowed so that juries may refuse to convict a person who is guilty when the criminal law violated is unjust or otherwise unacceptable.

♦ However, the jury may not be specifically instructed about this prerogative. Otherwise the prerogative could be overused and result in anarchy. The prerogative remains as a last resort, which will be used only in extreme circumstances.

Concurrence and dissent. If the jury has this prerogative, which it does, it should be properly informed to use it.

Chapter II
The Justification of Punishment

A. What is Punishment?

Although there are many explanations of the concept of punishment, it is generally considered to be the infliction of suffering by one with the authority to do so. Punishment presupposes that something blameworthy was done, and it expresses moral condemnation. Punishment for the violation of criminal laws subjects the offender to certain deprivations. A fine deprives the offender of property, and imprisonment deprives the offender of liberty and isolates him from society.

B. Blame and Punishment

1. Introduction

Blameworthiness takes into account the harm caused by the offense and the culpability of the offender. Criminal laws are enacted in recognition of the fact that certain types of conduct have the effect of disrupting social order and infringe on the rights of others. Some form of punishment is affixed to violations of the criminal laws, but the justification for such punishment is not always apparent.

2. Hunger Not an Excuse for Murder

Regina v. Dudley and Stephens
14 Q.B.D. 273 (1884).

Facts. Four shipwreck survivors in a lifeboat went days without food and water. Dudley and Stephens suggested killing the youngest member; the third person on board refused; finally, Dudley and Stephens killed the 17-year-old boy, who was too weak to resist or assent. The three fed off of the dead body. The jury found that the three survivors, who were picked up four days later, would not have survived otherwise. The legal effect of the fact-finding was left to the court.

Issue. Does the extreme necessity of saving one person's life justify taking another's?

Held. No. Hunger is not an excuse for taking the life of another person.

- ♦ The argument is only successful when protecting oneself against an offending party. Here, the victim was innocent of any wrongdoing toward his murderers.

- ♦ Comments.

- ♦ Although sentenced to die, the sentence was later commuted by the Queen to six months' imprisonment.

- ♦ What is the purpose of punishment in this type of situation? Will it deter such events in the future? Is the purpose restraint? Rehabilitation? Or is it simply retribution for a "wrong"?

C. Why Punish?

1. Retribution

The retribution theory of punishment states that a criminal must be punished for the "wrong he has committed." This theory of punishment looks to the past and not to the future, and rests solely upon the foundation of vindictive justice.

2. Deterrence

a. Introduction

Punishment serves many functions for society. One belief of penologists is that by punishing those who commit acts condemned by society, others will be deterred from committing similar acts for fear of the punishment that will result from their acts.

b. Value structure

Society's demand that certain acts be punished expresses its collective belief in the wrongfulness of some acts. Failure to punish these wicked acts has the effect of endorsing acts that are contrary to society's value structure of what is right and what is wrong.

c. Forms of deterrence

There are many possible forms. Social embarrassment is one (antitrust violators suffer social disgrace, for example); in other words, the sentence means little but the conviction means a lot. And, in murder cases, an indictment alone is often as much of a stigma as would be a conviction in some other crimes.

d. Summary comments on deterrence

Deterrence theories furnish the most widely accepted rationale of the practice of punishment. According to these theories, punishment should not be designed to exact retribution upon convicted offenders but to deter the commission of future offenses. However, most studies indicate that severity of punishment has only a slight effect in deterring crime. For example, white-collar business crimes and drug trafficking are two types of crimes for which there is no evidence that fear of lengthy incarceration affects any significant number of criminal decisions. More important in deterring crime is increased certainty of arrest, conviction, and imprisonment. Certainty and severity of punishment together operate as the most effective deterrents of crime. Either one alone is ineffective.

3. Rehabilitation

a. Introduction

Punishment has purposes in addition to retribution and/or crime deterrence. Penology also seeks to reform the criminal to become a useful member of society.

b. Conflicting purposes

Penology is in constant tension between the purposes or ends it seeks to serve. Should deterrence be given supremacy? Should rehabilitation? Should retribution? It would be a paradox if the main purpose of providing punishment for murder was to reform the murderer, not to prevent the murder. Yet, rehabilitation is an important, though elusive, goal.

4. Segregation

An additional goal of the criminal law is to protect society by segregating the criminal offender from general society, thereby limiting the number of people against whom he can commit further crimes.

5. Summary

The purpose of the criminal law is to protect the public interest by preventing certain undesirable conduct. There are differing theories of punishment. Retribution focuses primarily on the nature of the offense and its condemnation by society. Retribution has little support today, while rehabilitation, at least in theory, has become the chief goal of penology.

D. Assigning Punishment— Sentencing

1. Introduction

The philosophical debate over the purpose of punishment provides at best broad, generalized guidelines for determining an appropriate punishment in a particular case. Until recently, most of the sentencing responsibility rested with the trial judges. Modern trends disperse the sentencing authority through specific sentencing statutes, administrative sentencing guidelines, etc.

2. Sentence Length

United States v. Bernard L. Madoff
U.S. Dist. Ct. (S.D.N.Y. 2009).

Facts. Sentencing Transcript. At the sentencing hearing, Madoff's (D's) counsel requested a sentence of either 12–15 years, based on D's health, history and life expectancy (based on statistics)—just short of a life sentence; or a sentence of 15–20 years, which would leave D imprisoned until his 90s. D apologized to the Court. The prosecutor requested a sentence of 150 years for "carry[ing] out a fraud of unprecedented proportion over . . . more than a generation," and to promote the goal of deterrence.

Held. D shall be sentenced to a term of 150 years.

♦ The court is not bound by the guideline restriction of 150 years, the maximum sentences for each of the 11 counts when combined. Along with respectful consideration of the guidelines, an individual assessment must be made based on the factors in the statute, the facts and the circumstances. Over 20 years, D's fraud, albeit disputes range from $65 million to $13 million, was many times above the highest amount of $400 million provided in the sentencing guidelines offense level chart. Victims—individuals, charities, pension funds— have stated that they based life decisions based on false account statements. While some of the money was returned upon an investor's request to withdraw funds, a large amount was used by D for his family, friends, and others. D turned himself in only when he was not able to keep up with the payouts to investors who requested to withdraw, and D has not been helpful to the trustee overseeing the recovery of the funds. There are no financial fraud cases in this district comparable to the "scope, duration … and degree of betrayal" present in this case. Not one letter has been submitted in support of D from family, friends or colleagues. D puts forth a life expectancy analysis that, if correct, suggests that any sentence above 20–25 years would be symbolic. This symbolism is important, however, for retribution, that D is punished in proportion to his blame; for deterrence; and for the victims, people from all walks of life who have lost college funds, retirement income, and who had personal assurances from D that their money was safe with him. While they will not be given back their financial security, the victims' healing process may be helped by the knowledge that D has been punished to the full extent of the law.

3. Life Sentence Permissible

United States v. Jackson
835 F.2d 1195 (7th Cir. 1987).

Facts. Thirty minutes after he was released from prison, Jackson (D) robbed a bank while brandishing a revolver. He was sentenced to life without parole. D had been previously convicted of four armed bank robberies and one armed robbery. The statute in effect provides that anyone who possesses a firearm and has three previous felony convictions for robbery or burglary, or both, shall be fined and imprisoned for not less man 15 years without parole. D appeals.

Issue. May a life sentence be imposed on a defendant who commits armed robbery for the fifth time based on a statute that provides for imprisonment of "not less than 15 years"?

Held. Yes. Judgment affirmed.

- ♦ D's argument that the statute permits only a determinate number of years and not a life sentence is silly when one considers D's age (35) and a long prison term, for example, 60 years. The result is the same.

- ♦ The selection of a sentence within the statutory range is essentially free of appellate review.

Concurrence. Although the sentence is too harsh, there is no ground on which we are authorized to set it aside.

4. Shaming

United States v. Gementera
379 F.3d 596 (9th Cir. 2004).

Facts. Gementera (D) pled guilty to mail theft. Although D was only 24 years old, he already had a long criminal history, including misdemeanor criminal mischief, driving with a suspended license, misdemeanor battery, and possession of drug paraphernalia. The judge sentenced D to two months of incarceration and three years of supervised release. One condition of his release was that D perform 100 hours of community service by standing in front of a postal facility wearing a sandwich board that stated in large letters "I stole mail. This is my punishment." After D filed a motion to correct the sentence, the judge modified it. Instead of the 100-hour sandwich board requirement, the judge imposed a four-part condition. D had to observe postal patrons visiting the "lost or missing mail" window, write letters of apology to any identifiable victims of his crime, deliver several lectures at a local school, and perform one eight-hour day of community service wearing or carrying a two-sided sign stating, "I stole mail; this is my punishment," in front of a postal facility. D appeals.

Issue. Does the release condition requiring D to wear a sandwich board or to carry a sign that publicly announces his crime violate the Sentencing Reform Act?

Held. No. Judgment affirmed.

- The Sentencing Reform Act affords courts broad discretion in fashioning conditions of supervised release. Such conditions must serve legitimate objectives and be reasonably related to the nature of the offense and the history of the defendant. The three legitimate statutory purposes are (i) deterrence, (ii) protection of the public, and (iii) rehabilitation.

- Here, D argues that the sandwich board condition was imposed for the impermissible purpose of humiliation. However, the court was concerned that D did not understand the seriousness of his offense, and it intended to remove D's illusion that his crime was victimless. The court acknowledged that D would likely be humiliated, but it stated that the experience should bring him in touch with the serious nature of his crime and have a rehabilitative effect on him. In addition, it would serve as a deterrent to others unaware of the consequences of engaging in mail theft. Thus, the court imposed the condition for the stated and legitimate statutory purpose of rehabilitation and also for general deterrence and the protection of the public.

- D contends that the condition is not reasonably related to his rehabilitation and that shaming causes the offender to withdraw from society and inflicts psychological damage. He claims that no scientific evidence shows that shaming is rehabilitative. However, all criminal offenses and the penalties that accompany them cause shame and embarrassment. Such feelings signal a defendant's acknowledgement of his wrongdoing.

- Furthermore, the sandwich board condition was not a stand-alone condition. D was also required to write apologies to his victims and lecture at a school. These conditions were meant to promote D's social reintegration. The conditions were tailored to D's specific needs and are reasonably related to the legitimate statutory objective of rehabilitation.

Dissent. I believe that the sandwich board condition violates the Sentencing Reform Act and that it is bad policy. Public humiliation or shaming should not be a part of our system of justice.

E. What to Punish?

1. Crime and Sexual Misconduct

a. Introduction

The issue of the legitimacy of criminal enforcement of private morality has been the subject of long-standing debate. The United States Supreme Court has held that there is a "zone of privacy created by several fundamental constitutional guarantees." [Griswold v. Connecticut, 381 U.S. 479 (1965)] What bearing, if any, does this language have upon a state's power to use the law to enforce its moral judgments by prohibiting various forms of sexual practice in which consenting adults might engage?

b. The *Wolfenden Report*

The *Wolfenden Report* (1957) takes the view that the proper role of the criminal law is not to concern itself with private morals but only to restrict conduct that injuriously affects the rights of other citizens (*i.e.*, public solicitation for immoral purposes).

Chapter III
Defining Criminal Conduct—The Elements of Just Punishment

A. Introduction

1. Definition of a Crime

A crime is an act, or an omission to act, that is prohibited by law enacted for the protection of the public and made punishable in a judicial proceeding initiated by the state. It is important to understand that a crime is a "public" wrong, to be distinguished from "private" or "civil" wrongs to an individual.

2. Classification of Crimes

There are many ways to classify crimes (*e.g.*, on the basis of the quantum of punishment meted out for violation, on the basis of felony or misdemeanor, etc.).

a. Felonies and misdemeanors

Crimes are divided into these two classes depending on the grievousness of the offense and the severity of the punishment.

1) Felonies

a) Common law

The common law punished all felonies by total forfeiture of the offender's lands and goods, or alternatively, by death.

b) State law

Felonies are usually defined by statute to be those that are punishable by death or by confinement in the state prison.

c) Federal law

All offenses that are punishable by death or imprisonment for one year or more are felonies.

2) Misdemeanors

All crimes that are not felonies (or treason) are misdemeanors. They are normally crimes that are thought to be less serious in nature. Note also that misdemeanors may be further subdivided into misdemeanors and "petty" offenses (crimes of minor seriousness).

b. Crimes mala in se and mala prohibits

Sometimes crimes are also classified as "mala in se" or "mala prohibita."

1) Mala in se

These crimes are often said to be those acts or omissions to act that are wrong from their very nature (crimes such as murder, robbery, or rape).

2) Mala prohibita

Those crimes that are "mala prohibita" are wrong merely because they are prohibited by statute.

3. Merger of Crimes

The very same act may constitute more than one crime. For example, every murder necessarily includes an assault and battery.

a. Common law

At common law, if the offenses were not of the same degree (*i.e.*, if one were a felony and the other a misdemeanor) then there was a merger, but only if one of the crimes was necessarily included within the other. Therefore, one tried for a felony could not also or alternatively be convicted of a necessarily included misdemeanor.

b. Modern rule

Most jurisdictions no longer apply the merger doctrine in this way, so that a person indicted for a higher offense may be convicted of a lesser offense necessarily included therein.

4. Corpus Delicti—The Prima Facie Elements of a Crime

a. Preliminary elements

Before the state can attempt to prove that the defendant is the one who committed the alleged crime, it must first prove (i) that there has actually been an occurrence of some injury that constitutes a crime, and (ii) that somebody's criminal act is responsible (as opposed to the happening of a mere accident). Therefore, in a murder case the state would have to show that someone was dead and that somebody's criminal act was the cause of that death.

b. Criminal agent

After the state has proved the corpus delicti, it may then proceed to prove that the defendant is the one who has committed the crime (*i.e.*, that he is the criminal agent or cause).

1) General rule

As a general rule, the corpus delicti cannot be proved solely by resort to the out-of-court confession or admission of the defendant. Such admission or confessions should not be admitted into evidence until the corpus delicti has been established. However, improper prior admission is not reversible error on appeal.

2) In-court confessions or admissions

If the defendant takes the stand in court and confesses the crime, this may be used to prove the corpus delicti.

c. Standard of proof

Only "slight" evidence is needed to prove the corpus delicti (that is, the two requisite elements need not be proved "beyond a reasonable doubt"). Most states hold that circumstantial evidence, for example, is sufficient (*i.e.*, evidence from which the fact to be proven may be inferred).

B. Legality

1. Introduction

Statutes should give fair warning of what conduct is prohibited. Some statutes that fail to define clearly the prohibitions have been held to be void for vagueness. Certainty is a desired feature of any system of law, but it is not always possible to precisely define illegal conduct.

2. Fair Warning—The Problem of Open-Ended Criminality

a. Common law

At common law, absent a statute, the only conduct that was criminal was that which was deemed malum in se (inherently evil). The common law took a theological approach, which looked at the intrinsic quality of conduct.

b. Criminal codes

One of the reasons for the formulation of criminal codes is to safeguard conduct that is without fault from arbitrary condemnation as criminal and to give fair warning of the nature of the conduct that does constitute a criminal offense.

c. Common law offense not controlled by statute

Commonwealth v. Mochan
110 A.2d 788 (Pa. 1955).

Facts. Mochan (D) made numerous obscene telephone calls to Louise Zivkovich at any hour of the day or night. He referred to Louise as a lewd, immoral, indecent woman, and he propositioned sodomy. D was charged with intending "to debauch and corrupt, and further devising and intending to harass, embarrass and villify" Louise. D was tried, convicted, and sentenced by a judge without a jury. D appeals.

Issue. Can D be convicted under common law for actions that are not criminal offenses by statute?

Held. Yes. Judgment affirmed.

- In Pennsylvania, the common law of England as to crimes is in force except in so far as it has been abrogated by statute. There is no statute addressing D's conduct, and D contends that his conduct does not constitute a misdemeanor at common law. However, the absence of precedent for the crime is of no consequence because the test is whether the alleged crime could have been prosecuted and the offender punished under common law. Common law principles dictate that any act which injuriously affects public morality is a misdemeanor at common law.

- D's outrageously indecent behavior rises above the level of merely attempting to persuade a married woman to commit adultery. Furthermore, D's actions at least potentially injuriously affected public morality. At least two persons in the victim's household heard some of D's language, and the operator or anyone else on D's four-party telephone line could have listened in on the conversations. Thus, the offense is a common law misdemeanor.

Dissent. Although D's conduct was reprehensible, under our system of government, it is for the legislature, not the courts, to determine what constitutes a crime.

d. The reach of statutory language

McBoyle v. United States
283 U.S. 25 (1931).

Facts. McBoyle (D) was convicted of transporting an airplane, which he knew to have been stolen, from Illinois to Oklahoma. D was sentenced to three years in prison and was fined $2,000. The court of appeals affirmed. The Supreme Court granted certiorari.

Issue. Does the National Motor Vehicle Theft Act apply to aircraft?

Held. No. Judgment reversed.

- The National Motor Vehicle Theft Act provides that the term "motor vehicle" includes an automobile, truck, automobile wagon, motorcycle, "or any other self-propelled vehicle not designed for running on rails." Anyone who transports a motor vehicle in interstate or foreign commerce, knowing that it has been stolen, will be punished by a fine of not more man $5,000, or by imprisonment of not more man five years, or both.

- The meaning of the word "vehicle" in everyday speech refers to a thing that moves on land. The phrase "any other self-propelled vehicle not designed for running on rails" also indicates a vehicle that runs on land. Furthermore, aircrafts were not mentioned in the congressional reports and debates that accompanied passage of this statute.

- The words of a statute should give fair warning in understandable language of what the law will do if a certain line is passed.

e. Ambiguous statutory language

United States v. Dauray
215 F.3d 257 (2nd Cir. 2000).

Facts. When an officer approached Dauray's (D's) car in a state park, he found D in possession of pieces of magazine pages and photocopies of those pages which showed pictures of minors. D was charged with possessing child pornography in violation of 18 U.S.C. section 2252(a)(4)(B). The statute then in effect punished the possession of "3 or more books, magazines, periodicals, films, video tapes, or other matter" that had passed in interstate or foreign commerce and contained any visual depiction of a minor engaged in sexually explicit conduct. After a jury found D guilty, the court considered his pretrial motion to dismiss the indictment for failure to charge an offense. D argued that each photograph was, in itself, a "visual depiction" and thus could not be other matter that contained any visual depiction. The court denied D's motion and denied D's request to apply the rule of lenity. D was sentenced to three years in prison. D appeals.

Issue. Before it was amended, was the wording of section 2252(a)(4)(B) ambiguous when applied to the possession of three or more pictures?

Held. Yes. Judgment reversed.

♦ Congress provided no definition of the terms "other matter" or "contain" in the statute. One dictionary definition of the verb "to contain" is "to have within: hold." D claims that a picture is not a thing that contains itself. Thus, a magazine may contain pictures, but one cannot say a picture "contains" a picture.

♦ Another definition of "to contain" is "to consist of wholly or in part: comprise; include." The government argues that each piece of paper is "matter" that contains the picture printed on it. Applying this meaning, each picture, composed of paper and ink, is matter that contains its imagery.

♦ The term "other matter" also presents difficulty. Although a magazine is "matter" that "contains" visual images, no court that has construed section 2252(a)(4)(B) has considered whether a loose photograph clipped from such a magazine is itself "matter" that "contains" a visual image. A single negative film strip containing three images has been held to constitute only one piece of "matter" under section 2252(a)(4)(B). The case concerned the nature of singular "matter" containing multiple images, not whether each image, if separated from the container, could constitute prohibited "matter."

♦ Two canons of statutory interpretation inform our analysis of the meaning of "other matter." First, the meaning of doubtful terms or phrases may be determined by reference to their relationship with other associated words or phrases. Second, "where general words follow a specific enumeration of persons or things, the general words should be limited to persons or things similar to those specifically enumerated." Therefore, here, "other matter" should be construed to complete the class of items or things in the list preceding it, namely books, magazines, periodicals, films, or videotapes.

♦ D contends that the listed items make up a category of picture containers and that a picture taken from a picture container, such as a magazine, is not itself a picture container, but is a thing removed from its container. Hence, a picture in itself cannot be "other matter." On the other hand, the government argues that because the list is general enough and completed by the catch-all "other matter," it can be read to include any physical medium capable of presenting visual depictions. If a picture cut from a magazine is considered as paper and ink used to exhibit images, it can be said to contain an image or as many images as can be perceived.

♦ The Protection of Children Against Sexual Exploitation Act contains four substantive subsections: section 2252(a)(1) prohibits the interstate transportation of child pornography; (a)(2) prohibits the receipt or distribution of it; and (a)(3) prohibits its sale or possession with intent to sell. These sections prohibit "any visual depiction" of child pornography. Only section 2252(a)(4) specifies that the conduct forbidden involves "books, magazines, periodicals, films, video tapes or other matter" containing child pornography.

♦ D claims that the different drafting shows that Congress knew how to prohibit the possession of individual pictures if it wanted to do so. It is clear that D would have violated the law if he had transported, distributed, or sold the pictures he merely possessed. However, the government could argue that the transport, distribution, and sale of child pornography are more harmful to children and, thus, are prohibited regardless of medium or number of depictions and that Congress used different language in section 2252(a)(4) to assure that the accidental possessor of one piece of pornography would avoid liability while the collector would not.

- A statute should be construed to be consistent with subsequent statutory amendments. Here, Congress amended the statute by replacing "3 or more" with "1 or more" of the same list of books, magazines, or other matter and established an affirmative defense for a defendant who could show that he possessed less than three matters containing child pornography and promptly and in good faith took reasonable steps to destroy the pornography or report it to law enforcement officials without disseminating it to others.

- The government contends that because the list contains the catch-all of "other matter," it covers even an individual photograph. But that could have been accomplished by an amendment that prohibited possession of one or more "visual depictions," without including the list.

- A statute should be interpreted so as to avoid absurd results. Either party's interpretation here would produce absurd results. D's would prohibit the possession of three books containing one image each, but permit possession of stacks of unbound photographs. The government's reading would prohibit the possession of three individual photographs (unless they were mounted in a single album), but would permit the possession of two thick, illustrated books.

- Due process requires that a criminal statute gives fair warning of the conduct that it makes a crime. The rule of lenity stems from this requirement; it requires that ambiguities in a statute be resolved in the defendant's favor. Lenity is a doctrine of last resort and is reserved for situations in which a reasonable doubt persists about a statute's intended scope after looking to the language and structure, legislative history, and motivating policies.

Here, legislative history gives us no insight into what Congress intended the precise scope of "other matter" to be. The government did not show that the pictures were taken from more than one magazine. At the time of D's arrest, the statute did not forbid possession of one such magazine or give notice that removing several pictures from the magazine and keeping them was a crime. Thus, we must apply the rule of lenity and resolve the ambiguity in D's favor.

Dissent. Most statutes are ambiguous to some degree, and the rule of lenity should only be invoked when there is a grievous ambiguity. There is not a grievous ambiguity in the statute in this case. Given the statute's purposes, a photograph could be understood to contain a visual depiction.

f. Crime not within statute

Keeler v. Superior Court
470 P.2d 617 (Cal. 1970).

Facts. Five months after receiving a divorce decree, Keeler (D) saw his former wife, who was pregnant by another man. D kicked her in the stomach, and the baby was born dead. D was charged with murder. The action is a proceeding for a writ of prohibition.

Issue. May a person be guilty of murder for killing an unborn fetus when the law has not determined whether an unborn fetus is a "human being"?

Held. No. Writ should issue.

- The settled meaning of the term "human being" is a person born alive. Thus, D's act is not covered by current statute.

- There are no common law crimes in California.

- Due process prevents retroactive application of a penal statute even if the court had the power to rule that a fetus is a "human being."

Dissent. Medicine now makes it possible for most viable fetuses to be born alive. This fact should be taken into account in interpreting the statute.

g. Retroactive application

Rogers v. Tennessee
532 U.S. 451 (2001).

Facts. Rogers (D) stabbed Bowdery, causing him to go into cardiac arrest and a coma. Bowdery died 15 months after the attack from complications related to the coma. D was convicted in state court of murder. D appealed, asserting the common law "year and a day" rule, under which no defendant could be convicted of murder unless his victim had died by the defendant's act within a year and a day of the act. The Supreme Court of Tennessee affirmed D's conviction, finding that the original reasons for the "year and a day" rule no longer existed. The court abolished the rule and held that its abolishment of the rule in D's case did not violate D's right to due process or the Ex Post Facto Clauses of the state and federal constitutions. The Supreme Court granted certiorari.

Issue. Did the Tennessee Supreme Court's retroactive application to D of its decision abolishing the "year and a day" rule deny petitioner due process of law in violation of the Fourteenth Amendment?

Held. No. Judgment affirmed.

♦ In *Bouie v. City of Columbia*, 378 U.S. 347 (1964), this Court held that due process prohibits retroactive application·of any judicial construction of a criminal statute that is unexpected and indefensible by reference to the law which had been expressed prior to the conduct in issue.

♦ In this case, D contends that because the Ex Post Facto Clause prohibits the retroactive application of a decision abolishing the year and a day rule if accomplished by the Tennessee Legislature, due process should prevent the Supreme Court of Tennessee from accomplishing the same result by judicial decree. However, although *Bouie* does contain some expansive language that is suggestive of such a broad interpretation, this language is dicta. Our decision in *Bouie* was based on the due process concepts of notice, foreseeability, and the right to fair warning as those concepts bear on the constitutionality of attaching criminal penalties to what previously had been innocent conduct.

♦ The Ex Post Facto Clause does not apply to courts. In the context of common law doctrines, there often arises a need to clarify or reevaluate prior opinions as new circumstances or fact patterns present themselves. Strict application of ex post facto principles would impair the development of precedent, which is the foundation of the common law system. Thus, we conclude that a judicial alteration of a common law doctrine of criminal law violates the principle of fair warning only where it is "unexpected and indefensible by reference to the law which had been expressed prior to the conduct in issue."

♦ The supreme court's abolition of the year and a day rule was neither unexpected nor indefensible. The rule has been rendered obsolete by advances in medical science and has been legislatively or judicially abolished in a vast majority of jurisdictions. At the time of D's crime, the rule was not part of the statutory criminal code of Tennessee and never served as a ground of decision in any murder prosecution in the state. The court's decision was a routine exercise of common law decisionmaking that brought the law into conformity with reason and common sense.

Dissent (Scalia, J.). This opinion allows unelected judges to do what the elected representatives of the people cannot do—retroactively make murder what was not murder when the act was committed. There was no fair warning here; the idea of fair warning is not warning that the law might be changed, but warning of what constitutes a crime at the time of the offense. While many jurisdictions have abolished the "year and a day" rule, some have not, and others have abolished it legislatively and prospectively rather than through retroactive judicial rulings. Even if it was predictable that the rule would change, it was not predictable that it would do so in a retroactive manner.

3. Vagueness and Uncertainty of Prohibitions

a. Introduction

The law should be certain enough so that persons who want to determine the legality of their conduct can do so without acting and then being held responsible for something they believed permissible.

1) Obscenity

The standard of certainty can be an elusive one. For example, at one time the standard for "obscenity" as determined by the Supreme Court under the First Amendment provided as follows: "Obscene material is that which deals with the subject matter of sex in a manner appealing to prurient interests and is without redeeming social value (as tested by contemporary community standards)."

2) Novel construction

Generally, the Supreme Court construes state laws as they have been interpreted by the state's highest court. When a statute seems clear on its face, but the state supreme court applies a novel construction, thus making conduct criminal that otherwise was apparently outside the statute, the construction given cannot be applied retroactively. For example, in *Bouie v. City of Columbia*, 378 U.S. 347 (1964), *the* Court reversed a conviction under a state criminal trespass statute that referred to persons "coming onto another's land," but which the state supreme court construed as applicable to persons remaining on another's land after having been asked to leave.

3) Gang loitering statute

City of Chicago v. Morales
527 U.S. 41 (1999).

Facts. The City of Chicago's (D's) "Gang Congregation Ordinance" barred "criminal street gang members" from "loitering" with one another or with other persons in any public place. Violation of the statute required that: (i) a police officer must reasonably believe that at least one of the people present in a public place is a gang member; (ii) the persons must be loitering, *i.e.*, "remaining in any one place with no apparent purpose;" (iii) the officer must order all of the persons to disperse and leave the area; and (iv) a person must disobey the officer's order. Any person who refuses to leave, whether or not a gang member, is guilty of violating the ordinance. Two trial judges upheld the constitutionality of the ordinance, but 11 did not. The appeals court affirmed the invalidity and reversed the convictions in the other cases. The state supreme court affirmed. The United States Supreme Court granted certiorari.

Issue. Does the ordinance violate the Due Process Clause of the Fourteenth Amendment because it is unconstitutionally vague?

Held. Yes. Judgment affirmed.

♦ The ordinance goes beyond prohibiting intimidating conduct by gang members upon the public. It broadly covers a significant amount of activity, but there is uncertainty about the scope of that coverage.

♦ Vagueness will invalidate a law if it: (i) fails to provide notice, which would be understood by ordinary citizens, and (ii) it is susceptible to arbitrary and discriminatory enforcement.

- The ordinance does not give notice because its definition of "loiter" is not a commonly accepted definition. The statute fails to provide a standard by which the police can judge whether a person has an "apparent" purpose.

- Fair notice is required so citizens will have opportunity to conform their behavior to the law.

Concurrence (O'Connor, Breyer, JJ.). There are reasonable alternatives available to this vague ordinance. "Loiter" could be more narrowly construed.

Dissent (Thomas, J., Rehnquist, C.J., Scalia, J.). The ordinance is not vague and does not violate due process. The freedom to loiter for innocent purposes is not a protected activity. Police officers are also peace officers and this ordinance allows them to maintain the peace.

4) Vagrancy statute.

In *Papachristou v. City of Jacksonville*, 405 U.S. 156 (1972), the Court found that a broad, generalized vagrancy statute violated due process. In that case, Papachristou and her co-defendants were arrested for "prowling by auto" while driving from a restaurant to a nightclub. The Jacksonville vagrancy statute forbade various activities, including wandering without any purpose and being a habitual loafer. The Court reversed the conviction, holding that the statute failed to give adequate notice of unlawful conduct. Its wording could apply to a wide variety of innocent activity. The statute encouraged arbitrary arrests in that it allowed the police unfettered discretion. It allowed the police to treat as criminals those who did not present any threat to society.

C. Proportionality

1. Cruel and Unusual Punishment

The Eighth Amendment prohibits cruel and unusual punishment. This prohibition applies to inherently cruel punishments such as torture and execution by painful and lingering methods. It also prohibits punishments that, while conceptually permissible, are cruel and unusual in a given case because the punishment is so disproportionate to the crime. The courts must defer to legislative judgments as to what punishments are appropriate, but only up to a point; if the punishment is outrageously disproportionate in a given case, the courts may forbid enforcement of the punishment.

2. Sentence Not Grossly Disproportionate

Ewing v. California
538 U.S. 11 (2003).

Facts. Ewing (D) was a repeat felon who had been convicted of numerous misdemeanors and felonies, including robbery and residential burglary. While on parole from a nine-year prison term, D stole three golf clubs worth $399 each from a pro shop. He was convicted of felony grand theft and sentenced to 25 years to life under California's "three strikes" law. D appealed his sentence, arguing that it was disproportionate and violated the Eight Amendment's prohibition of cruel and unusual punishment. D argued that, under California law, grand theft was one of several crimes known as "wobblers," meaning that they could be classified as either felonies or misdemeanors. Thus, if theft of the golf clubs (the offense that "triggered" the three strikes law) had been treated as a misdemeanor, D would not have been sentenced under the three strikes law. The court of appeal affirmed, and the Supreme Court of California denied D's petition for review. The Supreme Court granted certiorari.

Issue. Does the Eighth Amendment prohibit a state from sentencing a repeat felon to a prison term of 25 years to life under the state's "Three Strikes and You're Out" law?

Held. No. Judgment affirmed.

- ♦ Under California's three strikes law, a defendant who is convicted of a felony and has two or more prior "serious" or "violent" felony convictions must be sentenced to "an indeterminate term of life imprisonment" with no eligibility for parole for at least 25 years. Although the Eighth Amendment prohibits imposition of a sentence grossly disproportionate to the severity of the crime, mis Court previously upheld a recidivism statute in *Rummel v. Estelle*, 445 U.S. 263 (1980).

- ♦ In *Rummel*, we held that sentencing a three-time offender to life imprisonment with the possibility of parole did not violate the Eighth Amendment. We noted mat, outside the context of capital punishment, successful challenges to the proportionality of sentences have been rare. However, in *Solem v. Helm*, 463 U.S. 277 (1983), we held that the Eighth Amendment prohibited a life sentence without possibility of parole for a seventh nonviolent felony. In *Solem*, we set out three factors relevant to determining whether a sentence is so disproportionate that it violates the Eighth Amendment. The court must consider: (i) the gravity of the offense and the severity of the penalty; (ii) the sentences of other criminals in the same jurisdiction; and (iii) the sentences imposed for the same crime in other jurisdictions.

- ♦ In a later case, *Harmelin v. Michigan*, 501 U.S. 957 (1991), which did not involve recidivism, Justice Kennedy, in his concurrence, explained that the Eighth Amendment does not require strict proportionality between the offense and the sentence, but prohibits sentences that are "grossly disproportionate" to the offense.

- ♦ The purpose of three strikes laws is to protect the public safety by isolating career criminals from society and deterring crime. We have a longstanding tradition of deferring to state legislatures in making and implementing such important policy decisions.

- ♦ D claims that his sentence is disproportionate to his "shoplifting" offense. However, the gravity of his offense was not merely shoplifting three golf clubs. He was convicted of felony grand theft for stealing $1,200 worth of merchandise after having previously been convicted of at least two "violent" or "serious" felonies. The state's interest lies in dealing more harshly with offenders whose acts have shown that they are not capable of conforming to society's norms as established by the criminal law. His sentence reflects a rational legislative judgment entitled to deference.

Concurrence (Scalia, J.). As the plurality acknowledges, "the Constitution does not mandate adoption of any one penological theory." The plurality shows that D's sentence is justified by the state's public-safety interest in incapacitating and deterring recidivist felons. But this has nothing to do with the principle of proportionality. Proportionality can only logically be tied to the penological goal of retribution. Once deterrence and rehabilitation come into the analysis, it is difficult to speak intelligently of proportionality.

Dissent (Breyer, Stevens, Souter, Ginsburg, JJ.).

- ♦ A "gross disproportionality" claim requires that the court first make a threshold comparison of the crime committed and the sentence imposed. Then the court should compare the sentence at issue to other sentences imposed on other criminals in the same or other jurisdictions. The court should consider: (i) the length of the prison term that the offender is likely actually to serve; (ii) the sentence-triggering criminal conduct; and (iii) the offender's criminal history.

- ♦ This Court held that the sentence of life imprisonment in *Rummel* did not violate the Eighth Amendment, but the life sentence in *Solem* did violate the Eighth Amendment. However, the third factor, the offender's criminal history, was worse in *Solem*. The second factor, the sentence-triggering criminal conduct, was about the same, in terms of actual monetary loss, in *Rummel* and *Solem*. The critical difference in these two cases was the third factor—the length of the prison term. In *Rummel*, there was the possibility of parole. In *Solem*, there was not.

♦ D's prior record is not significantly different from the defendant in *Solem*, and D's triggering crime is not significantly different from that of the defendants in *Solem* and *Rummel*. The length of the real prison term, the critical factor in *Solem* and *Rummel*, is what is important here. D's sentence amounts, in real terms, to at least 25 years without parole. Although that is considerably shorter than the sentence in *Solem*, it is more than twice as long as the sentence at issue in *Rummel*, which amounted, in real terms, to at least 10 or 12 years. And D, who was seriously ill when he was sentenced at age 38, will likely the in prison.

♦ Here, the crime triggering the sentencing was shoplifting, which, while serious in terms of the cost to retailers, is less serious than much other criminal conduct. These factors make D's gross disproportionality argument a strong one. A comparative analysis of D's sentence with sentencing practices in other jurisdictions and in California, outside the three strikes context, reveals that D's recidivist sentence is virtually unique in its harshness.

♦ Finally, the stated objective of this particular three strikes law is to reduce serious and violent crime. But the statute's definitions of both kinds of crime include crimes against the person, crimes that create danger of physical harm, and drug crimes, and do not include even serious crimes against property, such as obtaining large amounts of money through theft, embezzlement, or fraud. Also, the criminal law objectives of retribution and rehabilitation are not relevant, and in terms of deterrence, D's 25-year term is excessive.

3. Juveniles

Graham v. Florida
130 S.Ct. 2011 (2010).

Facts. At the age of 16, Graham (D) pleaded guilty to an armed robbery attempt and was sentenced to 3 years probation, the first year to be served in the county jail. Less than six months after his release, D, 34 days short of his 18th birthday, took part with Bailey and Lawrence in a home invasion robbery. On the same night, the three attempted a second robbery; Bailey was shot. D drove Bailey and Lawrence to the hospital and after dropping them off, failed to comply with a police officer's signal to stop his car. A high-speed chase ended with D crashing into a telephone and attempting to flee on foot. He was apprehended and three handguns were found in his car. After finding that D had violated his probation by committing the home invasion robbery, possessing a firearm and associating with persons engaged in criminal activity, the trial court imposed the maximum sentence—life imprisonment for the home invasion and 15 years for the attempted armed robbery. Florida has abolished its parole system, so D's life sentence was without the possibility of parole. D's motion challenging his sentence under the Eighth Amendment was deemed denied after the trial court failed to rule on it within 60 days. The Florida Court of Appeal affirmed. The Florida Supreme Court denied review. We granted certiorari.

Issue. Does the Eighth Amendment's Cruel and Unusual Punishment Clause prohibit the imposition of a life without parole sentence on a juvenile offender who did not commit homicide?

Held (Kennedy, J.). Yes. Judgment reversed; case remanded.

♦ Inherent in the ban against cruel and unusual punishments is the "precept . . . that punishment for crime should be graduated and proportioned to [the] offense."

♦ Our cases involving the proportionality standard involve two categories: whether the length of a term-of-years sentence is unconstitutionally excessive for a particular defendant's crime, or another in which we have applied certain categorical rules against the death penalty. In one sub-category, we have considered the nature of the offense, and in another, we have considered the characteristics of the offender.

- Where cases involve categorical rules, the we first consider "objective indicia of society's standards, as expressed in legislative enactments and state practice" to assess whether there is a national consensus against the sentencing practice at issue. Next, assessing the "the standards elaborated by controlling precedents and by the Court's own understanding and interpretation of the Eighth Amendment's text, history, meaning, and purpose," we determine in the exercise of our own independent judgment whether the punishment in question violates the Constitution,

- This case presents an issue we have not considered before, a categorical challenge to a term-of-years sentence; it addresses a particular type of sentence as it applies to an entire class of offenders who have committed a range of crimes; thus, the appropriate analysis is the categorical approach.

- We have prohibited death sentences for defendants who committed their crimes before 18 because we determined that because juveniles have "lessened culpability," they do not deserve the most severe punishments. We have held that defendants who do not intend to kill, who do not kill or who do not foresee a death will result are categorically less deserving of the most serious forms of punishment than are murderers. When compared to an adult murderer, a juvenile who did not intend to kill has a "twice diminished moral culpability." *Roper v. Simmons,* 543 U.S. 551 (2005).

- Like death sentences, life without parole changes a defendant's life by deprivation that is irrevocable; there is no hope of having one's basic liberties restored. The goals of retribution (addressed above), deterrence, incapacitation and rehabilitation do not justify such sentences. deterrence is unsupported. To assume a juvenile will forever be a danger to society, incorrigible, is a questionable judgment. The ideal of rehabilitation is foresworn. While there may be some juveniles who are incorrigible or "sufficiently depraved" to justify life without parole, we cannot say that courts can assess this on a case by case basis with sufficient accuracy.

- By their very nature, juveniles have a limited understanding of the workings of a court and criminal proceedings, of future consequences, and these factors might impair the quality of their representation. A categorical rule provides offenders with the opportunity to show maturity that can lead to reflection and serve as a basis for remorse and rehabilitation.

Concurrence (Roberts, C.J.). While I agree D's sentence violates the Eighth Amendment, I do not agree that a categorical ban in all juvenile non-homicide cases is the appropriate solution. While a case by case analysis may, as the Court states, not result in "sufficient accuracy" in juvenile cases, that is true in all cases. There is no such thing as perfect wisdom; judges apply reasoned judgment in all cases that come before them.

Dissent (Thomas, J.). Life without parole deters and incapacitates. Thirty-seven states allow this sentence for juveniles who have not committed homicides, and removing that sentence option available in certain cases illustrates how far the Court has reached to assure that its "sense of morality and retributive justice preempts that of the people and their representatives."

Comment. Even with the *Graham* ruling, challenges to individual sentences must meet the *Ewing*

test, and successful Eighth Amendment challenges are uncommon. However, some scholars have suggested that *Graham* may provide for challenges to extend its ruling to juvenile felony-murder cases and lengthy term of years sentences for nonhomicides.

D. Culpability

1. Introduction

There are two basic elements of every crime: (i) the actus reus, or the commission (or omission) of some act prohibited by law; and (ii) the mens rea, or some criminal state of mind. To constitute a crime, the act must concur with the intent; *i.e.*, the intent must accompany the doing of the act, and the actus reus must be attributable to the mens rea.

2. Actus Reus—The Forbidden Acts

a. Definition of an "act"

Some wrongful outward act or manifestation is required. Furthermore, an "act" is any event that is subject to the control of the will (although the will need not actually be exercised since omissions to act are also punishable); thus, to meditate is an act, but to dream is not.

b. Speaking or verbal acts

Such acts can be the subject of crimes; for example, solicitation.

c. Involuntary acts

1) Introduction

The act that is the subject of a crime must be "voluntary." Thus, reflexes, convulsions, and other acts done while sleepwalking or while in the middle of an epileptic fit, etc., are not voluntary acts.

2) Epileptic reflexes

In *People v. Decina*, 138 N.E.2d (N.Y.I 956), Decina, aware of his epileptic condition and the likelihood of being rendered unconscious as the result of a seizure, drove his vehicle on a public way. He suffered an attack and the car went up onto the sidewalk, killing four people. He was charged with criminal negligence in the operation of a vehicle. The court found his actions constituted criminal negligence because he deliberately chose to take a chance by driving alone while he was aware of his vulnerability to seizures and did so in disregard of the results that might follow. Note the necessity of prior knowledge; a disabling attack, without any prior knowledge, would be viewed differently.

3) Voluntariness

Martin v. State
17 So. 2d 427 (Ala. Ct. App. 1944).

Facts. Martin (D) was arrested at his home and taken onto a public highway, where he used loud and profane language and manifested a drunken condition with other persons present. He was convicted of drunkenness in a public place under a state statute.

Issue. May a person be guilty of a crime if his conduct was not voluntary?

Held. No. Conviction reversed.

♦ The statute presupposes that the defendant voluntarily appears in public in a drunken condition. D was brought to the public place involuntarily by the arresting officer.

4) Unconsciousness

People v. Newton
87 Cal. Rptr. 394 (Cal. Ct. App. 1970).

Facts. Newton (D), involved in an altercation with a police officer subsequent to his arrest, was shot in the midsection, but then managed to grab the gun and fired several shots at the officer, killing him. D testified that he remembered nothing after being shot (except for a few events in an emergency room) until recovering consciousness at a second hospital. Expert testimony established that a shock reaction (producing unconsciousness) could have resulted from the shot and could have lasted up to a half hour. The defense asked for an instruction to the jury on unconsciousness but the trial court refused. D was convicted of voluntary manslaughter. D appeals.

Issue. Is it error to fail to instruct the jury on the issue of unconsciousness as a defense?

Held. Yes. Judgment reversed.

- ♦ Unconsciousness, where not voluntarily induced, is a complete defense to murder.

- ♦ Unconsciousness includes situations where the defendant can act physically but is not conscious of what he is doing.

- ♦ D is entitled to a jury instruction on the consciousness issue even if the inference that he was unconscious arises from his own testimony. The jury must be allowed to consider whether D was in fact unconscious.

d. Status crimes

The "act" may involve simply the status or condition of an individual, such as those crimes punishing individuals for vagrancy or habitual drunkenness.

e. Prohibited acts

In all instances the "act" must be prohibited in order for a crime to exist. A person might intend to commit a crime by performing some act, but if that act is not prohibited, then there is no crime.

f. Negative acts or omissions to act

A defendant may be criminally liable for an omission or forbearance to act when there is a legal duty for him to so act.

1) Legal duty

A punishable negative act is a nonoccurrence involving a breach of defendant's legal duty to take positive action.

2) Contractual duty

Jones v. United States
308 F.2d 307 (D.C. Cir. 1962).

Facts. Green and her baby lived for some period of time with Jones (D). The baby died from neglect and malnutrition. D was charged with the death. At trial, conflicting evidence was presented as to whether Green had hired D to care for the baby or whether Green was staying with D and should have been taking care of the baby herself. D wanted an instruction that the jury must find beyond a reasonable doubt that D had a legal duty to care for the baby. The court failed to give the instruction and D was convicted of involuntary manslaughter. D appeals.

Issue. When a person is criminally charged with an omission to act, must the government prove there was a legal duty to act?

Held. Yes. Judgment reversed.

- Breach of a legal duty may arise in four situations:

   (i) Where a statute imposes the duty of care;

   (ii) Where one stands in a certain status relationship to another;

   (iii) Where one has assumed a contractual duty to care for another; or

   (iv) Where one has voluntarily assumed the care of another and has withdrawn the helpless person from others who could render aid.

- Criminal liability for failure to act must be based on more than just a moral duty to act. The government must prove that D had a legal duty to act. Although the facts would justify a finding that D had such a legal duty, the evidence is conflicting and the issue should have been given to the jury with appropriate instructions.

Comment. Legal duty and moral duty are *not* synonymous, although the trend is to equate one with the other.

3) Child neglect

Pope v. State
396 A.2d 1054 (Md. 1979).

Facts. Pope (D) took Norris and her three-month-old child into D's home because Norris had no place to go. Norris was mentally ill and occasionally would go into a violent religious frenzy. At D's home, Norris began beating and tearing at the child, believing that Satan was hidden within the child's body. D did not protect the child or seek police or medical assistance. Instead, she went to church with Norris and brought her back home. The child died that night from the beating. D was charged with child abuse and misprision of felony. D was convicted and appeals.

Issue. Does a person who charitably assumes partial support of a parent and her child become criminally responsible for child abuse committed by the parent on the child?

Held. No. Judgment reversed.

- The crime of child abuse consists of a person who is responsible for the supervision of a minor child causing, or being accountable for, whether by commission or omission, abuse to the child, including physical injury. D's failure to prevent the beating of the child and her failure to seek medical assistance constitute omissions that are cruel and inhumane treatment. She could therefore be convicted if she was a person "responsible for the supervision" of the child.

- D was not the child's parent, nor was she in loco parentis to the child. The prosecution claimed that D assumed responsibility for the child within the statute once she began to house, feed, and care for the child and Norris. However, Norris was always present. D could not usurp Norris's role as mother. It would be incongruous to impose criminal liability premised solely on acts of hospitality and kindness.

- D may have had a strong moral obligation to assist the child, but she had no legal obligation to do so. Accordingly, D was not in the class of persons that fall within the statute.

- The offense of misprision of felony has become obsolete and is no longer cognizable by the criminal law of this state.

4) Failure to continue life-support systems

Barber v. Superior Court
195 Cal. Rptr. 484 (Cal. Dist. Ct. App. 1983).

Facts. Herbert underwent surgery at the hands of Nejdl and Barber (Ds), who were surgeons. After the successful operation, Herbert suffered cardio-respiratory arrest and was placed on life-support equipment. Herbert lapsed into a coma from which he was not expected to recover. The family asked that the equipment be removed and Ds complied with the request. Herbert continued breaming, but had to be fed intravenously. After again consulting with the family, Ds removed the intravenous tubes and Herbert died a short while later. Ds were charged with murder, but the magistrate dismissed the complaint. The Superior Court reinstated the complaint and Ds appeal.

Issue. May a doctor be charged with murder for failure to continue to provide life-sustaining treatment?

Held. No. Judgment reversed.

- ◆ Historically, death consisted of the cessation of heart and respiratory function. By statute, death consists of irreversible cessation of all brain function. By either definition, Herbert was not dead when Ds ceased further treatment.

- ◆ Disconnecting mechanical life-support devices, including the IV tubes, is comparable to withholding manually administered injection or medication. Ds could have criminal liability only if they had a legal duty to continue to provide life-sustaining treatment. Under these circumstances, after coordinating with Herbert's wife and children, Ds had no duty to continue treatment.

5) Other applications

a) In *Airdale NHS Trust v. Bland*, All E.R. 821 (H.L. 1993), an insensate patient, with no hope of recovery, continued to live by means of artificial feeding and antibiotics. The House of Lords held that the treatment could lawfully be withheld even when withholding such treatment meant that the patient would shortly die. The House of Lords distinguished between a doctor's decision not to act, and the decision to actively administer a lethal drug to bring a patient's life to an end. A doctor who switches off a life support machine does not "act" but rather does not struggle to maintain life. This is not a breach of duty, because he is not obligated to continue in a hopeless case. The law does not permit a doctor to prescribe a lethal injection, however, because the law does not authorize euthanasia. *Note:* The court succinctly stated the common fear that "once euthanasia is recognized as lawful in these circumstances, it is difficult to see any logical basis for excluding it in others." However, it is difficult to justify the notion that one may legally withdraw feeding tubes, thus condemning a patient to literally starve to death, but one may not legally hasten that death.

b) In *People v. Beardsley*, 150 Mich. 206 (1907), the court refused to find a legal duty where the defendant failed to summon a physician for his weekend mistress when she took a fatal dose of morphine.

c) But in *Jones v. State*, 220 Ind. 384 (1942), the court found a duty to rescue where the defendant raped a child who then jumped into a creek and drowned (the court emphasizing the fact that the defendant had been the "cause" of the child's actions).

6) Knowledge

In general, no criminal act can be found *unless* the defendant is shown to have had knowledge of his legal duty to act.

a) Exceptions:

(1) Where the duty to act arises from a statute.

(2) Where negligence results in the imposition of criminal liability in exceptional cases where the potential risk of harm is very great. (For example, a railroad switchman was held criminally liable for failure to throw a switch even though his attention was distracted and he was unaware of danger.)

3. Mens Rea—The Mental State Accompanying the Forbidden Acts

a. Introduction

1) Definition

Mens rea is a guilty or wrongful purpose; a criminal intent. The intent required is *not* the same for all crimes (for example, negligence may be sufficient in some crimes).

2) Motive distinguished

Proof of motive is immaterial in establishing criminal liability. Motives create an intent to act, while intent itself is merely a determination to act in a certain way. An accused's motive may be relevant in proving the probability of his having committed the offense and/or of having had a certain type of intent when an act was committed. But failure to prove motive will not prevent a conviction.

b. Types of intent

1) Introduction

Each crime has its own standard as to the nature and quality of the intent required. At common law there were three types of mens rea: general mens rea, specific mens rea, and criminal negligence.

2) General intent

General intent requires only that the accused meant to do the act he committed (*i.e.*, that the prohibited result was substantially certain to flow from the intentional conduct, even if the result that occurred was not subjectively intended). For example, if A voluntarily fires a gun into the middle of a crowd, even if he does not want to injure someone, and B is killed thereby, A may be held for murder (*i.e.*, he intended to fire the gun into the crowd, and objectively speaking, the killing of a person was substantially certain to follow).

a) Proof of general intent

Intent is inferred by the results that occur. Therefore, general intent may be proved simply by showing that the prohibited result was caused by a voluntary act of the defendant.

b) Transferred intent

When a person has the required intent to commit one criminal act, he may be held responsible for results that he did not intend if he inflicts the kind of harm intended and if the injuries sustained do not require a different mens rea.

(1) Usually the intent from the first crime will only be transferred to the second where the first act was "malum in se." For example, if A attempts to hit B and unintentionally hits and injures C, A is guilty of assault on C.

(2) The transfer generally occurs only where the unintended result involves the same mens rea requirement as the intended act. Therefore, if A shoots at B, misses, and the bullet strikes an oil lamp, igniting a fire, A is not guilty of arson because arson requires that specific intent to start a fire be shown (specific intent is discussed below), and here A can only be held to have had *the* intent to do personal injury.

3) Malice

a) Introduction

Malice can refer to a specific criminal state of mind where the defendant is subjectively cognizant of the likely harmful results of his actions, yet inexcusably carries out these potentially harmful acts. Malice may also be inferred where the defendant acts recklessly or with wanton disregard for the consequences of his actions. Finally, malice may be used in its dictionary meaning, as in the crime of malicious mischief (defendant acting out of resentment or hatred of the owner of the injured property).

b) Unforeseeable result

Regina v. Cunningham
2 Q.B. 396 (1957).

Facts. Cunningham (D) tore the gas meter from the wall in a house in order to steal the money contained therein. He did not turn off the gas and it leaked into the next house and asphyxiated an elderly lady. D was convicted under a statute for "maliciously causing another to take noxious things." D appeals.

Issue. May a person be convicted under a statute that requires malicious intent when he did not actually intend to do the harm done and did not foresee the result?

Held. No. Conviction reversed.

- ♦ "Maliciously" requires that the defendant act recklessly with foresight of the actual consequence, or it requires actual intent to do the particular harm done. Recklessness is where the defendant foresees that such harm might occur but does the act anyway.

- ♦ Malice does not require that ill will toward the person injured be shown, nor does it require that the act done in itself be unlawful (as the stealing of the gas meter was here).

- ♦ The jury instructions by the trial judge were thus erroneous; the jury should have been left to decide whether D foresaw possible injury occurring from his act.

4) Accidental collateral act

In *Regina v. Faulkner*, 13 Cox Crim. Cas. 550, 555, 557 (1877), the court reversed a sailor's conviction for the malicious destruction of a ship, which was the result of an accidental fire caused by the sailor while stealing rum. Although the court agreed that the sailor was culpable for the theft of the rum, it held that he was not responsible for every unintended result caused by the theft.

5) Acting willfully

This term usually requires only a general mens rea but may be elevated to a standard of specific intent if expressly required by the terms of a statute.

6) Wanton or reckless conduct

This type of conduct consists of the intentional failure to take reasonable care when confronting a known risk. Such a failure may be subjective (i.e., the defendant having been actually aware of the probable consequences of his actions) or objective (a reasonable person would have known of the risk).

7) Criminal negligence

Criminal negligence is a flagrant and reckless disregard for the safety of others. The test applied, whether it is an act of omission or commission, is what a reasonable person would do under like circumstances?

a) Degree of negligence required

The lack of due care required for criminal liability is greater than that required for tort liability. How much greater is not always certain because both are supposedly measured by the same standard.

b) Criminal sanction under civil negligence standard

State v. Hazelwood
946 P.2d 875 (Alaska 1997).

Facts. Hazelwood (D) was the captain of an oil tanker that ran aground and leaked 11 million gallons of oil into Prince William Sound in Alaska. D was convicted of negligent discharge of oil. The court of appeals reversed on the ground that D should have been tried under a criminal negligence standard rather than a civil negligence standard. The state appeals.

Issue. May a person be convicted of criminal negligence based on a standard of negligence that is civil in nature?

Held. Yes. Judgment reversed.

- ♦ Under both criminal negligence and civil negligence standards, a person acts negligently when he fails to perceive a substantial and unjustifiable risk that a particular result will occur, but criminal negligence requires a greater risk. Criminal negligence involves a risk of such a nature and degree that the failure to perceive it constitutes a gross deviation from the standard of care that a reasonable person would observe in the situation. The negligence must be so gross that it merits not only damages, but also punishment. It does not require recklessness, and there is no requirement that the defendant be aware of the risk of harm. But it does require a more culpable mental state than ordinary negligence.

- ♦ Those who would abolish objective fault crimes assume that legal regulations can operate only through the offender's conscious reason. However, even when an offender does not realize that his conduct is wrongful, he may be made to take care. This can serve important social aims.

- ♦ The negligence standard is the minimum for a criminal offense because it assures that criminal penalties will be imposed only when the conduct at issue is something society can reasonably expect to deter.

Dissent. Due process requires something more than "failure to act reasonably" before a defendant may be imprisoned. Mere negligence is insufficient to justify a punitive damages award; thus it is difficult to accept that it may result in imprisonment.

c) Model penal code reforms

The Model Penal Code's response to problems set forth by common-law mens rea terminology and its interpretation resulted in a new approach. The MPC set out to mitigate the difficulties of mens rea analysis by providing manageable categories, precise definitions, and convenient default rules. It replaces the ten or more varieties of common law mens rea with four mental states: purpose, knowledge, recklessness, and negligence, and provides a clear definition for each. Applicable MPC provisions are:

Sect. 2.02(1)—Sets forth the minimum requirements of culpability;

Sects. 2.02(2) (a)–(d) Defines the kinds of culpability;

Sects. 2.02(3)–(4) Provides the default rules.

Model Penal Code § 2.02. General Requirements of Culpability.

"(1) Minimum Requirements of Culpability. Except as provided in Section 2.05, a person is not guilty of an offense unless he acted purposely, knowingly, recklessly or negligently, as the law may require, with respect to each material element of the offense.

"(2) Kinds of Culpability Defined

"(a) Purposely.

"A person acts purposely with respect to a material element of an offense when:

"(i) if the element involves the nature of his conduct or a result thereof, it is his conscious object to engage in conduct of that nature or to cause such a result; and

"(ii) if the element involves the attendant circumstances, he is aware of the existence of such circumstances or he believes or hopes that they exist.

"(b) Knowingly.

"A person acts knowingly with respect to a material element of an offense when:

"(i) if the element involves the nature of his conduct or the attendant circumstances, he is aware that his conduct is of that nature or that such circumstances exist; and

"(ii) if the element involves a result of his conduct, he is aware that it is practically certain that his conduct will cause such a result.

"(c) Recklessly.

"A person acts recklessly with respect to a material element of an offense when he consciously disregards a substantial and unjustifiable risk that the material element exists or will result from his conduct. The risk must be of such a nature and degree that, considering the nature and purpose of the actor's conduct and the circumstances known to him, its disregard involves a gross deviation from the standard of conduct that a law-abiding person would observe in the actor's situation.

"(d) Negligently.

"A person acts negligently with respect to a material element of an offense when he should be aware of a substantial and unjustifiable risk that the material element exists or will result from his conduct. The risk must be of such a nature and degree that the actor's failure to perceive it, considering the nature and purpose of his conduct and the circumstances known to him, involves a gross deviation from the standard of care that a reasonable person would observe in the actor's situation.

"(3) Culpability Required Unless Otherwise Provided. When the culpability sufficient to establish a material element of an offense is not prescribed by law, such element is established if a person acts purposely, knowingly or recklessly with respect thereto.

"(4) Prescribed Culpability Requirement Applies to All Material Elements. When the law defining an offense prescribes the kind of culpability that is sufficient for the commission of an offense, without distinguishing among the material elements thereof, such provision shall apply to all the material elements of the offense, unless a contrary purpose plainly appears."

8) Deliberate ignorance

United States v. Jewell
532 F.2d 697 (9th Cir. 1976).

Facts. Jewell (D) was convicted of knowingly transporting marijuana from Mexico to the United States, concealed in a secret compartment in his car. D testified he did not know that the marijuana was present. The evidence showed that D might have known of the marijuana, or that he might have deliberately avoided such positive knowledge. The court instructed the jury that "knowingly" could mean actual knowledge or deliberate avoidance of actual knowledge. D appeals his conviction.

Issue. Are deliberate ignorance and positive knowledge equally culpable?

Held. Yes. Conviction affirmed.

♦ One can "know" facts without being absolutely certain of them. "Knowingly," therefore, can mean an awareness of the high probability of the existence of a fact.

Dissent. The majority justifies the "conscious purpose" jury instruction as an application of the "willful blindness" doctrine. But the instruction makes no mention of "high probability" that D knew of the marijuana, nor does it state that "actual belief" could thwart a conviction. The jury instruction also wrongly indicates that ignorance or not actually being aware could still lead to a conviction.

c. Mistake of fact

1) Introduction

"Mistake of fact" is an unconscious ignorance of a material fact. It is a common defense challenging the mens rea necessary to convict.

2) Crimes requiring specific intent—actual belief

If the defendant makes an honest and reasonable mistake of fact and his conduct would not be criminal if the facts were as he supposed them to be, then his mistake of fact is a defense to a crime requiring that *specific* intent be shown. However, mistake of fact is not a defense to a crime requiring only general intent.

3) Mistake as to ages

a) Reasonable belief

Regina v. Prince
2 Cr. Cas. Res. 154 (1875).

Facts. Prince (D) was convicted of having sexual relations with an unmarried female under 16 in violation of a statute. The girl was 14 but told D she was 18. D appeals.

Issue. Is a reasonable but mistaken belief as to age a defense urder these circumstances?

Held. No. Judgment affirmed.

- D's belief was reasonable, but it was irrelevant because it did not constitute a defense to this crime. The statute forbids taking a girl out of the possession of her parents or another having legal charge of her. Whoever does this act does so at the risk of her being under 16. D had the mens rea to do the forbidden act, although he did not know the girl's true age. If D did not know the girl was in someone's possession, or thought he had permission, he would not have had mens rea.

Dissent. Because D would not have committed an offense if the facts had been as he thought, he had no intent to commit an offense and is not guilty.

b) Good faith belief

People v. Olsen
685 P.2d 52 (Cal. 1984).

Facts. Two months before her 14th birthday, Shawn was permitted by her parents to sleep in the family's camper in the driveway. She claimed that after she had locked the door and fallen asleep, she was awakened by Garcia, who was in the trailer and had a knife. Garcia then called to Olsen (D), who entered the trailer as well. Garcia told Shawn to let D have intercourse with her or he would stab her. During the act, Shawn's father came in and grabbed D. Garcia stabbed Shawn's father and they escaped. At D's trial for rape, Shawn admitted that she had told Garcia and D that she was older than 16. Garcia testified that he in fact had had intercourse several times with Shawn the night before the incident, pursuant to Shawn's invitation. Shawn had invited D and Garcia back, and asked to have sex with D first. At his trial, D claimed the defense of good faith belief. After the court rejected the defense of good faith belief, D was convicted of statutory, but not forcible, rape. D appeals.

Issue. Is a good faith belief that the female is over 16 years old a valid defense to a statutory rape charge?

Held. No. Judgment affirmed.

- In a prior case, this court adopted a defense to statutory rape based on an accused's good faith and reasonable belief that the victim was at least 18 years old. Despite that holding, at least one court of appeal in this state refused to recognize the defense in the context of a charge of offering marijuana to a minor.

- In the statute defining lewd or lascivious conduct, the legislature provided for probation for accused persons who "honestly and reasonably believed the victim was 14 years old or older." This demonstrates that the legislature did not intend to approve the honest and reasonable belief defense; otherwise, there would be no need to provide for probation, because the person would not be convicted.

- The legislature has determined that persons under age 14 need special protection. Those who commit sexual offenses with such young persons are punished more severely than those who do so with older persons under age 18. Recognition of the defense in cases involving victims under age 14 would undermine the legislative purpose and cannot be permitted.

Concurrence and dissent. It is unfair for a person to be sentenced to prison when he committed the offending act only because his belief about the facts of the victim's age were incorrect. Strict liability may be applied for regulatory offenses, but traditional crimes should require at least some proof of fault. The legislature could impose a strict standard of what is reasonable, such as reasonable inquiry, but once the belief becomes reasonable as measured by a legitimate standard, there should be no criminal liability.

c) Honest belief

B (A Minor) v. Director of Public Prosecutions
1 All E.R. 833 (2000).

Facts. A 15-year-old boy (D) repeatedly asked a 13-year-old girl to perform oral sex. D was charged, under the Indecency with Children Act 1960 ("Act"), with inciting a child under 14 to commit an act of gross indecency. D pleaded not guilty on the basis that he had honestly believed that the girl was over 14. He changed his plea to guilty, preserving his right to appeal, after the justices ruled that his mistake was not a defense. D appeals.

Issue. Is an honest but mistaken belief as to age a defense under the Act?

Held. Yes.

- ◆ Where Parliament has proscribed prohibited conduct only in terms of proscribed physical acts, mens rea is an essential ingredient of the offense unless Parliament has indicated otherwise. This common law presumption has been expressed traditionally to the effect that an honest mistake does not help a defendant unless it was made on reasonable grounds. However, during the last 25 years, several important cases have emphasized the subjective nature of mens rea and rejected the "reasonable belief approach in favor of the "honest belief approach.

- ◆ If a man believes that the girl with whom he is committing a grossly indecent act is over 14, he does not have the intent to commit the act with a girl under 14. To determine whether such an intention is an essential ingredient of the Act, we must properly construe it.

- ◆ The more serious the offense, the greater is the weight to be attached to the presumption requiring mens rea. The Act created a new and serious offense. The punishment upon conviction is a maximum of 10 years' imprisonment. The proscribed behavior may be depraved or may be relatively innocuous. This reinforces the application of the presumption.

- ◆ The statutory context of the Act gives no indication that Parliament intended to displace the application of the common law requirement of the mental element. The necessary mental element is the absence of a genuine belief by the accused that the victim was 14 years of age or older. The burden of proof rests with the prosecution.

- ◆ *Regina v. Prince, supra*, must now be read in light of this decision.

d) Mistake-of-age defense not allowed

Garnett v. State
632 A.2d 797 (Md. 1993).

Facts. Garnett (D), a retarded man with an I.Q. of 52, was 20 years old when he engaged in consensual sexual intercourse with a 13-year-old girl. Later, the victim gave birth to D's son. D was tried for second degree rape under a Maryland statute prohibiting sexual intercourse between a person under 14 and another at least four years older than the complainant. The defense offered evidence that the victim and her friends had told D that the victim was 16 years old and that D had acted with that belief on the night in question. Because the trial court considered the matter a strict liability offense, it excluded the evidence as immaterial. D was convicted and sentenced to five years in prison; the sentence was suspended and D was placed on probation and ordered to pay restitution to the victim and her family. D appeals.

Issue. Is mistake of age a defense under the Maryland statute?

Held. No. Judgment affirmed.

♦ Both the plain language of the statute and its legislative history lead us to conclude that it defines a strict liability offense that does not require the state to prove mens rea and does not allow for a mistake-of-age defense.

♦ Our interpretation is consistent with the traditional view of statutory rape, and the majority of states have statutes that impose strict liability for sexual acts with underage complainants. Even some of the states that provide for a mistake-of-age defense in some instances do not permit the defense where the sex partner is 14 years old or less. Here, the victim was 13.

Dissent. To hold that the statute does not require proof of the necessary mental state, or that the defendant may not litigate that issue, renders meaningless the presumption of innocence and the right to due process.

d. Strict liability

There are crimes where the accused is criminally liable regardless of fault. Mistake of fact cannot serve as a defense to strict liability crimes.

1) Rationale

Mistake of fact in strict liability crimes is not a defense because of the traditional rule that, regardless of the mistake, the accused's conduct is still "morally wrong" and should be punished. Hence, there is no mens rea requirement. There is a minority trend away from strict liability, especially with the more serious offenses.

2) Modification of common-law rule

In *United States v. Balint*, 258 U.S. 250 (1922), the defendants were convicted of selling narcotics without obtaining written permission from the IRS as required by the Narcotics Act of 1914. They claimed that they did not know the drugs they were selling were narcotics. The Supreme Court rejected the defendants' argument that punishing a person for a violation when he is ignorant of the facts which make his conduct a violation denies him due process and upheld the indictment. The Court explained that although the general rule at common law was that scienter was a necessary element even where statutory language did not include it, that view had been modified with respect to statutes the purpose of which would be obstructed by such a requirement. The purpose of the Narcotics Act was to require every person dealing in drugs to find out whether what he was selling came within the prohibitions of the statute, and if he sold a prohibited drug in ignorance of its nature, to penalize him. The Court stated that Congress weighed the possibility of punishing an innocent seller against the possibility of exposing innocent buyers to danger and concluded that it was better to avoid the latter.

3) Mens rea and public safety

In *United States v. Dotterweich*, 320 U.S. 277 (1943), a company that purchased drugs from manufacturers and shipped them, repacked under its own label with the manufacturers' description of the drugs, shipped misbranded products on two occasions. As a result, the corporation and Dotterweich, the president and general manager, were prosecuted for violating the Federal Food, Drug and Cosmetic Act by shipping misbranded products in interstate commerce. The corporation was acquitted, but Dotterweich was convicted. The Supreme Court affirmed, finding that no mens rea and no awareness of a wrongdoing was required by the statute, which, in the interest of the larger good, put the burden on the person standing in responsible relation to a public danger.

4) Mens rea requirement in "true crimes"

Morissette v. United States
342 U.S. 246 (1952).

Facts. Morissette (D) entered an Air Force bombing area and appropriated some old, rusty bomb casings. He flattened out the metal and sold it as scrap for $84. He was indicted and convicted of violating a federal law that makes it a crime to "knowingly convert" government property. His defense was that he honestly thought the government had abandoned the casings. The trial court took the view that this was no defense because the federal statute does not explicitly require the intent to steal. Thus, the trial court viewed the crime as one of strict liability in which mens rea was unnecessary. D's conviction was subsequently affirmed. The Supreme Court granted certiorari.

Issue. Can a person be held criminally responsible on a strict liability basis for a codified crime, which at common law required proof of bad intent?

Held. No. Conviction reversed.

♦ There is a difference between true crimes such as conversion of property and public welfare offenses (such as violation of the liquor code). Where the criminal law, as in this case, is entirely statutory and the statute makes no mention of a mens rea requirement, mens rea will be deemed inherent in any offense that is a codification of a common law crime.

♦ At common law all crimes were mala in se. Thus, all crimes required mens rea. Today public welfare offenses dispense with the mens rea requirement. But codifications of common law crimes do require the existence of a bad intent.

Comment. When a statute is merely a codification of a common law crime, mens rea usually remains an element whether it is mentioned in the statute or not. However, despite the commitment of traditional Anglo-American law to the mens rea requirement, there have been departures in a number of instances (*e.g.*, the felony-murder and misdemeanor-manslaughter rules, bigamy, and sex offenses with minors).

5) Act silent as to mens rea

Staples v. United States
511 U.S. 60 (1994).

Facts. Staples (D) was convicted of violating the National Firearms Act by possessing a weapon capable of automatically firing more man one shot with a single pull of *the* trigger. The rifle was not manufactured as an automatic weapon, but had been altered to allow automatic firing. D contended that he never knew the rifle could fire automatically. D appealed; the court of appeals affirmed. The Supreme Court granted certiorari.

Issue. Can a defendant be convicted of possession of an automatic weapon without proof that he knew that his rifle could fire automatically?

Held. No. Judgment reversed and case remanded.

♦ The Act is silent concerning a mens rea requirement. Silence, however, does not mean Congress intended to dispense with the element of mens rea.

♦ We require some indication of congressional intent to dispense with mens rea; absent such an indication, it will be presumed to be required.

♦ Our previous analysis in *United States v. Freed*, 401 U.S. 601 (1971), was premised on the assumption that the defendant knew he possessed a particularly dangerous item. That assumption is not warranted here.

♦ We will not ease the path to convicting persons whose conduct would not even alert them to the chance that they were violating the Act.

Concurrence (Ginsburg, O'Connor, JJ.). Even though the word "knowingly" does not appear in the Act, the general rule is that absent a contrary indication, it will be assumed that Congress intended to retain the mens rea requirement.

6) Limitation on vicarious criminal liability

State v. Guminga
395 N.W.2d 344 (Minn. 1986).

Facts. Two undercover officers accompanied a 17-year-old woman into a restaurant owned by Guminga (D). The three ordered alcoholic drinks, and when the waitress brought them, the minor paid. The officers verified that the drinks were alcoholic and then arrested the waitress. D was later charged with violating the law against serving underage persons. The law held employers vicariously liable for violations by employees. D was unaware of the entire incident. D moved to dismiss the charges as denying him due process. The trial court denied the motion, but D appealed. The court of appeals certified the issue to the state supreme court.

Issue. Is a statute consistent with due process if it imposes vicarious criminal liability on an employer for the acts of his employee in serving alcoholic beverages to underage customers?

Held. No. The statute deprives D of due process.

- The penalty D faced if convicted of the gross misdemeanor included up to one year of imprisonment or payment of a fine of up to $3,000, or both. D could also lose his liquor license. Even though D might not receive these penalties, he still faces a possible gross misdemeanor conviction, which would give him a criminal record.

- Due process requires a balancing between the public interests behind a statute and the private interest in liberty. Alternative means to achieving the public purpose must also be evaluated.

- The statute in this case assists in deterring violation of the liquor laws, while D has a private interest in liberty, his reputation, and other effects of criminal prosecution, such as a longer sentence if ever convicted in the future. The infringements on private interests are not justified by the public interest in this case. The state could use other alternatives, such as civil fines or license suspension, to accomplish the same ends. The statute does not distinguish between employers who properly train their employees and those who do not; it simply imposes vicarious liability without consideration of the employer's degree of responsibility.

Dissent. The state has a strong public interest in deterring drinking by minors. The potential criminal sentences are reasonably related to the purpose of enforcing the law. The legislature could rationally conclude that, without criminal sanctions, owners such as D would be less likely to insure that their employees do not violate the law. Most other states have upheld imposition of vicarious liability in this type of case.

7) Standards for a defense under strict liability

State v. Baker
571 P.2d 65 (Kan. Ct. App. 1977).

Facts. Baker (D) was convicted of speeding. He wanted to introduce evidence that the excessive speed was due to the malfunction of his car's cruise control and that he had subsequently had the defective cruise control repaired. The trial court sustained the State's (P's) motion to suppress D's offered evidence, and D appeals.

Issue. Under a strict liability criminal statute, is the malfunction of a nonessential component of an automobile a defense to criminal liability for the consequences of the malfunction?

Held. No. Judgment affirmed.

- Even if D had been able to prove that the malfunction caused him to speed, such proof would not constitute a defense to strict liability because he himself activated the cruise control. This is a case of delegation of partial control of the car, which differs significantly from failure of an essential component of a car such as a brake or a throttle.

- To be valid, a defense to strict liability must show that the violation was the result of an unforeseen occurrence or circumstance, not caused by D and not preventable by him.

8) Absolute liability in Canada

In *Regina v. City of Sault Ste. Marie*, 85 D.L.R.3d 161 (1978), the Supreme Court of Canada noted that the basic justifications for absolute liability in public welfare offenses—the need for a strong incentive and administrative efficiency—do not override the violation of fundamental principles of penal liability. There is no empirical evidence of the incentive rationale, and it is clear that even if the penalty is relatively small, a significant stigma attaches to a conviction. Administrative convenience is an insufficient justification. Rather than the extremes of defining crimes as requiring either full mens rea or absolute liability, the Court noted the availability of offenses in which mens rea need not be proved, but the accused retains the option of avoiding liability through proof that he took all reasonable care. Such a category of offenses would include public welfare offenses. In 1985, relying on the *Sault Ste. Marie* reasoning, the Supreme Court of Canada held that the doctrine of absolute liability was unconstitutional. Specifically, it held that imprisonment for an absolute liability offense is a deprivation of liberty guaranteed by the Canadian Charter of Rights and Freedoms.

e. Mistake of law

Ignorance or mistake of law arises in two entirely different contexts: (i) those in which, because of ignorance or mistake as to a collateral law, the defendant lacked the mental state required for a conviction; and (ii) those in which the defendant had the requisite mental state but claims he was unaware that his conduct was proscribed by the criminal law.

1) Mistake as to collateral law

Some crimes involve a particular belief concerning a legal matter. If the defendant was ignorant or mistaken as to that legal matter, he lacked the necessary mens rea. This is a mistake not regarding the criminal statute itself, but a collateral law. For example, if a person mistakenly believes that he owns certain property that he finds, when in fact he does not, he could not be convicted of larceny if he keeps the property.

2) Mistake as to criminal statute

Criminal mens rea requires only that the defendant intended to do the prohibited act. Ignorance or mistake of the law is not a defense, on the theory that such a defense would undermine the enforcement of laws. The rule encourages the public to learn the laws. There are exceptions, however.

a) Statute later held unconstitutional

A defendant who acted in good faith reliance upon a statute that permitted her conduct may assert this reliance as a defense, even though the statute was later invalidated.

b) Judicial decision

If a judicial decision held that the particular conduct was not criminal, a defendant who relied on the decision may assert that reliance as a defense. In most jurisdictions, the decision does not need to be that of the highest state court.

c) Official interpretation

Reliance upon an official interpretation of the law by one responsible for administering or enforcing the law may constitute a defense.

d) Advice of private counsel not a defense

Unlike the exceptions set forth above, the courts have held that a person who in good faith relies on the advice of private counsel may not assert that reliance as a defense.

3) Irrelevance of mistake when intent is not an element of the offense

People v. Marrero
507 N.E.2d 1068 (N.Y. 1987).

Facts. Marrero (D) was a federal corrections officer. D carried a loaded .38 caliber automatic pistol, but he was not licensed to do so. He was arrested for violating the unlicensed possession law. By its terms, the law did not apply to "peace officers," which was defined to include corrections officers of any penal correctional institution. D claimed he was exempt from the law because of his status, but he was charged with the violation. The trial court dismissed the indictment, but the appellate court reversed and reinstated the indictment. At his trial, D requested a jury instruction that would have led to an acquittal if the jury found that D reasonably believed the exemption applied to him. The court refused the instruction, and the appellate court affirmed. D appeals.

Issue. Is a misinterpretation of a statute a valid defense to a crime that does not require an intent to violate the statute?

Held. No. Judgment affirmed.

♦ When intent is an element of the crime, a mistake of law may constitute a defense. In a kidnapping, for example, if the defendant believed that he seized the victim with authority of law, he could not have the necessary intent to confine another without authority of law. In this case, however, liability for weapons possession is imposed regardless of the defendant's intent, so a mistake of law is no defense.

♦ The mistake of law defense applies when the defendant has relied on an official statement of the law contained in a statute or an official interpretation of the statute. D claims that his reasonable but mistaken interpretation of the statute should constitute a defense. However, the proper rule is that the defense applies when the defendant relies on an official statement of the law that is thereafter determined to be invalid or incorrect. It applies only when the statute in fact authorizes the conduct, not when a defendant incorrectly reads the law.

♦ The narrow defense of mistake of law is intended to encourage respect for and adherence to the law. D's proposed approach would instead encourage mistakes about the law. Defendants could in many cases come up with reasonable but mistaken interpretations of criminal statutes that would constitute a defense.

Dissent. A person should not be convicted for committing an act that is not inherently wrong or immoral, but is a crime solely because of a statute, if the person acted in good faith but mistakenly believed that the act was not an offense because of the wording of the statute. Such a person has not knowingly committed an offense, so there is no rationale for punishment. The common law notion was formed when crimes were acts that by their nature were evil. That approach should not be carried forward to apply to conduct that would be lawful but for a criminal statute. This is the basic difference between acts malum in se and malum prohibitum. In this case, D's interpretation of the statute was certainly reasonable. The more just approach would be to permit a defense based on a defendant's good-faith but mistaken belief based on a well-grounded interpretation of an official statement of the law contained in a statute.

4) Requirement of "willful" violation

Cheek v. United States
498 U.S. 192 (1991).

Facts. Cheek (D) was convicted of "willfully" evading taxes and failing to file a return. D's defense was that he believed that he owed no taxes and that the tax laws were unconstitutional. While deliberating, the jury indicated they were divided as to D's honest and reasonable belief that he owed no taxes. The judge gave further instructions that "an honest but unreasonable belief does not negate willfulness." "[a]dvice or research resulting in the conclusion that wages . . . are not income or that tax laws are unconstitutional is not objectively reasonable," and "[p]ersistent refusal to acknowledge the law does not constitute a good faith misunderstanding of the law." D appealed. The court of appeals affirmed. The Supreme Court granted certiorari.

Issue. Was the trial court correct in instructing that only an objectively reasonable misunderstanding of the law negates the requirement of willfulness?

Held. No. Remanded for further proceedings.

- ♦ We have long held that ignorance of the law is no defense, but because of the proliferation of laws, Congress has lessened the burden by requiring specific intent to violate certain tax laws.

- ♦ In *United States v. Murdoch*, 290 U.S. 389 (1933), the Court held that an accused was entitled to an instruction with respect to whether he acted in good faith based on his actual belief.

- ♦ As it has evolved, "willful" means the "voluntary, intentional violation of a known legal duty." It requires proof that: (i) the law imposed a duty on D; (ii) D knew of his duty; and (iii) D voluntarily and intentionally violated that duty.

- ♦ One cannot "know" of a duty if there is a good faith misunderstanding of that duty. However, a good faith misunderstanding is not the same as a researched conclusion that is wrong. Such a taxpayer may not ignore his duty without risking criminal prosecution.

5) Knowledge of regulation

In *Liparota v. United States*, 471 U.S. 419 (1985), Liparota owned a sandwich shop that was not authorized to accept food stamps. On three occasions, Liparota purchased food stamps from an undercover agent for less than their face value. This was a violation of food stamp regulations. Federal law provided that anyone who knowingly uses, transfers, acquires, alters, or possesses coupons in any manner not authorized by the regulations is guilty of an offense. Liparota was tried for illegally acquiring and possessing the food stamps. The Court found that in the absence of a contrary purpose in the language or legislative history of a statute forbidding knowing conduct, the government must prove that the defendant knew his conduct to be unauthorized by law. The statute itself requires "knowing" conduct, but does not specify what element that knowledge relates to. Criminal statutes that do not require mens rea generally have a disfavored status. When it is not clear that Congress intended the statute not to require mens rea, the courts will construe the statute to require mens rea. Thus, the government had to prove that Liparota knew his acquisition or possession of food stamps was in a manner unauthorized by statute or regulations.

6) Knowledge of or intent to violate the law not required

Defendant in *United States v. Ansaldi*, 372 F.3d 118 (2d Cir. 2004), was charged with selling the controlled substance GBL, a chemical compound that is converted to the "date rape" drug GHB when metabolized by the body. Defendant claimed he did not know GBL was a controlled substance. The relevant statute provides that it is "unlawful to 'knowingly or intentionally ... distribute ... a controlled substance.'" The court stated that the drug law is different from the tax evasion statute that requires knowledge of the law for conviction. Without further explanation, the court stated knowledge of or intent to violate the law was not an element of this crime.

7) Knowledge of wrong but not of specific law required

In *United States v. Overholt*, 307 F.3d 1231 (10th Cir. 2002), defendant was charged with "willful" violation of the Safe Water Drinking Act by unlawfully dumping contaminated waste water. While the jury was instructed that it must find that the defendant knew he was doing something in violation of the law, the judge refused to instruct that the jury must find the defendant knew of the specific law he was violating. The conviction was upheld on appeal; the court found that *Liparota* and *Cheek* did not govern, but *International Minerals & Chemical Corp.*, 402 U.S. 558 (1971), did. Defendant in *International* knowingly transported corrosive liquids. The Court held that the defendant did not have to know of the existence and meaning of applicable regulations, but only that the actions defendant knowingly committed violated the regulation. The Court said that environmental laws were complex, and that Congress did not intend that those handling dangerous chemicals be burdened by having to inform themselves of what the law required. The word "willful" in the statute did not require proof of knowledge of the regulation allegedly violated.

8) Ignorance of laws imposing a duty to act

Lambert v. California
355 U.S. 225 (1957).

Facts. Lambert (D) was convicted under a Los Angeles ordinance that required convicted felons to register with the police. The ordinance defined "convicted person" as any person who had been convicted of a felony in California, or convicted of any offense in any other state, which, if committed in California, would have been punishable as a felony. Another section of the ordinance required any convicted person who stayed more than five days in the city or who had visited the city more than five times in a 30-day period to register with the police. Failure to register was a continuing offense, each day's failure to register being treated as a separate offense. D was arrested on suspicion of another crime and charged with violating the registration ordinance. She appeals her conviction.

Issue. Does a city ordinance that requires convicted persons to register with the police violate the Due Process Clause when it is applied to a person who had no actual knowledge of her duty to register?

Held. Yes. Judgment reversed and case remanded.

♦ It is a general maxim of criminal law that ignorance of the law is no excuse; however, the conduct prohibited by the city ordinance here is passive. Mere presence in the city constitutes the violation and there is no requirement that the convicted person have any knowledge of the registration ordinance.

♦ It is true that the police power is broad, but due process places some limits on its exercise. Notice is a key part of due process and the principle of notice is appropriate where a person, wholly unaware of any wrongdoing, is brought before a court in a criminal case.

♦ The ordinance's only purpose is for the administrative convenience of the police. But when D became aware of the existence of the law, it was already too late; she was given no chance to comply and thereby avoid punishment.

♦ Therefore, to comply with due process, it must be shown that D had actual knowledge of the duty to register, or that there was a probability of such knowledge. Otherwise, D cannot be punished for conduct that would have been innocent if done by other members of the community.

Dissent (Frankfurter, Harlan, Whittaker, JJ.). Numerous laws enacted under the police power of the state require no knowledge of the existence of the law on the part of the defendant. The majority bases its decision on an untenable distinction between affirmative and passive acts.

Comment. The rule that ignorance or mistake of law is no defense is less strictly applied when the accused's crime is one of omission. The Model Penal Code expresses this principle more generally, providing that ignorance or mistake of law is a defense when "the statute or other enactment defining the offense is not known to the actor and has not been published or otherwise reasonably made available prior to the conduct alleged." [Model Penal Code §2.04(3)(a)].

Chapter IV
Rape

A. Introduction

Laws concerning rape have evolved along with the place of women in society. In a real sense, such developments reflect changes in our view of the victims rather man the crime. Unlike victims of other crimes, women were long held responsible for avoiding rape. Whether women were criticized for how they were dressed, or where they were walking, or the establishments they patronized, they were held accountable for their own victimization. For many years, various state penal codes defined rape as sexual intercourse under various circumstances "with a female not the wife of the perpetrator." This traditional exemption for husbands who forcibly raped their wives was only one of the failings found in many state penal codes. Others included the gender-specific nature of the crime, as well as the degree of force or resistance required.

B. Actus Reus

1. Introduction

The offense of rape generally consists of forcible nonconsensual sexual penetration. In the absence of force or threat of force, nonconsensual sexual intercourse was traditionally a criminal offense only if the victim was underage, unconscious, or mentally incompetent. However, a minority of states now treat all nonconsensual intercourse as a criminal offense.

2. Reasonableness of Victim's Fears

State v. Rusk
424 A.2d 720 (Md. 1981).

Facts. The prosecuting witness, Pat, met Rusk (D) at a bar. D knew Pat's friend. Pat said she was leaving, and D asked her for a ride home. Pat drove D to his house in a neighborhood Pat was unfamiliar with. D invited Pat to come into his house, but Pat declined. D reached over, turned off the car engine, and took the keys, repeating his invitation. Pat was afraid that D would rape her by the way D looked at her, but she went with D into his house. She made no attempt to leave when D momentarily left the room. She asked D if she could leave, but D told her he wanted her to stay. Pat begged to leave and told D he could get other girls, but D became insistent. Pat started to cry and D put his hands on her throat, lightly choking her. Pat asked D if he would let her go if she did what he wanted; D said yes, and Pat proceeded to perform the sex acts D wanted. Afterwards, D returned Pat's car keys and Pat left. She immediately reported the incident to the police. D and two friends testified to the effect that Pat willingly accompanied D, and D stated that Pat got upset only after the sex acts. D was convicted of second degree rape, but the court of appeals reversed the conviction on the ground that Pat did not resist and did not possess fear great enough to overcome an attempt to resist. The State (P) appeals.

Issue. Is the reasonableness of a rape victim's fear a factual question for the jury?

Held. Yes. Judgment reversed.

- ♦ Lack of consent is established through proof of resistance or by proof that the victim failed to resist because of fear. The victim must have actual and reasonable fear. The reasonableness of the victim's fear is a question of fact for the factfinder, based on the evidence.

- ♦ The evidence in this case is sufficient to allow a reasonable jury to conclude that Pat's fear was reasonable and prevented her further resistance. The appellate court erred in substituting its own judgment for the jury's.

Dissent. All essential elements of a crime must be sustained by the evidence. There is no evidence that D did anything to create Pat's fears or made any intimidating threats. Pat may have actually feared D, but D did nothing reasonably calculated to give rise to such fear.

3. Nonphysical Threats

a. In *State v. Thompson*, 792 P.2d 1103 (Mont. 1990), a high school principal was charged with forcing a student to engage in sexual intercourse by threatening to prevent her from graduating. The charges were dismissed, and the dismissals were affirmed on appeal. The reasoning was that the victim was not "forced" to submit to sexual intercourse because there was no physical compulsion, and no use or threat of imminent bodily harm. While agreeing that the victim had been intimidated, the court declined to include intimidation (fear, apprehension) within the definition of force.

b. In *Commonwealth v. Mlinarich*, 498 A.2d 395 (Pa. Super. 1985), a 14-year-old victim was lawfully removed from a juvenile detention center by the defendant. Once she was at his home, the victim submitted to defendant's sexual demands because he threatened to return her to the detention center if she refused. The defendant was convicted of rape "by threat of forcible compulsion." The conviction was reversed by the superior court. The reversal was upheld on the grounds that qualifying nonviolent acts as forcible compulsion would result in an ambiguous, generic definition of force, which would create a wholly elastic definition of rape. In his dissent, one judge cogently pointed out that "force" has more than one common and approved meaning. Within those meanings, "to constrain or compel by physical, moral, or intellectual means or by the exigencies of the circumstances" would clearly include the defendant's action.

4. Eliminating the Force Requirement

a. Meaning of "physical force"

State in the Interest of M.T.S.
609 A.2d 1266 (N.J. 1992).

Facts. C.G., a 15-year-old girl, lived with her family and M.T.S., a 17-year-old boy. C.G. claimed to have awakened with D on top of her, having already penetrated her. C.G. slapped D and told him to get off her and leave, which D did. D claimed that the encounter had started consensually. At trial, the court did not find that C.G. had been sleeping, but that she had not consented, and that second degree sexual assault had been proven. The verdict was overturned by the appellate division. The state petitioned for certiorari.

Issue. Does the statutory requirement of "physical force" mean the use of force to overcome lack of consent?

Held. No. Appellate division reversed.

- ♦ To require that the element of force be extrinsic to the sexual act would not only reintroduce a resistance requirement into the sexual assault law, but would also immunize many acts of criminal sexual contact short of penetration. Further, it would be fundamentally inconsistent with the legislative purpose underlying the relevant statute to eliminate any consideration of whether the victim resisted or expressed nonconsent.

- Any penetration done without the affirmative and voluntary consent of the victim to the specific act of penetration constitutes the offense of sexual assault.

Comment. The court concedes that "cases such as this are inherently fact sensitive, and depend on the reasonable judgment and common sense of judges and juries." Does that make the standard unconstitutionally vague?

b. Coercive circumstances

M.C. v. Bulgaria
15 Eur. Ct. H.R. 627 (2003 WL 23721668).

Facts. M.C. (P), a Bulgarian national, alleged that she was raped when she was 14 years and 10 months old. She had gone with two men she knew and their friends to a disco bar. On the return ride home, over P's objections, the group stopped for a swim at a reservoir. P remained in the car. One of the men returned to the car and had sex with her. P claimed that she tried to push him away but that she was forced to have sex, was scared, and did not have the strength to scream. Later, the group stopped at a house where another man forced her to have sex with him. P claimed that she did not have the strength to resist violently but begged him to stop. When P returned home, her mother took her to the hospital. The medical examiner found that her hymen had been freshly torn and she had four small oval-shaped bruises on her neck. After a criminal investigation was launched, the accused men claimed that the sex was consensual. The investigation was halted when prosecutors found insufficient proof of the allegations. Two appeals were dismissed. P then filed a complaint against the Bulgarian government under the European Convention on Human Rights.

Issue. Did the government violate its positive obligations under the European Convention on Human Rights?

Held. Yes. Damages to be paid to P by the Bulgarian government for the psychological trauma resulting at least partly from the shortcomings in the Bulgarian authorities' investigation and approach.

- The relevant Convention provisions are: Article 3, "No one shall be subjected to torture or to inhuman or degrading treatment or punishment"; Article 8, "Everyone has the right to respect for his private . . . life"; and Article 13, "Everyone whose rights and freedoms as set forth in [the] Convention are violated shall have an effective remedy before a national authority."

- On appeal, it was held that there was no criminal act unless the alleged victim resisted and was coerced by physical force or threats. P argues that the local law requirement of proof of the victim's physical resistance leaves certain acts of rape unpunished. P also argues that by setting the age for consent at 14 and then limiting prosecution for rape to cases of violent resistance, Bulgaria leaves children with insufficient protection against rape.

- The rape statutes of most European countries require proof of violence or threat. However, in Europe and some other parts of the world, there has been a trend toward abandoning traditional, narrow interpretations of the law. The statutes of European countries no longer require the victim to resist physically, and in case law and legal theory, lack of consent, not force, is considered an essential element of rape. It has been recognized in international criminal law that force is not an element of rape and that taking advantage of coercive circumstances is also punishable. And courts in the United States are increasingly taking into account social science data indicating that some women become frozen with fear at the start of a sexual attack and cannot resist.

- Although under the European Convention member states may choose the means to secure compliance with Article 8 of the Convention, the states have an obligation to enact criminal law provisions that effectively punish any nonconsensual sexual act, even in the absence of physical resistance by the victim, and to apply them through effective investigation and prosecution.

- In this case, little was done to assess the credibility of the alleged rapists, including one's claim that 14-year-old P started caressing him minutes after having sex for the first time with another man. The prosecutors apparently believed that without direct proof of rape, such as traces of violence and resistance, they could not infer proof of lack of consent. It also appears that they thought that without proof of resistance, it could not be concluded that the perpetrators had understood that P had not consented. The prosecutors failed to attempt to prove mens rea by assessing all of the circumstances, such as evidence that the perpetrators had deliberately misled P and taken her to a deserted area, creating an environment of coercion.

- The government argues that the legal system provides for the possibility of a civil action for damages against the perpetrators, but effective protection against rape requires criminal law measures.

5. Deception

a. Ambivalent statements of threat

People v. Evans
379 N.Y.S.2d 912 (1975).

Facts. Evans (D) met a petite 20-year-old college student at the airport. D told her he was a psychologist doing a magazine article and proceeded to ask her various questions. D took her to a bar for a "sociological experiment" where he observed her reaction to the people there. Then he took her to his apartment and, after a time, began to undress her. She resisted and D told her he was disappointed that she failed the test. He then told her, "Look where you are. You are in the apartment of a strange man. I could kill you. I could rape you. I could hurt you physically." The girl became afraid as she realized her situation. Then D began telling her about his lost love who had died and how much the girl reminded D of the lost love. D thereby engaged her sympathy, and several sex acts followed throughout the night. There is no evidence that the girl resisted. D was charged with rape and brought to trial.

Issue. May a man be convicted of rape on the basis of allegedly threatening statements that may be consistent with either guilt or innocence?

Held. No. D is acquitted.

- There can be no rape that is achieved by fraud, trick, or stratagem. As long as there is actual consent to the act, fully understood by the victim, there is no rape.

- Seduction has been made a statutory offense in some states. In New York, there are no existing penal sanctions against seduction.

- The question is whether D's statements undermined the victim's will. The words could be interpreted as a threat, or as a mere statement of the position the girl was in and of the harm that could have come to her had she been with someone other than D. Because a crime is charged, the criminal intent of D must be shown beyond a reasonable doubt. The ambiguity of D's statements falls short of proof beyond a reasonable doubt.

b. Fraud in the inducement

Boro v. Superior Court, 210 Cal. Rptr. 122 (1985), deals with a rape victim who was tricked into having intercourse in the belief that it was part of a medical procedure. The court held that it would not find that deception vitiated consent because the legislature had not specifically included such a principle in the rape statute. If the deception causes a misunderstanding as to the fact itself, *i.e.,* having intercourse (fraud in the factum), there is no legally recognized consent because what happened is not that for which consent was given. If the deception goes to a collateral matter (fraud in the inducement) (here the victim was told she had to engage in intercourse to cure her dangerous, possibly fatal disease), the consent is as effective as any other consent.

C. Mens Rea

1. Introduction

Rape is a difficult crime for the judicial system to address. Because it is one of the most violent and despicable crimes, fairness to victims and society in general requires effective enforcement. However, it is difficult to distinguish between truthful and false complainants. The necessary mens rea is not easily articulated, nor are the rules easily applied to specific cases. *[See, e.g.,* Commonwealth v. Sherry, *infra]*

2. Subjective Belief that Victim Consented

Commonwealth v. Sherry
437 N.E.2d 224 (Ma. 1982).

Facts. A registered nurse who worked with Sherry (D), a doctor at the same hospital, was at a party with D. While there, the nurse met Hussain and Lefkowitz (Ds). At various times during the party, each of Ds made sexual advances toward the nurse. Ds then grabbed the nurse and took her outside, saying they were going to Rockport. The nurse protested but did not physically resist, because she believed they were kidding and would leave her alone. Ds took her to Lefkowitz's home. They toured the house, and in a bedroom, Ds began to remove their clothes. The nurse protested, but each D in turn had intercourse with her. They then made the nurse bathe. Eventually, they returned her to her car. At their trial, Ds testified that the nurse voluntarily accompanied them and consented to the acts of intercourse. Ds moved to dismiss for lack of force or threat of bodily injury, but the trial judge denied the motions. The jury convicted each D of rape. Ds appeal.

Issue. Does the accused's subjective belief that the victim did not object to intercourse constitute a defense to the crime of rape?

Held. No. Judgment affirmed.

- The evidence in the case supports the jury's verdict. A rape victim need not use physical force to resist, as long as the resistance used demonstrates an honest and real lack of consent.

- Ds' request for an instruction that the jury had to find they had actual knowledge of the victim's lack of consent was properly rejected by the judge. This instruction essentially raised a defense of good faith mistake as to consent, although it was not based on a reasonable good faith mistake of fact and therefore could not be given.

- The crime of rape essentially requires the victim's lack of consent. A victim's statement of "no" can imply nothing but nonconsent. Even if the perpetrator does not believe the statement, he should be convicted. The subjective belief of the aggressor cannot constitute a defense.

3. Jury Instruction Regarding Consent

Commonwealth v. Fischer
721 A.2d 1111 (Pa. Super. Ct. 1998).

Facts. Both Fischer (D) and the victim testified that a couple of hours before the incident at issue, they went to D's dorm room and engaged in intimate contact. The victim testified that the contact was limited to kissing and fondling. D claimed they engaged in "rough sex," which culminated in the victim performing fellatio on him. D claimed the victim acted aggressively by holding his arms above his head, biting his chest, stating, "You know you want me," and initiating oral sex. After a brief separation, the students met up again and went to D's room. The victim testified that D locked the door, pushed her onto the bed, straddled her, held her wrists above her head, and forced his penis into her mouth. She claimed she struggled throughout and repeatedly stated she did not want to engage in sex. She said that D ignored her pleas, and said, "Nobody will know where you are." When the victim tried to leave, D blocked her path. After striking D in the groin with her knee, the victim was able to escape. D claimed the victim consented to "a quick one." D said he began to engage in the same type of behavior the victim had exhibited in their previous encounter. D admitted that he held the young woman's arms above her head, straddled her, and placed his penis at her mouth. When she replied, "no," D answered, "No means yes." After another verbal exchange wherein the victim said she had to leave, D insisted that "she wanted it." D claimed when she answered, "No, I honestly don't," he stopped. D claimed the two then lay side by side on the bed and continued to kiss and fondle one another. D claimed the victim enjoyed his actions, but at one point stood up and said she had to leave. When D tried to touch her thigh, she said she was "getting pissed," and before D could ready himself to walk her to her room, she abruptly left. Evidence at trial showed the victim had been treated by a physician, and her friends testified she was nervous, upset, and shaken after the incident. D's attorney argued that D was sexually inexperienced and, relying on the first encounter, thought he was acting with the victim's consent. D was convicted on all counts and appeals.

Issue. Did the court err in affirming the trial court's finding that trial counsel was not ineffective for failing to request that the trial court provide a specific jury instruction concerning petitioner's "reasonable mistake as to consent"?

Held. No. Conviction affirmed.

- To prove ineffectiveness of counsel, D must establish: (i) there is an underlying issue of arguable merit, (ii) there was an absence of a reasonable strategy on the part of prior counsel in acting or failing to act, and (iii) counsel's action or inaction resulted in prejudice.

- D is not entitled under our state law, by which we are bound, to the defense of reasonable mistake as to consent. His lawyer was not entitled to that instruction at the trial.

- The relief D seeks is a significant departure to our current law. We cannot announce a new rule of law and then find counsel ineffective for failing to predict the law would be changed.

4. Rejection of the Marital Exception

People v. Liberta
474 N.E.2d 567 (N.Y. 1984).

Facts. New York's rape statute included an exception for married persons. For purposes of the exception, a husband and wife were considered to be "not married" if at the time of the sexual assault they were living apart pursuant to a valid and effective court order that required living apart, a decree or judgment of separation, or a written agreement of separation. Liberta (D) was living apart from his wife pursuant to a family court order. D forcibly raped his wife during a visit with their son. D was convicted of rape, and the appellate court affirmed. D appeals, claiming that the marital exception creates a violation of equal protection because it burdens differently males who do not fall within the marital exception.

Issue. Is the marital exception to the crime of rape unconstitutional?

Held. Yes. Judgment affirmed.

- ♦ There is no rational basis for distinguishing between marital and nonmarital rape. The traditional notion that a married woman gives irrevocable implied consent does not justify the distinction. Rape is not simply a nonconsensual sexual act; it is a degrading, violent act that causes severe harm. Consent to such an act cannot be implied. Therefore, the rape statute applies to all males, whether they are married to their victims or not.

- ♦ A married woman has the same right to control her own body as does an unmarried woman, and a husband who feels aggrieved by his wife's refusal to engage in sexual intercourse must find relief in the courts governing domestic relations, not in forceful self-help.

- ♦ Another former rationale for the distinction between marital and nonmarital rape was that the married woman was the property of her husband, but a marriage license is not a license for a husband to forcibly rape his wife. The modern justification for the marital exception is that it protects against invasion of marital privacy. But the marital exception does not facilitate reconciliation, since a marriage subjected to forcible rape is hardly susceptible to reconciliation. Marital rape is no less serious than other types of rape and should be equally subject to prosecution.

D. Problems of Proof

1. Introduction

Because of the special difficulties involved in proving or disproving rape, the rules of evidence have been carefully considered in this area. Instructions about the complainant's credibility are carefully worded. Some corroboration of the complaint may be required. Special limitations on cross-examination also apply.

2. Corroboration

United States v. Wiley
492 F.2d 547 (D.C. Cir. 1974).

Facts. Wiley (D) and a co-defendant were tried for an alleged sexual assault on a 12-year-old victim. They were charged with carnal knowledge and taking indecent liberties with a minor. After D's jury trial, the indecent liberties charge was dismissed and the carnal knowledge charge was submitted to the jury. D was found guilty. D appeals.

Issue. Was there sufficient corroborative evidence to take the case to the jury?

Held. No. Judgment reversed.

- ♦ The law in this jurisdiction is that a person may not be convicted of a "sex offense" on the uncorroborated testimony of the alleged victim.

- ♦ No medical testimony was presented at trial although the victim had been examined by a doctor. With only the victim's accusation, the traditional purpose of the corroboration requirement—to avoid fabricated charges—requires reversal of D's conviction.

Concurrence. While it is an ancient rule that the testimony of a single witness is inadequate to prove a crime, the common law gradually moved away from that rule in all cases except perjury. Thirty-five states have rejected the requirement for rape. This jurisdiction retains the requirement in the absence of legislation. Traditionally, rape was considered a charge easily made, but once made, difficult to defend against, even if the defendant was innocent. The court here adopted the rule whereby independent corroborative evidence is regarded as sufficient when it would permit a jury to conclude beyond a reasonable doubt that the victim's version of what happened was not fabricated. The following are some of the policies behind requiring corroboration:

(i) False rape charges are more common than false charges of other crimes. This notion arises from the contention that women may fantasize rape or may have motives to fabricate charges, such as revenge, explanation for pregnancy, etc. However, rape is actually one of the most underreported crimes because of the treatment a victim receives in society.

(ii) Rape is unusually difficult to defend against: This policy stems from the usual absence of eyewitnesses and the supposed sympathy juries feel for the victim. However, the low rate of convictions where there is no corroborating evidence suggests that juries are actually skeptical of rape accusations.

(iii) Rape convictions result in severe sentences: Corroboration is sometimes required because of the severity of punishment imposed, yet more lenient punishment would not reflect the serious nature of the offense.

(iv) Racial and sexual discrimination: In the past, rape accusations may have been used to discriminate against blacks, who were disproportionately convicted of the offense. Corroboration was considered necessary to protect against this form of racism. It was also used to some extent to discriminate against women. Both forms of discrimination are disappearing in society.

3. Cross-Examination of the Victim

a. Introduction

Generally, character evidence is not admissible to prove conduct. Federal Rule of Evidence 608 allows such evidence for impeachment of a witness, but only under narrow restrictions. Formerly, a rape victim's character trait of unchastity could be used. Today, most jurisdictions have adopted "rape shield" laws that generally bar evidence of the victim's unchastity on the issue of consent. Most jurisdictions also do not allow proof of unchastity by specific instances of consensual intercourse with persons other than the defendant. Some jurisdictions have reached the same result by judicial decision.

b. Prior bad acts

State v. DeLawder
344 A.2d 446 (Md. Ct. Spec. App. 1975).

Facts. DeLawder (D) was charged with statutory rape of a girl less than 14 years old. D desired to discredit the prosecuting witness's testimony by revealing her possible biases, prejudices, or ulterior motives in making the allegations she did. D wanted to show that at the time of the alleged incident the girl thought she was pregnant by someone else and that she claimed D raped her because she was afraid to tell her mother that she had voluntarily had sexual intercourse with others. D would show that she had previously had sexual intercourse. The trial court sustained objections to this line of questioning and D was convicted. On appeal, the conviction was upheld. Then the United States Supreme Court decided *Davis v. Alaska*, 415 U.S. 308 (1974), which discussed the Confrontation Clause of the Sixth Amendment. The Court held that "the exposure of a witness's motivation in testifying is a proper and important function of the constitutionally protected right of cross-examination." The Court held that this principle outweighed the interests of protecting the confidentiality of juvenile adjudications of delinquency, the issue in the *Davis* case. In light of *Davis*, D seeks postconviction relief.

Issue. May a defendant use evidence of prior bad acts when such evidence may directly reveal the witness's biases, prejudices, or ulterior motives in testifying?

Held. Yes. Conviction overturned.

- The rationale for not allowing evidence of prior bad acts was that consent was not an issue in a statutory rape prosecution, and any bad reputation for unchastity was immaterial as an excuse.

- The prosecution's case here relied entirely on the girl's veracity. D should have been able to show her biases or ulterior motives. His inability to cross-examine as to these questions was a denial of the right to confrontation. The desirability of allowing the girl to perform her public duty of testifying free from embarrassment or damage to her reputation must yield to D's right to seek out the truth in his defense.

c. Psychiatric examination

Government of the Virgin Islands v. Scuito
623 F.2d 869 (3d Cir. 1980).

Facts. Scuito (D) was convicted of forcible rape. D and the victim told similar stories about the circumstances of the sex acts, the difference being whether D forced the woman. D sought a psychiatric examination of the woman because of her reputation for drug abuse and strange countenance and interests. The trial court refused to allow the exam. D appeals.

Issue. Does a trial judge have discretion as to whether to order a psychiatric examination of an alleged rape victim?

Held. Yes. Judgment affirmed.

- There are no evidence rules governing the use of a psychiatric examination, but many of the considerations regarding evidence of a rape victim's prior sexual conduct apply. [*See* Fed. R. Evid. 412] Both situations involve embarrassment to the victim, which may deter complaints and testimony by victims. The judge has discretion to allow the introduction of such evidence and to order such exams. The objective sought by D in this case could have been met by direct testimony of others in the community who observed the victim's behavior.

Chapter V
Homicide

A. Introduction

Homicide is the killing of one human by another. Homicide is not necessarily a crime, but it is a material element for the crimes of murder and manslaughter.

1. Types of Homicide

There are three types of homicide.

a. Justifiable homicide

A homicide is justifiable if it is commanded or authorized by law, such as when committed in execution of a sentence of death, in preventing an escape, or in pursuit of a dangerous fleeing felon.

b. Excusable homicide

Excusable homicide may be either accidental or in self-defense.

1) Accidental

For accidental homicide, the person must have committed the homicide while performing a lawful act with due care and without any intention of hurting the other.

2) Self-defense

Self-defense involves killing another upon sudden affray, merely in one's own defense or in defense of one's spouse, child, or parent, and not from any vindictive feeling.

3) Comment

Other homicides are excusable as a result of the status of the person committing the act (infants, feeble-minded persons, etc.), or because of an actual and reasonable mistake of fact.

c. Criminal homicide

Criminal homicide is the killing of another human being but without justification or excuse. The two important classifications here are "murder" and "manslaughter."

2. Elements of Criminal Homicide

a. Corpus delicti (the body of the crime)

The corpus delicti of a criminal homicide consists of two elements:

(i) A person is deceased; and

(ii) The death is a result of someone's criminality.

1) The victim

There is controversy whether an unborn infant was "living" at the time of the act that purportedly resulted in its death.

a) Majority view

The majority view presumes a child to be dead until proven otherwise. The proof of life required is that the child be expelled from the mother and using its own circulatory system.

b) Minority view

The minority view holds that the killing of a fetus is homicide.

2) Omission to act

Where there exists a legal duty to act, an omission to so act will constitute criminal homicide if such omission results in the killing of another human being. For example, the court found a legal duty existed where two elderly women lived together and one became incapacitated; the other did nothing to help her, creating culpable negligence when the first woman died.

b. Time limit

At common law, the death had to occur within one year and a day after the defendant's unlawful act causing the injury or there could be no prosecution for murder. This is still the law in most jurisdictions.

c. Criminal state of mind

Determination of the mental element (mens rea) is usually more difficult to establish than the physical element (actus reus). The classification of the mens rea distinguishes murder from manslaughter and the various degrees thereof.

B. Grading of Intended Killings— Murder

Murder is the unlawful killing of a human being by another human being with malice aforethought. This malice may be actual or may be implied by law.

1. Malice Aforethought

a. Introduction

The term "malice aforethought" does not approximate its literal meaning. Rather than relying on this misleading phrase, it is more appropriate to consider the various types of mens rea for murder that the common law came to recognize and that exist today in most jurisdictions:

1) Intent to kill

Conduct, accompanied by an intent to kill, that causes another's death constitutes murder, unless there are mitigating circumstances present, or the homicide is either justifiable or excusable.

2) Intent to inflict serious bodily harm

Conduct coupled with an intent to do serious bodily injury but without an intent to kill, which causes another's death, constitutes murder.

3) Depraved heart

Reckless conduct that a reasonable person would realize creates a high degree of risk of death or serious bodily injury to another, which actually causes the death of another, may constitute murder.

2. First and Second Degree Murder

a. Introduction

At common law, there were no degrees of murder. All homicide with "malice aforethought" was murder and punished by death. In order to reduce the punishment for less grievous homicides, most states classify murder. The typical classification is into first degree (homicide with "premeditation") and second degree (without "premeditation") murder.

b. First degree murder

First degree murder is all homicide with malice aforethought that is either (i) encompassed within the felony-murder rule of the jurisdiction (usually heinous felonies), or (ii) willful, deliberate, and premeditated.

1) Willful

The defendant must actually intend to kill.

2) Deliberate

The defendant must be possessed of a cool mind that is capable of reflection.

3) Premeditated

The defendant, having a cool mind, must in fact reflect before his act of killing. The defendant's state of mind is decisive during the length of time between the formation of the idea to kill and the actual killing.

4) Proof of state of mind

Premeditation, deliberation, and willful intent are subjective states of mind. The existence of these elements must be determined from the defendant's conduct in light of the surrounding circumstances.

5) Presumption of premeditation for certain homicides

Homicides perpetrated by poison or torture or after lying in wait for the victim, etc., are presumed by common law to have been premeditated.

a) "Irresistible impulse" does not preclude premeditation

Commonwealth v. Carrol

194 A.2d 911 (Pa. 1963).

Facts. Carrol (D) was convicted of first degree murder after he took a gun from near the bed and shot his wife twice in the back of the head while she was lying on the bed with her back to him. D's wife suffered from mental disorders and was allegedly sadistic and nagging. A psychiatrist testified that, in his opinion, D's act was an impulsive automatic reflex homicide as opposed to an intentional premeditated homicide. D appeals, claiming that his crime was at most second degree rather than first degree murder.

Issue. May a person be guilty of first degree murder when acting out of an "irresistible impulse"?

Held. Yes. Judgment affirmed.

- ◆ The intent to kill necessary to first degree murder may be found from D's own words or conduct or the surrounding circumstances together with all reasonable inferences therefrom, and may be inferred from the intentional use of a deadly weapon on a vital part of another's body.

- ◆ Whether the time period between forming the intent to kill and committing the killing was short or long is immaterial if the homicide was in fact intentional, willful, deliberate, and premeditated. The fact that D may not have established a plan to dispose of the body or escape is no defense if he acted deliberately.

- ◆ A psychiatrist's testimony that there was no premeditation need not be believed by the jury and was entitled to little weight since it was contradicted by D's own testimony that he "remembered the gun, took it down, and fired two shots" into the head of his sleeping wife.

- ◆ The relationship between D and his wife leading up to the murder may have created an irresistible impulse or an inability of D to control himself, but could not excuse his deliberate act.

b) Elements of proof

State v. Guthrie

461 S.E.2d 163 (W. Va. 1995).

Facts. Three co-workers, dishwashers, were joking in the restaurant kitchen and Farley poked fun at Guthrie (D), who was in a bad mood. Farley told D to "lighten up" and snapped him with a dishtowel. When the dishtowel hit D's nose, D became enraged, moved toward Farley, pulled a knife from his pocket, and stabbed him in the neck. D also stabbed Farley in the arm as he fell to the floor. Farley looked up and cried: "Man, I was just kidding around." D responded: "Well, man, you should have never hit me in my face." Upon his arrest, D confessed. The police described him as calm and cooperative. D experiences up to two panic attacks daily and was being treated for them at the time of the killing, he suffers chronic depression, an obsession with his nose (body dysmorphic disorder) that began when he was 17 (he was 29 at the time of the trial), and borderline personality disorder. D testified he suffered an intense panic attack just before the stabbing. D said he avoided the boisterous activity in the kitchen, that he was quiet and kept to himself, but Farley kept irritating him. At trial, D did not understand his overreaction. All witnesses testified that D was not attacked, Farley was just playing around. Contrary to his written statement, D testified that he could not recall stabbing Farley, and that he "lost it" when Farley hit him in the nose. A psychiatrist testified that D was sane at the time of the killing because he knew the difference between right and wrong and could have conformed his actions accordingly. The jury was instructed that murder in the first degree is when one person kills another person unlawfully, willfully, maliciously, deliberately, and premeditatedly. In its effort to define these terms, the trial court gave three instructions. Instruction No. 8 stated: "The Court instructs the jury that to constitute a willful, deliberate and premeditated killing, it is not necessary that the intention to kill should exist for any particular length of time prior to the actual killing; it is only necessary that such intention should have come into existence for the first time at the time of such killing, or at any time previously." Instruction No. 10 stated: 'The Court instructs the jury that in order to constitute a 'premeditated' murder an intent to kill need exist only for an instant." Instruction No. 12 stated: "The Court instructs the jury that what is meant by the language willful, deliberate and premeditated is that the killing be intentional." D was convicted of first degree murder. D appeals.

Issue. Were the jury instructions, when given together, wrong and confusing?

Held. Yes. Judgment reversed and case remanded.

- These instructions fail to adequately inform the jury of the difference between first and second degree murder and provide no guidance as to what constitutes premeditation. Also of concern is the manner in which the instructions confuse premeditation with the intent to kill.

- The definition of premeditation and deliberation is confusing, if not meaningless. To allow the state to prove premeditation and deliberation by only showing that the intention came "into existence for the first time at the time of such killing" completely eliminates the distinction between the two degrees of murder.

- Although premeditation and deliberation are not measured by any particular period of time, there must be some period between the formation of the intent to kill and the actual killing, which indicates the killing is by prior calculation and design. This means there must be an opportunity for some reflection on the intention to kill after it is formed.

- When the state seeks a conviction of first degree murder based on premeditation and deliberation, the trial court should instruct the jury that first degree murder consists of an intentional, deliberate, and premeditated killing, which means that the killing is done after a period of time for prior reflection. The accused must kill purposefully after thinking about the intent to kill. The time required for reflection is any interval between forming the intent and execution, which is of a sufficient duration for the accused to be fully conscious of what he intended.

c. Second degree murder

In most states, murder not falling within the first degree murder category is second degree murder.

1) No premeditation

Those murders committed with the intent to kill but lacking premeditation and deliberation are of the second degree.

a) Intentional

Both first and second degree murder include "intentional" homicide. Since it may actually be impossible for the mind to function in a way so that an intentional homicide occurs without at least some premeditation, the only difference between first and second degree murder exists in the degree of the premeditation (a difficult distinction to make).

b) Voluntary manslaughter

However, if the rationale of second degree murder is that it does not involve premeditation, then a conflict between it and intentional (voluntary) manslaughter inevitably arises. Voluntary manslaughter does not include malice (since it is a homicide that arises from a sudden passion and on adequate provocation); therefore, it seems that the difference between voluntary manslaughter and second degree murder is in the adequacy of the provocation that causes the killer's act—a more substantial provocation must be required to classify the homicide as voluntary manslaughter.

2) Felony-murder

Those felony-murders where the felony in question is not enumerated in the first degree murder statute are considered to be second degree murder.

3) Wanton disregard for human life

Killings that indicate the defendant's wanton and willful disregard for human life are also second degree murder (*e.g.*, playing "Russian roulette" with a loaded revolver).

a) This standard seems to approach the negligence standard, but in order for second degree murder to exist, the defendant's act must be sufficiently wanton to imply malice.

b) Involuntary manslaughter may also arise from criminal negligence (although sufficient wantonness is not present to imply malice aforethought). Here again, the distinction between second degree murder and involuntary manslaughter is a difficult one to draw.

c) Criminal negligence, even of a wanton nature, cannot ever amount to first degree murder because negligence necessarily rules out the possibility of premeditation.

d) The element of provocation, which is discussed *infra* in connection with manslaughter, may reduce murder to manslaughter.

e) The character of the defendant (*e.g.*, personal turpitude) may also have an effect on whether the murder is held to be first or second degree murder.

3. Provocation

a. Common law reasonable person test

At common law, sufficient provocation is that which causes a reasonable person to lose his normal self-control. Although a reasonable person who has lost control over himself would not kill, his homicidal reaction to the provocation is at least understandable. The provocation defense is available only if the offender moves quickly (*i.e.*, succumbs to the provocation right away); too much delay can lose the defense.

b. Traditional common law limits on provocation

Girouard v. State
583 A.2d 718 (Md. 1991).

Facts. During an argument with his wife, Girouard (D) stabbed her 19 times after she graphically disparaged his sexual ability, said she did not love him, demanded a divorce, and told him she had filed charges to have him court-martialed. D then non-fatally slit his own wrists and called the police. Police found D wandering around, despondent and tearful. D was convicted of second degree murder and sentenced to 22 years in prison, 10 of which were suspended. D appeals.

Issue. Should the mitigating factor of provocation be limited only to the traditional circumstances of: extreme assault and battery upon a defendant; mutual combat; illegal arrest; injury or serious abuse of a close relative; or sudden discovery of a defendant's spouse committing adultery?

Held. Yes. Judgment affirmed.

- This state holds, as do most jurisdictions, that words alone, even "fighting words," do not constitute provocation adequate to reduce the crime of murder to manslaughter.

Comment. Most cases of provocation involve inflammatory words being used by one person to another, who reacts with force. What if the disparaging remarks in this case were said to other people about D and in D's presence? Or, what if the remarks were made to D, but loudly enough for others to hear? Would the added factor of "humiliation" tip the scales?

c. Provocation out of presence of defendant

Maher v. People
10 Mich. 212 (1862).

Facts. Maher (D) was convicted of assault with intent to kill. D tried to kill a man he had been told had had sexual intercourse with his wife. The trial court excluded evidence of provocation on the rule that the provocation had to be committed in the presence of the defendant. D appeals.

Issue. To be admissible, must provocation have been committed in D's presence?

Held. No. Judgment reversed.

- The evidence should have been admitted. The acts amounting to the provocation need not be committed in D's presence. Adequate provocation is that which would provoke a reasonable person, before a reasonable time has elapsed for the passion to cool, and is the result of temporary excitement.

- Here, D seeing his wife and another man go into the woods, and being told that his wife had had sexual relations with the man the day before, was sufficient evidence to go to the jury on the issue of provocation. A new trial is granted.

Comment. The common law did not permit a jury to find provocation in any and all situations in which the jury could find the circumstances reasonably provocative. The more lenient approach in *Maher* is recognized in most states today.

d. Model Penal Code

People v. Casassa
404 N.E.2d 1310 (N.Y. 1980).

Facts. Casassa (D) became infatuated with Lo Consolo, who rejected D's advances. D eavesdropped on Lo Consolo's apartment. Finally, D took several bottles of liquor to Lo Consolo's apartment, but she rejected his offer. D then stabbed her to death. D eventually confessed and was charged with second degree murder. D claimed as a defense that he acted under the influence of extreme emotional disturbance based on his obsession with Lo Consolo. A state witness testified that D's mental state was the result of stress he created within himself. The trial court found D guilty on the ground that the test of extreme emotional disturbance was objective, not subjective, and that D's emotional state was so peculiar to him that it could not be considered reasonable. D appeals.

Issue. Does the defense of extreme emotional disturbance require a completely subjective evaluation of reasonableness?

Held. No. Judgment affirmed.

- Under the criminal statute, D has the burden of proof as to the affirmative defense of extreme emotional disturbance. The defense is broader than the traditional "heat of passion" defense that it replaced, because extreme emotional disturbance need not be spontaneous; it can be one that affects the accused's mind for a substantial period of time before becoming manifest. It requires a mental infirmity short of the level of insanity but sufficient to render the accused less culpable for his actions.

- There are two elements to the defense: (i) an act done under the influence of extreme emotional disturbance; and (ii) a reasonable explanation for the disturbance as viewed by a person in the defendant's situation under the circumstances as the defendant believed them to be.

- D claims that the extreme emotional disturbance defense is based on a subjective standard of reasonableness. The first element of the defense is clearly subjective, but the second requires an objectively reasonable explanation. The jury evaluates the defense by viewing the accused's internal situation and his perception of the external circumstances, and then determining whether from that viewpoint the explanation for the emotional disturbance was reasonable. By this means, an accused has a fair opportunity for mitigation, while the fact finder is not required to find mitigation whenever emotional disturbance exists.

- The trial court applied the correct standard when it considered D's mental disability but found that D's excuse was so peculiar to him that it did not merit mitigation. D acted out of malevolence, not pursuant to an understandable human response that deserves mercy.

C. Grading of Unintended Killings

1. Manslaughter

Manslaughter is a catch-all category that includes homicides that are not bad enough to be murder but that are too bad to be of no criminal consequence whatever.

a. Voluntary manslaughter

Voluntary manslaughter is an intentional homicide committed under extenuating circumstances that mitigate but do not justify or excuse the killing. The principal extenuating circumstance is that the defendant acted in a state of passion engendered by adequate provocation.

1) Heat of passion. The elements of heat of passion are:

a) There must have been a reasonable provocation.

b) The defendant must have been in fact provoked.

c) A reasonable person so provoked would not have cooled off in the interval of time between the provocation and the delivery of the fatal blow.

d) The defendant must not in fact have cooled off during that interval.

b. Involuntary manslaughter

Involuntary manslaughter is an unintentional homicide committed without excuse, justification, or malice. Involuntary manslaughter may result from the commission of a lawful act in a negligent manner, or from the commission of an unlawful act that is not a felony (the misdemeanor-manslaughter rule).

1) Criminal and tort negligence compared

Most states require a higher degree of negligence for criminal liability than that required for ordinary (tort) negligence. The negligence required is either one or both of the following two elements:

(a) The defendant's conduct must involve a high degree of risk of death or serious bodily injury, in addition to the unreasonable risk required for ordinary negligence.

b) Whatever the degree of risk required, the defendant must be aware that his conduct creates this risk.

c) Note that if both are required, then "recklessness" is a more appropriate term than negligence.

2) Hazardous business conditions

Commonwealth v. Welansky
55 N.E.2d 902 (Mass. 1944).

Facts. Welansky (D) was hospitalized for an illness. At the same time, in a nightclub D owned, a 16-year-old employee used a lighted match in trying to see to replace a burned-out light bulb. In so doing, he lit some flammable decorations. The fire spread throughout the club and several customers died. D was convicted of manslaughter because he permitted the flammable decorations, defective wiring, overcrowding, and absence of suitable means of escape, all of which proximately led to the deaths. D appeals.

Issue. May a person be convicted of manslaughter merely for permitting hazardous conditions to exist on his business premises?

Held. Yes. Judgment affirmed.

♦ Involuntary manslaughter consists of death resulting through wanton or reckless conduct. If there is a duty of care for the safety of business visitors invited to premises that D controls, wanton or reckless conduct may consist in intentional failure to take such care in disregard of the probable harmful consequences to them.

♦ Knowing facts that would cause a reasonable person to know the danger is equivalent to knowing the danger, even if the person is so heedless as to not actually know the danger. Even if D actually thought he was careful, the facts showed the risk was so great that his inaction was wanton and reckless.

♦ D was more than just negligent or even grossly negligent. Fire in a public place is always a danger, and D's disregard for the safety of his patrons in the event of a fire from any cause was wanton and reckless.

3) Homicide through the use of automobiles

a) Simple negligence

In *State v. Barnett*, 63 S.E.2d 57 (S.C. 1951), Barnett was convicted of involuntary manslaughter because of a homicide resulting from his negligent operation of a car. He appealed, claiming that the court erred in charging that ordinary negligence is sufficient for conviction. The court held that ordinary negligence in the handling of a dangerous instrumentality is equivalent to culpable negligence. Generally, involuntary manslaughter requires that the accused's negligence be "gross." However, because of the inherent danger of an automobile, simple negligence is sufficient for an involuntary manslaughter conviction.

b) Special statutes

Some states, such as California, provide for a special category of manslaughter—manslaughter in the operation of a motor vehicle:

(1) It is a felony to unintentionally kill a person while operating an automobile in a criminally negligent manner.

(2) It is a misdemeanor to kill a person while operating an automobile in a negligent manner.

4) Sufficient evidence for felony reckless manslaughter

People v. Hall
999 P.2d 207 (Colo. 2000).

Facts. While skiing on Vail Mountain, Hall (D) flew off of a knoll and collided with Cobb. Cobb sustained traumatic brain injuries and died. D was charged with felony reckless manslaughter. At a preliminary hearing, it was determined that D's conduct "did not rise to the level of dangerousness" required under Colorado law to uphold a manslaughter conviction and the county court dismissed the charges. The district court affirmed. It determined that in order for D's conduct to have been reckless, it must have been "at least more likely than not" that death would result. The court determined that skiing too fast for the conditions is not likely to cause another's death; thus it found that D's conduct did not constitute a "substantial and unjustifiable" risk of death. The Supreme Court of Colorado granted certiorari.

Issue. Did the state present sufficient evidence to establish probable cause that D committed reckless manslaughter?

Held. Yes. Judgment reversed and case remanded.

- The district court erred in its construction of "recklessness," finding that for the risk to be "substantial," it must "be at least more likely than not that death would result." However, depending on the circumstances of a particular case, a risk of death that has less than a 50% chance of occurring may be a substantial risk. Because this case was dismissed at the preliminary hearing, we consider the facts in the light most favorable to the prosecution.

- Specific facts support a reasonable inference that D created a substantial and unjustifiable risk that he would cause another's death. Eyewitnesses said that D was skiing too fast for the conditions, lacked control, and used improper technique for skiing bumps. D admitted that he first saw Cobb when D was airborne and that he could not stop when he saw people below him just before the collision. Thus, in addition to finding that D was skiing at a very high rate of speed, a reasonable person could have concluded that D was unable to anticipate or avoid a potential collision with a skier on the trail below him and that the extent of the injuries that might result from such a collision included the possibility of death.

- D's extremely fast and unsafe skiing served only his own enjoyment. Thus, a reasonable person could have found that D's creation of a substantial risk was unjustifiable.

- D is a trained ski racer and was an employee of a ski area. We must determine whether D's conduct constituted a "gross deviation" from the standard of care that a reasonable law-abiding ski racer and resort employee would have observed in the circumstances.

- A Colorado statute imposes upon a skier the duty to avoid collisions with any person or object below him. While this statute may not form the basis of criminal liability, it establishes the minimum standard of care and, for the purposes of civil negligence suits, creates a rebuttable presumption that the skier is at fault whenever he collides with skiers on the slope below him. An extreme violation of a skier's duty, such as here, may be evidence of a "gross deviation" from the standard of care imposed by statute for civil negligence. D was travelling so fast and with so little control for some time over a considerable distance that he could not possibly have respected his obligation to avoid other skiers.

- Furthermore, D's knowledge and training could give rise to the reasonable inference that he was aware of the possibility that by skiing so fast and out of control he might collide with and kill another skier unless he regained control and slowed down.

- Therefore, a reasonably prudent and cautious person could have found that D consciously disregarded a substantial and unjustifiable risk that by skiing exceptionally fast and out of control he might collide with and kill another person on the slope. The prosecution presented sufficient evidence to establish probable cause that D committed reckless manslaughter.

Comment. On remand, the jury convicted D of negligent homicide, rather than reckless manslaughter.

c. Objective and subjective standards

State v. Williams
484 P.2d 1167 (Wash. Ct. App. 1971).

Facts. The Williamses (Ds), husband and wife, were both Indians who did not graduate from high school. The wife had two children from a prior marriage, the younger of whom was 17 months old. This child developed a toothache from an abscessed tooth. Within a two-week period, an infection of the mouth and cheeks developed and became gangrenous. Because he could not eat, the child's resistance was lowered and he contracted pneumonia, from which he died. During this time, Ds knew the child was ill and they gave him aspirin. They did not take him to a doctor for fear that the authorities would keep him because of his condition. The autopsy surgeon testified that, even if the child had seen a doctor in the last week, the child's life could not have been saved. Ds were charged with manslaughter for negligently failing to provide necessary medical attention. Ds were convicted and now appeal.

Issue. May simple negligence suffice to render a person criminally liable?

Held. Yes. Judgment affirmed.

♦ The common law rule required more than ordinary or simple negligence for a determination of involuntary manslaughter; gross negligence was essential. A Washington state statute has modified the law by imposing criminal liability where death is the proximate result of only simple or ordinary negligence.

♦ Ds were required to exercise ordinary caution. They knew that the child was sick while there was still time to take him to a doctor and save his life. They had taken him to a doctor previously. They could see that his condition was deteriorating. Ds breached their duty of caution, and the child died as a proximate result of the breach; thus, they are guilty.

d. Distinguishing murder and manslaughter

1) Intent to do a dangerous act

Commonwealth v. Malone
47 A.2d 445 (Pa. 1946).

Facts. Malone (D), age 17, was convicted of second degree murder for killing his friend, age 13, during a game of "Russian poker." D and the victim were on friendly terms; both had consented to play, neither intending harm to the other. D appeals, contending that he is only guilty of manslaughter.

Issue. Is malevolence toward the victim an essential element of malice?

Held. No. Judgment affirmed.

♦ When an individual commits an act of gross recklessness for which he must reasonably anticipate that death to another is likely to result, he exhibits that wickedness of disposition, hardness of heart, and a mind regardless of social duty that proves that he possessed malice.

Comment. D did not intentionally kill the victim. He did act in a "maliciously reckless" manner, however.

2) Insufficient evidence

In *People v. Prindle*, 944 N.E.2d 1130 (N.Y. 2011), defendant led officers on a high speed chase after stealing a snowplow blade. After running five red lights and repeatedly driving into oncoming traffic, defendant crashed into another vehicle and killed its driver. A divided court reversed defendant's conviction for depraved indifference murder, finding sufficient evidence to support only reckless manslaughter. The dissent found defendant's conduct so devoid of regard for the lives of others as to render him as culpable as one whose conscious objective was to kill.

3) Malice based on reckless and wanton conduct

United States v. Fleming
739 F.2d 945 (4th Cir. 1984).

Facts. Fleming (D) had a blood alcohol level of .315 and was driving in the wrong direction on a one-way road at between 70 and 80 miles per hour. The speed limit was 30 miles per hour. D lost control of his vehicle and collided with a car driven by Mrs. Haley. The impact killed Mrs. Haley. D was convicted of second degree murder. D appeals, claiming that the evidence did not show malice aforethought, so he could be convicted at most of manslaughter.

Issue. May a person be convicted of murder for a death caused by reckless driving while intoxicated?

Held. Yes. Judgment affirmed.

- ♦ Malice aforethought is the element that makes a homicide a murder instead of manslaughter. Such malice does not require an intent to kill or injure, nor does it require ill will against the victim or other persons. Evidence of reckless and wanton conduct that is a gross deviation from a reasonable standard of care, sufficient to support an inference that the accused was aware of a serious risk of death or serious bodily harm, may demonstrate malice.

- ♦ In this case, the prosecution only had to prove that D intended to drive the way he did without regard for the life and safety of others. The evidence presented supports the verdict.

- ♦ D claims that if he could be convicted of murder without proof that he intended to cause death or injury, then all drunk driving homicides would be murder. However, the difference between malice for murder and gross negligence, which only supports manslaughter, is a difference of degree. D's conduct is markedly different in degree from most vehicular homicides. While the typical drunk driver puts others in danger simply by attempting to drive, in this case, D was drunk but also drove in a reckless manner that was especially dangerous because he was drunk.

2. Felony-Murder Rule

At common law, any homicide committed while perpetrating or attempting to perpetrate a felony was murder. Most jurisdictions have limited this rule.

a. The basic rules

1) Types of felonies

Some jurisdictions have amended the felony-murder rule to hold that it will be applied only to certain types of felonies (*e.g.*, rape, robbery).

2) "In perpetration of felony"

The homicide must occur "in the perpetration of the felony. Most courts interpret this to mean that it is sufficient if the homicide takes place at any time within the "res gestae" of the other felony, and this includes all acts in the immediate preparation, actual commission, and immediate escape. A few courts require that the homicide occur at the actual moment of technical perfection of the felony (if the felony is burglary, it must occur during the breaking and entering).

3) Dangerous felony

Regina v. Serné
16 Cox Crim. Cas. 311 (1887).

Facts. Serné (D) insured his property and the life of one of his boys. While the family was sleeping, D allegedly set fire to the house. Everyone but D's two boys escaped. D was charged with murder, and the judge gave instructions to the jury.

Issue. Does the felony-murder doctrine apply regardless of the dangerous nature of the felony involved?

Held. No. D is not guilty.

♦ Malice aforethought includes knowledge that the act will probably cause the death of a person as well as acts done with an intent to commit a felony. However, the common law rule is too broad unless it is limited to dangerous felonies. The felony-murder rule should only apply when the act is known to be dangerous to life and likely in itself to cause death, and is done for the purpose of committing a felony and does cause death.

Comment. In *People v. Stamp*, 82 Cal. Rptr. 598 (1960), the victim died from a heart attack partially brought on by fright when he was robbed at gunpoint by the defendant. The defendant's conviction of first degree murder was affirmed on the grounds that a felon is strictly liable for all killings committed by him in the course of the felony and takes his victim as he finds him.

b. Inherently dangerous requirement

People v. Phillips
414 P.2d 353 (Cal. 1966).

Facts. Phillips (D) was convicted of second degree murder by application of the felony-murder rule based on his commission of grand theft. D, a chiropractor, induced the victim's parents not to allow an operation, representing falsely that he could treat her. D charged them a substantial sum, but the child died. D appeals his conviction.

Issue. Must the felony D is charged with be an "inherently dangerous" one in order to apply the felony-murder rule?

Held. Yes. Judgment reversed.

♦ Grand theft is not inherently dangerous to life, and only such dangerous felonies will support a felony-murder conviction. No prior case has applied the doctrine when the death resulted from felonious perpetration of a fraud.

♦ It makes no difference that the acts of D may themselves have been inherently dangerous. The court must look in the abstract to the felony with which D is charged. Otherwise there would be no limitation on the doctrine, which has been severely criticized.

♦ There is no proof that D acted with conscious disregard for life in this case. The felony-murder rule allowed a conviction without proof of express or implied malice.

Comment. In *People v. Satchell*, 489 P.2d 1361 (Cal. 1972), the court found that the felony possession of a concealable weapon by an ex-felon was not a "felony inherently dangerous to human life." Looking to the genus of crimes known as felonies, the court determined that it could not conclude that the "possession of a concealable firearm by one who has been convicted of *any crime* *within that genus* is an act inherently dangerous to human life which, as such, justifies the extreme consequence (*i.e.*, imputed malice) which the felony-murder doctrine demands."

c. Convicted felon's possession of a firearm

Hines v. State
578 S.E.2d 868 (Ga. 2003).

Facts. While turkey hunting with friends and relatives, Hines (D) thought he heard a turkey gobble, shot through heavy foliage, hit his friend, and killed him. D was convicted of felony murder based on the underlying crime of possession of a firearm by a convicted felon. D appeals.

Issue. Was D's violation of the prohibition against convicted felons possessing firearms an inherently dangerous felony that could support a felony-murder conviction?

Held. Yes. Judgment affirmed.

- D argues that a convicted felon's possession of a firearm while turkey hunting is not one of the inherently dangerous felonies required to support a conviction of felony murder. A felony is "inherently dangerous" when it is "dangerous per se" or "by its circumstances creates a foreseeable risk of death." Depending on the facts, possession of a Firearm by a convicted felon can be an inherently dangerous felony.

- In *Ford v. State*, 423 S.E.2d 255 (Ga. 1992), we reversed a conviction for felony murder based on felonious possession of a firearm where a convicted felon killed the occupant of the apartment below him while he was unloading a gun and it accidently discharged. Our reversal was based on the absence of evidence showing that the defendant knew that there was an apartment below him or that the victim was present.

- Here. D had been drinking before and while he was hunting. D knew that there were other hunters in the area whose exact location he did not know. He took an unsafe shot at dusk at a target he had not positively identified. Thus, D's possession of a firearm created a foreseeable risk of death, and his violation of the prohibition against convicted felons possessing firearms was an inherently dangerous felony that could support a felony-murder conviction.

Dissent. I do not find that the circumstances surrounding D's felony of possessing a firearm were inherently dangerous based on our decision in *Ford*. For purposes of our felony-murder doctrine, a felony is inherently dangerous if it carries a high probability that death will result. The facts may show that D was negligent, but they do not establish that his acts created a high probability that death would result or that he had a life-threatening state of mind. Also, although D may not have positively identified his target as a turkey, he had to make a split-second decision. His failure to identify his target beyond doubt did not carry a high probability that a person would be killed. The sanction of life in prison for murder should be reserved for cases in which the defendant's moral failings warrant such punishment.

d. The merger doctrine

People v. Burton
491 P.2d 793 (Cal. 1971).

Facts. While committing an armed robbery, Burton (D) killed someone. The trial judge instructed the jury on first-degree felony murder. D was found guilty. D appeals.

Issue. In the circumstances of this case, was it error to instruct the jury on first-degree felony murder, because the underlying felony was armed robbery?

Held. No. Judgment reversed on other grounds.

- D claims that armed robbery is an offense included in fact within the offense of murder and that under our decision in *People v. Ireland*, 450 P.2d 580 (Cal. 1969), as applied in *People v. Wilson*, 462 P.2d 22 (Cal. 1969), such offense cannot support a felony-murder instruction.

- In *Ireland*, the defendant shot his wife with a gun. His defense was that his mental state at the time of the act, affected by cumulative emotional pressure and ingestion of alcohol and prescribed medications, was not that required for murder. The jury instruction on the felony-murder rule used assault with a deadly weapon as the supporting felony. Based on the instruction, the jury could have inferred that the intent element of assault with a deadly weapon was not affected by diminished capacity. And the jury would have been relieved from considering the issue of malice aforethought, since malice was imputed. The net effect would be to consider all intentional killings accomplished by means of a deadly weapon as murder, regardless of the circumstances, and they could never be mitigated to manslaughter. We found this kind of bootstrapping impermissible. We held that a second-degree felony-murder instruction may not properly be given when it is based upon a felony which is an integral part of the homicide and which the evidence shows to be an offense included in fact within the offense charged.

- In *Wilson*, burglary (*i.e.*, entry coupled with the intent to commit assault with a deadly weapon) was the underlying felony that supported the felony-murder instruction. *Ireland* involved second-degree felony murder, but *Wilson* involved first-degree felony murder because of the entry. We found no meaningful distinction between assaults with deadly weapons indoors and outdoors. Thus, we excluded burglary from the operation of the felony-murder rule where the intended felony was assault with a deadly weapon.

- D argues that under *Ireland* and *Wilson*, armed robbery cannot support a felony murder instruction because armed robbery includes, as a necessary element, assault with a deadly weapon. He reasons that robbery is accomplished by means of force or fear, and thus, robbery is assault coupled with larceny, which when accomplished by means of a deadly weapon necessarily includes in fact assault with a deadly weapon; therefore, any charge of murder with respect to a killing arising out of armed robbery necessarily includes in fact assault with a deadly weapon and cannot support a felony-murder instruction.

- To accept D's argument would be to eliminate the application of the felony murder rule to all unlawful killings that are committed by means of a deadly weapon, since in each case the homicide would include in fact assault with a deadly weapon. We reject this argument.

- There is a great difference between deaths resulting from assaults with a deadly weapon, where the purpose of the defendant's conduct was the very assault which resulted in death, and deaths resulting from conduct for an independent felonious purpose, such as robbery or rape, which happened to be accomplished by a deadly weapon. In *Ireland* and *Wilson*, the purpose of the action which resulted in homicide was assault with a deadly weapon—the infliction of bodily injury upon the person of another, which was not satisfied short of death. Thus, there was a single course of conduct with a single purpose.

- As for other felonies that support a felony-murder instruction, there is an independent felonious purpose. For example, the independent purpose of armed robbery is to acquire another's money or property. Once a person has set out on a course of conduct for one of the enumerated felonious purposes, if a death results from the commission of the felony, it will be first-degree murder.

- The purpose of the felony-murder rule is to deter felons from killing negligently or accidentally by holding them strictly responsible for killings they commit. The legislature has indicated that this deterrent purpose outweighs the normal legislative policy of examining the individual state of mind. One who perpetrates or attempts to perpetrate one of the enumerated felonies is no longer entitled to such consideration, but will be deemed guilty of first-degree murder for any homicide committed in the course of the felony.

- D set out to commit armed robbery and brought himself within the class of persons the legislature has determined must avoid causing death or bear the consequences of first-degree murder.

e. Assaultive crimes

People v. Chun
45 Cal.4th 1172, 203 P.3d 425 (2009).

Facts. Three individuals, one of whom was the brother of a man considered by the police to be a highly ranked member of the Asian Boys street gang, were the victims of a drive-by shooting. One person was killed and the others injured. The surviving victims identified Chan, a member of the Tiny Rascals street gang, as the driver of the Honda from which the shots were fired. He was never found. Two months after the incident, Chun (D) was arrested and admitted he was in the back seat of the Honda and that he fired a gun but did not point it at anyone and intended only to scare the victims. D was charged with murder, attempted murder, and shooting into an occupied vehicle; the jury was also instructed regarding second degree felony murder based on the shooting into an occupied vehicle. D was found guilty of second degree murder, but acquitted of both counts of attempted murder.

Issue. Do all assaultive-type crimes, such as a violation of section 246 in this case, merge with the charged homicide, thus being precluded from serving as the basis for a second degree felony-murder instruction?

Held. Yes. The trial court erred in instructing the jury on the second-degree felony-murder charge, but the error was not prejudicial. Reversed and remanded.

- An assaultive felony is one that involves the threat of immediate violent injury.

- To determine merger, a court looks to the elements of the crime and not the facts of the case. If the elements have an assaultive aspect, the crime merges with the underlying homicide.

- Where the elements involve both assaultive and nonassaultive conduct (*e.g.,* child abuse), under our approach, that, too, would merge.

- We overrule *People v. Robertson* 34 Cal.4th 156 (2004), where a divided court held that the *Ireland (supra)* "merger" doctrine did not bar submission of grossly negligent discharge of a firearm (Pen. Code § 246.3) as a predicate for second-degree felony-murder.

Concurrence and dissent. Although the majority has improved it, the second degree felony murder rule should be abolished; it is a court-created rule, unsupported by statute. It is not necessary because by the majority's logic it was not needed to reach a conviction of second degree murder; and it is unfair, because it imposes a presumption of malice rather than allowing the "wisdom of juries" to recognize those situations where a defendant commits second degree murder by killing during the commission of a felony that is inherently dangerous to life.

f. Killing by nonfelons

1) No liability for death of a co-felon

State v. Canola
374 A.2d 20 (N.J. 1977).

Facts. Canola (D) and three others were robbing a store when shooting started. The store owner shot and killed one of the robbers and was, in turn, killed by another of the robbers. D was indicted on two counts of murder and was convicted of both counts. On appeal, the conviction for the murder of the store owner was upheld but the homicide of the co-felon prompted a petition of certification to the New Jersey Supreme Court.

Issue. May a felon be guilty of murder for the killing of a co-felon by a victim of the felony?

Held. No. The count relating to the death of the co-felon is dismissed.

- The applicable statute states simply that "if the death of anyone ensues from the committing" of a felony, then the felon may be guilty of murder. The common law felony-murder rule was never applied to hold a felon guilty of the death of his co-felon at the hands of the intended victim. Nor have any of the states so held, although some, at times, have imposed criminal liability on the felons for the killing of nonfelons by police or victims.

- The statute uses broad language that could include the death of a co-felon. The language could also mean to include accidental deaths or any death within the res gestae of the felony. Because of multiple possible interpretations, public policy must guide the application of the statute.

- The general doctrine of felony murder is based on an agency theory, because one may not be criminally liable for acts not actually or constructively his own. Thus, the statute should not be construed to expand the rule beyond the common law notion.

Concurrence. The statute was clearly intended to impose liability for any killing that ensues during the felony, even though not committed by any of the felons. The only exception would be the killing of a co-felon by other than another co-felon, which is justifiable homicide.

D. The Death Penalty

1. Introduction

Under common law, crimes were classified as treason, felony, and misdemeanor. Crimes classified as felonies under common law were punishable by the death penalty. Although the penalties have changed, the offenses have generally retained that status under modern statutes. The type of penalty used today to distinguish a felony from a misdemeanor is usually the type of prison to which the offender may be sent, or the length of sentence that can be imposed. Two other classifications continue in modern times: capital/noncapital crimes, and infamous/noninfamous crimes.

2. Capital Punishment Constitutional

Gregg v. Georgia
428 U.S. 153 (1976).

Facts. Gregg (D) was found guilty of murder and sentenced to death under Georgia law. In an earlier case, *Furman v. Georgia*, 408 U.S. 238 (1972), the Supreme Court had held the Georgia capital punishment statute unconstitutional because it allowed imposition of the death penalty in a capricious and arbitrary manner. D challenges the state statute as amended.

Issue. Is capital punishment per se "cruel and unusual punishment" and therefore unconstitutional under the Eighth and Fourteenth Amendments?

Held. No. Judgment affirmed.

- Although unappealing to many, capital punishment is essential to an ordered society that requires reliance on the legal process instead of self-help. On a number of occasions, we have both assumed and asserted the constitutionality of capital punishment. In fact, 35 states enacted capital punishment statutes since the *Furman* decision, indicating continued public acceptance of capital punishment.

- Because statistical attempts to evaluate the deterrent effect of the death penalty have been inconclusive, the resolution of this complex factual issue properly rests with state legislatures.

- Under Georgia's sentencing procedure, the jury's discretion is always circumscribed by legislative guidelines. The death penalty is available for only six categories of crime: murder, kidnapping for ransom or where the victim is harmed, armed robbery, rape, treason, and aircraft hijacking. After a verdict of guilty, a separate sentencing hearing is conducted, and the jury must find that one of 10 specified aggravating circumstances exists before imposing the death penalty. This satisfies the concerns of *Furman* as to those defendants who were being condemned to death capriciously and arbitrarily.

Dissent (Marshall, J.). The death penalty is unnecessary to promote the goal of deterrence or to further any legitimate notion of retribution, and is thus "cruel and unusual punishment."

3. Death Penalty for Mentally Retarded Criminals Unconstitutional

Atkins v. Virginia
536 U.S. 304 (2002).

Facts. Atkins (D) and Jones, carrying a semiautomatic handgun, abducted Nesbitt, robbed him, drove him to an automated teller machine, withdrew his cash, drove him to an isolated location, and shot him eight times. D was convicted of abduction, armed robbery, and capital murder. During the penalty phase, a forensic psychologist who had evaluated D before trial testified that, based on interviews with people who knew D, a review of school and court records, and the administration of a standard intelligence test, which indicated that Atkins had a full-scale IQ of 59, D was "mildly mentally retarded." Nevertheless, the jury sentenced D to death. The Supreme Court granted certiorari.

Issue. Are executions of mentally retarded criminals "cruel and unusual punishments" prohibited by the Eighth Amendment?

Held. Yes. Judgment reversed and case remanded.

- What is excessive punishment is judged by the current prevailing standards. The dignity of man is the basic concept underlying the Eighth Amendment, and the standards of decency of our maturing society have evolved.

- Relying on legislation enacted around the country as the clearest and most reliable objective evidence of contemporary values, we have held that the death penalty is excessive punishment for the rape of an adult and for a defendant who did not and never intended to take a life. We have also acknowledged that the Constitution contemplates that our own judgment will be brought to bear in deciding the acceptability of the death penalty under the Eighth Amendment.

- In *Penry v Lynaugh*, 492 U.S. 302 (1989), we upheld the constitutionality of the death penalty for criminal defendants who were mentally retarded. We determined that the two states which then prohibited execution of such defendants, even when added to the 14 states which prohibited the death penalty altogether, did not establish a national consensus against such executions. Since then, however, 17 more states have joined the original two. It is not so much the number of states that have enacted legislation, but the direction of the change. Where execution of the mentally retarded is permitted, it is rare; since *Penry*, only five states have executed offenders possessing an IQ of less than 70.

- Mentally retarded defendants have diminished capacities to understand and process information, to learn from experience, to engage in logical reasoning, or to control impulses. Thus, the justifications for the death penalty—retribution and deterrence of capital crimes— do not apply to the mentally retarded. As for retribution, the severity of the appropriate punishment depends on the culpability of the offender, and the lesser culpability of the mentally retarded offender does not merit death. As for deterrence, it is less likely that a mentally retarded person can process the information of the possibility of execution as a penalty and control his behavior based on that information.

♦ Another reason for a categorical rule making these offenders ineligible for the death penalty is the risk that the death penalty will be imposed in spite of factors that may call for a less severe penalty. A mentally retarded person is more likely to confess to crimes he did not commit, may be unable to give his counsel meaningful assistance, and may be a poor witness. Death is not a suitable punishment for a mentally retarded criminal.

Dissent (Scalia, J., Rehnquist, C.J., Thomas, J.).

♦ The fact that 18 states, fewer than half of those that permit capital punishment, have very recently barred the execution of mentally retarded criminals does not establish a national consensus. The Court contends that the infrequency of such executions is evidence of a national consensus against the execution of the mentally retarded. But this can be explained by the fact that the retarded constitute only a tiny fraction of society, and mental retardation is a constitutionally mandated mitigating factor at sentencing. The Court also mentions the views of professional and religious organizations and respondents to public opinion polls. But these views are not always those of the people.

♦ What really underlies today's decision is shown by the Court's words that "our own judgment" will be brought to bear in deciding the acceptability of the death penalty under the Eighth Amendment. Thus, it is the feelings and intuition of a majority of the justices that count.

♦ The Court reasons that the execution of mentally retarded offenders is excessive because their diminished capacities raise a serious question as to whether retribution and deterrence would be served. However, culpability and deservedness of the most severe retribution depends not only on the mental capacity of the criminal, but also on the depravity of the crime. Thus, the sentencer must weigh the degree of retardation and the depravity of the crime in each particular case.

♦ With respect to deterrence, the Court contends that a mentally retarded person is less likely to process the information of the possibility of execution as a penalty and control his behavior based on that information. But this leads to the conclusion that, because mentally retarded persons are less deterred, they are more likely to kill, which neither I nor society believes. And even if the mentally retarded offender is less likely to be deterred, if the death penalty successfully deters many, it is adequately vindicated.

4. Statistical Challenges to the Fairness of the Death Penalty

McClesky v. Kemp
481 U.S. 279 (1987).

Facts. McClesky (D) was convicted of murder for killing a white police officer during the course of a robbery. D was black. D was sentenced to death based on the aggravating circumstances that the murder was committed during the course of an armed robbery and the victim was a police officer who was performing his duties. The state courts upheld the conviction and sentence. D then petitioned for a writ of habeas corpus in federal court, claiming that the capital sentencing process was racially discriminatory. To support his claim, D produced a statistical study that showed that a black person convicted of killing a white victim was significantly more likely to be sentenced to death than a white person convicted of killing either a white person or a black person. The district court dismissed the petition and the court of appeals affirmed. D appeals.

Issue. May an accused rely on statistical evidence of racial disparity in sentencing to prove that the sentencing procedure is unconstitutional?

Held. No. Judgment affirmed.

- A defendant claiming deprivation of equal protection must prove purposeful discrimination that had a discriminatory effect on him. D failed to prove that the decisionmakers acted with discriminatory purpose in this case. Instead, D relied on the statistical study. While statistics may be useful in some types of cases, they are inapplicable to capital sentencing decisions.

- Sentencing procedures require consideration of innumerable factors that depend on the facts of each particular case. An appropriate inference that would apply to a specific decision may not be drawn from general statistics. The sentencing procedure, as well as the entire criminal justice system, relies on discretion as a basic principle, and the exercise of such discretion should not be overturned by resort to general statistical analysis.

- Even if the procedure in individual cases results in statistical disparities, this does not show that the state had a discriminatory purpose in using the system. There is no evidence that the state legislature adopted the capital punishment statute to further a racially discriminatory purpose.

- D also claims the sentencing system violates the Eighth Amendment. This attack on the discretionary nature ignores the substantial benefits to a defendant that accrue from the discretion in the system, such as the jury's ability to exercise leniency. The system is designed to minimize racial bias, while preserving the fundamental value of a jury and the benefits of discretion.

- Another problem with D's approach is that there is no limiting principle. Any statistical disparity based on an arbitrary variable, including physical attractiveness or facial characteristics as well as race, would support an attack. D's claims are matters for the legislature, not the courts.

Dissent (Brennan, Marshall, Blackmun, Stevens, JJ.). The fact in this case is that D's chance of a death sentence was more likely because he was black. The Court has in the past been concerned with the risk of an arbitrary sentence, even if the accused cannot prove racial bias in any particular sentencing decision. The statistical study shows that race is more likely than not to influence the sentence. If a conviction is not permissible if the chance of error is less likely than not, then a death sentence should not be imposed if the chance of irrational imposition is more likely than not. While discretion is important, it is a means, not an end.

Dissent (Blackmun, Marshall, Brennan, Stevens, JJ.). The Court is applying a lesser standard of scrutiny in this capital punishment case than it ordinarily applies to equal protection challenges. The statistical study shows that race better explains differential treatment than any other grounds.

Dissent (Stevens, Blackmun, JJ.). The racial disparity shown by D is contrary to the Court's prior requirement that capital punishment not be imposed unless it is done fairly and with reasonable consistency. The state could limit capital punishment to those serious offenses in which it can be shown that the sentence is not influenced by race.

Chapter VI
The Significance of the Resulting Harm

A. Causation—Accountability for the Results of Conduct

1. Introduction

Criminal culpability generally requires not only conduct but also a specified result of that conduct.

a. Some crimes do not require a specific result; for example, conspiracy.

b. The causation question is conveniently divided into two topics: actual causation and proximate causation.

2. Actual Cause

a. "But for" rule

The defendant's act must have actually caused the unlawful result before he can be held criminally liable. The defendant is the cause if "but for" his antecedent conduct the result would not have occurred.

b. Foreseeability

People v. Acosta
284 Cal. Rptr. 117 (Cal. Ct. App. 1991).

Facts. Acosta (D), driving a stolen motor vehicle, led the police on a 48-mile chase, driving recklessly much of the time. Two police helicopters, assisting in the chase, collided with each other, killing three occupants. Expert testimony at trial indicated the crash was due to pilot error and was not affected by ground activity. D was convicted of three counts of second degree murder. D appeals.

Issues.

(i) Was there sufficient evidence that D's conduct was the proximate cause of the deaths?

(ii) Was there sufficient evidence of malice?

Held. (i) Yes. (ii) No. Judgment reversed.

- The crash was not a "highly extraordinary result," which would absolve D. Rather, it was foreseeable that in the heat of the chase, a pursuer might act negligently or recklessly. But for D's conduct, the crash would not have happened.

- There was no malice, however, because no showing was made that D consciously disregarded the risk to the helicopter pilots.

Concurrence. D certainly represented a threat to other vehicles on the road, but to extend that responsibility to persons in the air, whose role was to merely observe D's movements, defies common sense.

c. Exclusive and sole cause not required

People v. Arzon
401 N.Y.S.2d 156 (N.Y. Sup. Ct. 1978).

Facts. Arzon (D) set fire to a couch in an abandoned multistory building. Firefighters responded to the resulting fire but were unable to control it. When they decided to leave the building, they were engulfed in smoke from a separate fire on a lower floor. The added smoke made evacuation more dangerous, and one firefighter received fatal injuries. D was charged with second degree murder for his reckless conduct and with second degree felony murder. D seeks to have these charges dismissed for lack of a causal connection.

Issue. Must a defendant's actions be the sole cause of another's death in order to support a murder conviction?

Held. No. Motions denied.

- When a person acts with "depraved indifference to human life," it is not necessary that the ultimate harm be intended by the actor. As long as the ultimate harm should have been foreseen as being related to the action taken, criminal liability may exist. The conduct must be an actual cause of the death; however, it need not be the sole and exclusive factor.

- Here, D's conduct indicated a depraved indifference to human life. The response of the firefighters was easily foreseeable, as was their exposure to a life-threatening danger. The spread of the fire further increased the danger and placed the firefighters in a position of particular vulnerability to the separate and independent fire on a lower floor. Therefore, D's conduct was a sufficiently direct cause of the death to make D liable. The ultimate harm was a result foreseeably related to D's acts.

d. Sufficiently direct cause

In *People v. Warner-Lambert Co.*, 414 N.E.2d 660 (N.Y. 1980), Warner-Lambert and its officers were indicted for manslaughter after an explosion at one of its chewing gum factories. The company used potentially explosive substances in the manufacturing process and had been warned by its insurer of the explosion hazard. There was no hard proof of what triggered the explosion. The court found the evidence before the grand jury was not legally sufficient to establish the foreseeability of the immediate, triggering cause of the explosion and dismissed the indictment. The court stated: "We subscribe to the requirement that the defendants' actions must be a *sufficiently direct cause* of the ensuing death before there can be any imposition of criminal liability . . . ."

e. Substantial factor test

The test here is: "Was the defendant's conduct a substantial factor in bringing about the forbidden result?" If the result would not have occurred "but for" the defendant's conduct, this conduct is a substantial factor in bringing about the result, but the defendant's conduct will sometimes be a substantial factor even though not a "but for" cause.

f. Example

A is falling from a window; midway down B shoots her dead. Is B to be held? Did he cause A's death? B certainly sped it up. The decision to hold B is not as easy as in tort cases where the courts would simply give damages for the worth of A's life at the time she was shot. In the criminal law, it is an all-or-nothing proposition. B is either guilty or not guilty. [See People v. Ah Fat, 48 Cal. 61 (1874)—he is guilty]

g. Neglect or maltreatment of injury

The defendant remains responsible for the death of another if he wounds or injures another and such injury results in death. It is irrelevant that the death is only an indirect result of a chain of natural causes or the result of unskilled or improper medical treatment. All persons are criminally liable for the consequences of their acts even though other causes produced the fatal result.

1) Improper medical treatment

In *Hall v. State*, 159 N.E. 420 (Ind. 1927), the defendant struck several blows to the head of the deceased, fracturing his skull. However, the cause of death was determined to be blood poisoning resulting from the skull fracture. Further evidence was presented indicating that the wounds to the head received improper medical treatment. Consequently, the defendant appealed his conviction of first degree murder. The court sustained the conviction, holding that the defendant would not be relieved of responsibility even though improper medical treatment aggravated the wound and contributed to the death.

h. Subsequent injury inflicted by another

When one willfully and with malice aforethought wounds another with a deadly weapon, and immediately thereafter a third person willfully and maliciously inflicts another wound and thereby accelerates or hastens the victim's death, both offenders can be found guilty of murder under the majority view.

1) Subsequent human actions

People v. Campbell
335 N.W.2d 27 (Mich. Ct. App. 1983).

Facts. Campbell (D) and Basnaw were drinking heavily. D, angry at Basnaw for having had sex with D's wife, encouraged Basnaw to kill himself, giving Basnaw his own gun and five bullets. After D left, Basnaw shot himself. D was charged with murder. D moved to quash the information and dismiss. The motion to quash was denied. D appeals.

Issue. Does providing a weapon to one who subsequently uses it to commit suicide constitute murder?

Held. No. Judgment reversed and case remanded with instructions to quash.

- The prosecution and trial court relied on *People v. Roberts*, 178 N.W. 690 (Mich. 1920), in which a husband left a poisoned brew within reach of his terminally ill wife who knowingly ingested it. Roberts was convicted of murder in the first degree.

- We hold that *Roberts* no longer represents the law of Michigan.

- "Homicide" involves the killing of another. "Suicide" by definition cannot include homicide. Inciting someone to commit suicide cannot qualify as a homicide because D did not kill another.

- D hoped Basnaw would commit suicide, but hope does not provide the degree of intent required for murder.

2) Physician-assisted suicide

People v. Kevorkian
527 N.W.2d 714 (Mich. 1994).

Facts. Approximately a year before Michigan enacted a statute prohibiting giving assistance in a suicide, Kevorkian (D) allegedly assisted in the deaths of Miller and Wantz. D was indicted on two counts of murder, but the charges were dismissed; the court concluded assisting in suicide does not fall within the crime of murder. The appeals court reversed. D appeals.

Issue. Does the common law definition of murder encompass the act of intentionally providing that means by which a person commits suicide?

Held. No. Judgment reversed and case remanded.

- The appeals court relied on *People v. Roberts (supra)* in which a husband left a poisoned brew within reach of his terminally ill wife who knowingly ingested it. Roberts was convicted of murder in the first degree.

- We overrule *Roberts* to the extent that it can be read to support the view that the common law definition of murder encompasses the act of intentionally providing the means by which a person commits suicide.

- Only where there is probable cause to believe that death was the direct and natural result of a defendant's act can the defendant be properly bound over on a charge of murder. If a defendant merely is involved in the events leading up to the death, the proper charge is assisting in a suicide, which may be prosecuted as a common law felony under the saving clause in the absence of a statute that specifically prohibits assisting in a suicide.

Concurrence and dissent. Without standards to distinguish between those that are terminally ill and rationally wish to die and those who are not, there is no way to protect against abuse.

i. Intervening act

Stephenson v. State
179 N.E. 633 (Ind. 1932).

Facts. Stephenson (D) abducted the deceased and took her to a train, on which he assaulted her with the intent to rape. D and his accomplice then took her to a hotel room. D permitted her to leave with his accomplice to buy a hat. The deceased also bought poison, which she took back at the hotel. After she became ill, D took her home. She died about a month later as a result of the combination of shock, loss of food and rest, infection from the wounds D inflicted, the effects of the poison, and the failure to obtain prompt medical attention. None of these factors alone would have caused death. D was convicted of second degree murder. D appeals.

Issue. May a person be convicted of murder for inflicting an injury that contributes substantially to a death, even though other causes also contributed to the death?

Held. Yes. Judgment affirmed.

- All of D's actions were so closely connected that they constitute one transaction. D's actions, taken as a whole, make him criminally responsible for the homicide.

- The fact that the deceased took poison is directly related to D's conduct. The deceased was under D's control at all times. The poisoning was part of the attempted rape because of the effect the assault had on the deceased.

Comment. A victim's voluntary self-infliction of harm may break the causation unless the victim is rendered irresponsible by the defendant's acts. The *Stephenson* case has been criticized, though, because the motive for taking the poison appeared to be to escape the shame and disgrace of what had happened, rather than to escape further assault.

3. Proximate Cause

Even though A's conduct may actually cause B's death, this conduct is not necessarily the "legal" or proximate cause of B's death.

a. Direct causation

Where direct causation exists, courts will hold that there is proximate cause also. In other words, if a reasonable person standing in the position of the defendant at the time of the act could have foreseen the result which in fact occurred (absent intervening forces), the defendant will be held responsible.

1) Comparison to tort law

Commonwealth v. Root
170 A.2d 310 (Pa. 1961).

Facts. Root (D) and the deceased were in a drag race on a highway, going about 90 miles per hour, when the road narrowed to two lanes at a bridge. The deceased tried to pass D and hit an oncoming car. D was convicted of involuntary manslaughter and appeals.

Issue. Do tort concepts of proximate cause apply equally in criminal cases?

Held. No. Conviction reversed.

- ◆ The deceased was aware of the risk and caused his own death by his own independent, reckless act. D's conduct was not a sufficiently direct cause of the death.

- ◆ The tort concept of proximate cause is inapplicable in criminal cases, where a more direct causal connection is required. Otherwise the expansion of tort liability principles could extend criminal liability to those whose conduct is not generally considered to present the likelihood of a resultant death.

Dissent. D's unlawful conduct was a direct cause of the death. The decedent's action was a natural reaction to the situation.

Comment. This case tends to distort the meaning of legal cause. The true reason for the court's holding is probably the feeling that D should not be held liable for the death of the deceased, who was an equally willing and foolhardy participant in the drag race that caused his death. The court pointed out that if the tort principles applied in criminal cases, the conduct of the deceased would have to be considered to determine whether it superseded D's conduct. The deceased's attempt to pass would be a superseding cause.

2) Sufficiently direct cause

People v. Kern, 545 N.Y.S.2d 4 (N.Y. App. Div. 1989), involved a racially motivated attack that ended in a death. After a group of white teenagers assaulted three black men whose car had broken down in the white neighborhood of Howard Beach, one of the men attempted to escape the bat-wielding teenagers by running across a highway. He was hit by a car and killed. The court of appeals upheld the defendants' convictions for second-degree manslaughter, finding that the defendants' actions were a "sufficiently direct cause" of the ensuing death. Running across the highway to escape a group shouting racial epithets and carrying weapons had been the only reasonable alternative left to the victim.

3) Foreseeable result

In *People v. Matos*, 83 N.Y.2d 509 (N.Y. 1994), a police officer fell down an airshaft to his death while pursuing an armed robbery suspect over Manhattan rooftops. The defendant's felony murder conviction was upheld because the officer's death was the foreseeable result of the robbery and the attempted escape.

4) Proximate cause/vicarious liability

State v. McFadden
320 N.W.2d 608 (Iowa 1982).

Facts. McFadden (D) and Sulgrove engaged in a drag race on a city street. Sulgrove lost control of his vehicle, swerved into oncoming traffic, struck a third vehicle, and killed six-year-old Ellis. Sulgrove was also killed. D's vehicle did not impact with either of the other cars. D was charged with two counts of involuntary manslaughter. After a bench trial, D was convicted and sentenced. D appeals.

Issue. Is there sufficient causation to uphold a conviction of involuntary manslaughter of a defendant who participates in a drag race with another person who strikes another vehicle and kills someone, when the defendant did not impact with any other cars?

Held. Yes. Convictions affirmed.

♦ The trial court found D guilty under three separate theories: (i) aiding and abetting; (ii) vicarious responsibility; and (iii) proximate cause.

♦ While vicarious liability would support D's conviction as to Ellis, it would not support the conviction as to Sulgrove. D could not be guilty of vicarious liability as to Sulgrove's death because there is a statutory requirement of proof that the perpetrator caused the death of another.

♦ Sulgrove's voluntary participation does not, in itself, bar D's conviction.

♦ The civil standard of proximate cause, *i.e., that* there be a sufficient causal relationship between the defendant's conduct and a proscribed harm to hold him criminally responsible, may be properly applied to criminal matters, since there are no specific policy differences that would justify a different standard.

5) Causation established

Commonwealth v. Atencio
189 N.E.2d 223 (Mass. 1963).

Facts. Atencio (D), his friend (D), and the deceased played a game of "Russian roulette." Each D placed the gun to his own head and pulled the trigger once before the deceased took his turn. The gun fired when the deceased pulled the trigger. Ds were convicted of manslaughter. Atencio appeals.

Issue. When a person shoots himself to death as part of a game of Russian roulette, are the other players criminally liable for the death?

Held. Yes. Judgment affirmed.

♦ Ds' concerted action and cooperation in the game constituted wanton or reckless conduct, which brought about the death. The deceased's act was not an intervening act so as to exculpate Ds; it was part of a joint enterprise.

♦ Ds may not have had a duty to prevent the deceased from playing, but they had a duty not to participate and thereby encourage him.

♦ This case differs from the drag racing cases in which the death results from lack of skill or judgment. Here, the outcome is a certainty and mere luck determines who will die.

Comment. Compare this case to *Commonwealth v. Malone, supra*, in which the defendant was found guilty of murder.

b. Intervening causes

1) Introduction

A defendant's criminal responsibility terminates if, subsequent to his act, a new and independent force that was neither contemplated nor reasonably foreseeable supersedes and itself becomes the proximate cause of the injury.

2) Examples

a) If A receives a nonmortal wound at the hands of B, is negligently treated by Doctor C, and dies, B will be held for homicide. Such negligent treatment is a reasonably foreseeable risk; the opposite is true when the negligence amounts to gross negligence.

b) If the defendant assaults someone, leaving him helplessly lying on the highway, and a car then runs the victim over, killing him, the defendant must be held for the death (the intervening force was certainly foreseeable).

c. Summary on proximate cause

Note that if a court finds that there is proximate cause, this is simply a determination by the court that, weighing all the facts of the case, it minks that responsibility is sufficient to find the defendant guilty as charged. Other hypotheticals:

1) A shot the victim, inflicting a mortal wound that would produce death in an hour. Then the victim took a knife and cut his own throat, which also would cause death in five minutes. The court held that concurrent causes existed and found A guilty.

2) A mortally wounds B; C comes along and kills B. C is held. If A materially increased the risk to B by putting him in a position to be killed, A may also be held. Similarly, both may be held if A and C are working in concert.

3) A gave B a poison pill. She attempted to swallow it and choked on the pill, dying of suffocation. Here there is "but for" causation, but the result is certainly bizarre. But since B would have died from the pill anyway, A is liable.

B. Attempt

1. Introduction

Both at common law and under most modern statutes, it is a crime to attempt the commission of any felony or misdemeanor. Merely taking steps toward the completion of a crime, if done with the requisite intent, may be a crime itself. Attempt consists of (i) a specific intent to commit a crime and (ii) an act in furtherance of that intent, which goes far enough toward completion of the crime.

2. Mens Rea

The mens rea of attempt has two components: (i) the intent to commit the acts or cause the result constituting the crime; and (ii) the intent necessary for the completed crime. Therefore, if the crime allegedly attempted requires specific intent, such as burglary, the defendant must have had the specific intent to commit burglary.

a. No permissible inference

Smallwood v. State
680 A.2d 512 (Md. 1996).

Facts. Smallwood (D) was diagnosed with HIV and told by his social worker that he should practice "safe sex." On three occasions, D robbed at gunpoint and raped women without wearing a condom. D was charged with the attempted second degree murder of each of his victims. D pled guilty to attempted first degree rape and robbery with a deadly weapon. In a nonjury trial, D was convicted of assault with intent to murder, reckless endangerment, and three counts of attempted second degree murder. D appeals.

Issue. May the trier of fact infer an intent to kill based solely on the fact that D exposed his victims to the risk that they might contract HIV?

Held. No. Conviction reversed.

♦ We have discussed AIDS and HIV in previous cases and described HIV as a retrovirus that attacks the human immune system, weakening it, and ultimately destroying the body's capacity to ward off disease. We also noted that the virus may be latent for as long as 10 years during which the victim shows no symptoms of illness, and that medical studies have indicated most people who carry HIV will progress to AIDS.

♦ The intent required in assault with intent to murder and attempted murder is the specific intent to murder, *i.e.*, the specific intent to kill under circumstances that would not legally justify or excuse the killing or mitigate it to manslaughter. D argues that he was properly found guilty only if the trier of fact could reasonably have concluded that he possessed a specific intent to kill at the time he assaulted each of the three women.

♦ An intent to kill may be proved by circumstantial evidence, by established facts that permit inference of its existence. It may be inferred from an accused's conduct, words, or the use of a deadly weapon directed at a vital part of the body (a gun fired at the driver's window).

♦ The state argues that because D knew the infection leads to death and he knew he would be exposing the victims to risk of HIV transmission, a permissible inference can be drawn that D intended to kill each of his victims.

♦ When a gun is fired at a vital part of the body, there is high risk of killing the victim. Here, there is no similar proof that death by AIDS is a probable result of D's actions. Without this evidence, it cannot be concluded that death by AIDS was "sufficiently probable" to support an inference that D intended to kill his victims.

♦ D made no explicit statements and took no specific action showing his intent.

3. Preparation Versus Attempt

a. Introduction

The actus reus of attempt is an act that progresses sufficiently toward the commission of the offense. Whether a defendant has done enough in furtherance of his intent to have committed attempt is not subject to any precise rule. Various approaches have been used.

b. Traditional approach

Some courts hold that the defendant's acts must have gone beyond mere "preparation" into the zone of "perpetration." However, because there is much confusion as to when preparation ends and perpetration begins, this formula is not always useful.

c. Alternative approaches

The difficulty in applying the traditional approach in a consistent and fair manner has led some courts to apply alternative analyses.

1) The last step

In *King v. Barker*, N.Z.L.R. 865 (1924), the court cited the rule stated in *R. v. Eagleton*, 169 E.R. 826 (1855): "the accused must have taken the last step which he was able to take along the road of his criminal intent."

2) Physical proximity test

Some have suggested that the defendant's conduct must be physically proximate to the intended crime, the focus being on what remains to be done as opposed to what was already done. In applying this test, courts may take into account such factors as the seriousness of the crime, the time and place at which it is to occur, and the uncertainty of the result.

3) Control over all indispensable elements

An alternative test requires that the defendant go far enough to have obtained control over all factors that are indispensable to the commission of the crime. Thus, nothing must be left undone that would prevent the defendant from committing the crime.

4) "Probable desistance" test

Another approach is to find an attempt only when the act is such that in the ordinary course of events it would lead to completion of the crime in the absence of intervening outside factors. Thus, the emphasis here is upon the likelihood that the defendant would cease his efforts to commit the crime, given the conduct he has already committed.

5) "Equivocality" or "res ipsa loquitur" test

Still another variation suggests that an act amounts to attempt only if—when considered alone—it firmly shows the actor's intent to commit the crime. Hence, the accused's behavior is considered without reference to other evidence that may demonstrate criminal intent (such as a confession); the act relied upon to constitute attempt must "speak for itself in establishing intent.

6) Act falling short of an attempt punishable by statute

People v. Rizzo
158 N.E. 888 (N.Y. 1927).

Facts. Rizzo (D) and three other men planned to rob Rao (or whoever replaced him) of a payroll valued at about $1,200, which he was to carry from the bank for the United Lathing Company. Two of the other men had firearms. They started out in a car, looking for Rao. D was to point him out to the others, who were to do the actual holding up. The four drove around looking for Rao, and at some point were watched and followed by two police officers. At a United Lathing Company building, when Rizzo jumped out of the car and ran into the building, all four were arrested. D was taken out from the building where he had been hiding. Neither Rao nor his replacement was in the building. No one had been identified by D.

Issue. Does this constitute the crime of an attempt to commit robbery in the first degree?

Held. No. Judgment reversed.

♦ There is no doubt D had the intention to commit the robbery.

- The relevant law provides: "An act, done with intent to commit a crime, and tending but failing to effect its commission, is 'an attempt to commit that crime.'" The word "tending" is very indefinite.

- "Tending" means to exert activity in a particular direction. The law makes a distinction between remote acts and proximate acts. The law considers those acts only as tending to the commission of the crime that are so near to its accomplishment that in all reasonable probability the crime itself would have been committed but for timely interference.

- Here, D was still looking for Rao when the police arrested him. No attempt could be made to rob Rao until he at least came in sight. He was not in the building and there was no one else there with the payroll. D had planned to commit a crime and was looking for an opportunity to commit it, but the opportunity never came.

Comment. New York attempt statute, N.Y. Pen. Law Sect. 110.00 (2011), now requires the a defendant "engage in conduct 'which tends to effect the commission' of the crime." The New York court of appeals has held that this language makes no change in the law, which continues to be that stated in *Rizzo*.

7) Lingering as attempt

McQuirter v. State
63 So. 2d 388 (Ala. Crim. App. 1953).

Facts. McQuirter (D), a black man, was sitting in the cab of his truck one evening. Mrs. Allen, who was white, and her children walked by, and D got out of his truck. D walked behind Mrs. Allen down the street. Mrs. Allen stopped at a friend's house for 10 minutes while D passed by. When she left, D came toward her. Mrs. Allen then went to another friend's house, and D turned and walked back down the street, then leaned on a stop sign for about 30 minutes. After D finally went back toward his truck, Mrs. Allen went home. D was charged with assault with intent to rape. At the trial, three police officers testified that D claimed that he intended to get a white woman that night and that he intended to take Mrs. Allen into a nearby cotton patch. D denied having made these statements and gave an innocent explanation for his actions. He was found guilty of an attempt to commit an assault with intent to rape. D appeals.

Issue. May a person be convicted of an attempt to commit an assault with intent to rape if he merely follows the victim and lingers near her home, as long as he later expresses his intent to "get" her?

Held. Yes. Judgment affirmed.

- An attempt to commit an assault with intent to commit rape is merely an attempt to commit rape that has not proceeded far enough to constitute an assault. To justify a conviction of attempt to assault with intent to commit rape, the jury must find beyond a reasonable doubt that D intended to have sexual intercourse with the woman against her will.

- If the jury was satisfied beyond a reasonable doubt that D intended to have sexual intercourse with Mrs. Allen against her will, by force or by putting her in fear, then the conviction was not improper. Intent is a jury question, and the evidence here was sufficient to sustain the verdict.

Comment. Attaching criminal liability merely for manifesting an intent in one's actions comes very close to violating the fundamental criminal law requirement of an actus reus.

d. Model Penal Code approach

1) Basic approach

Departing from the approaches considered above, the Model Penal Code would require an act constituting a "substantial step" in the course of conduct intended to result in the crime. In addition, the conduct must be "strongly corroborative" of the defendant's criminal purpose, although it need not establish purpose by itself.

2) Last proximate act not required

United States v. Jackson
560 F.2d 112 (2d Cir. 1977).

Facts. Jackson (D) and Allen were contacted by Hodges to help her carry out a bank robbery. The group planned to enter the bank with the manager on Monday morning and take the weekend deposits. They armed themselves and drove to the bank, but did not rob it because they had arrived late. They decided they needed another man and went and got Scott. They returned to the bank. Allen entered to check for cameras and D made a false license plate. Because customers were in the bank, the group decided to wait until the next Monday. In the meantime, Hodges was arrested for a separate crime and began cooperating with the government, warning them of the imminent robbery. Allen told Hodges he would not rob the bank, but on Monday morning the three men, heavily armed and otherwise prepared, went to the bank, alternately parking and driving around for about an hour. During this time, D removed the front license plate (the false plate had been placed over the rear plate). When making a pass by the bank, the men detected the government agents and sped off. They were arrested and convicted of attempted robbery. Ds appeal.

Issue. May a defendant be convicted of attempt when he did not commit the last proximate act necessary to effect a particular result that is an element of the offense?

Held. Yes. Judgment affirmed.

- ◆ Commission of the "last proximate act" is sufficient, but not necessary, to constitute an attempt.

- ◆ To be convicted, D must have (i) been acting with the kind of culpability otherwise required for conviction of a crime, and (ii) taken a "substantial step" toward the commission of the crime.

- ◆ The substantial step must "strongly corroborate" the firmness of the defendant's criminal intent. The substantial step, in addition to an affirmative act, can be an omission or possession. The substantial step requirement eliminates remote preparation from criminal liability.

- ◆ This approach assures firmness of criminal design while allowing apprehension of dangerous persons without risking the ultimate harmful result.

- ◆ The evidence here supports the findings made at trial that D's acts were substantial. The steps taken were not "insubstantial" as a matter of law.

3) Model Penal Code result

MPC Sect. 5.01(1)(c) provides that the actus reus of attempt can include "an act or omission constituting a substantial step...." In *United States v. Joyce*, 693 F.2d 838 (8th Cir. 1982), Joyce was contacted by government informant Gebbie and told cocaine was available for purchase in St. Louis. The two agreed on a price and Joyce flew from Oklahoma City, where he met Gebbie and undercover officer Jones; the three went to a hotel room where Jones told Joyce the cocaine was not there, but that it could be obtained if Joyce was interested in dealing, rather than just talking. Joyce said he was interested and Jones listed prices for various amounts of cocaine. Joyce said he could "handle" a pound for $20,000. Jones obtained the cocaine from his office. When Jones returned to the hotel, he gave Joyce a plastic-wrapped package encased in duct tape that he said contained cocaine. Joyce did not unwrap the package, but returned it to Jones, stating he could not see the cocaine. Jones unwrapped about half of the package, but Joyce refused it and asked Jones to open the package so he could examine it. Jones said he would do so only when Joyce showed the money he intended to use to buy the drug. The two argued and Joyce finally said he would not deal with Jones no matter how good the cocaine was. Jones told Jones to leave; he did, with no intent to return at a later time. As Joyce left the hotel, he was arrested by DEA agents who later obtained a search warrant and found $20,000 in cash. Joyce's conviction of attempting to purchase cocaine with intent to distribute was reversed. Applying the MPC test, the court determined that whatever intent Joyce had to purchase cocaine was abandoned before the commission of a necessary and substantial step to effectuate the purchase. Joyce never produced the money necessary to purchase and ultimately possess the cocaine, and he never accepted or opened the package said to contain the cocaine. The only thing that took place here was a preliminary discussion that broke down.

4. Solicitation

a. Common law

At common law, it is a misdemeanor to counsel, incite, or induce another to commit or to join in the commission of any offense, whether that offense is a felony or a misdemeanor.

1) Mens rea

The common law crime of solicitation apparently requires a showing that the defendant acted volitionally and with the intent or purpose of causing the person solicited to commit the crime.

2) Actus reus

The only act required for the commission of the crime is the counseling, inciting, or inducing of another to commit the offense. The crime of solicitation is complete upon the performance of this act.

b. Modern statutes

While statutes traditionally have not dealt comprehensively with solicitation, the tendency has been to limit the crime to the incitement, counseling, etc., of serious offenses, such as murder, rape, kidnapping, robbery, and so forth. A lesser penalty is generally imposed for solicitation man for the commission of the crime itself, an attempt to commit it, or even a conspiracy to commit it.

c. Comparison with attempt

Unlike solicitation, attempt requires that the defendant have progressed far enough in his criminal scheme to have gone beyond mere preparation. Generally, a person who does the bare minimum that suffices for solicitation will not be liable for attempt. At the same time, however, if the defendant continues to assist the person solicited, he may well incur liability as a party to an attempt to commit the crime.

d. Solicitation alone is not overt act

State v. Davis
6 S.W.2d 609 (Mo. 1928).

Facts. Davis (D) was convicted of attempted murder for paying an undercover police officer to kill the husband of his lover. D had given the officer various maps and photographs of the house and its occupants. D appeals.

Issue. Does solicitation of a planned murder amount to a perpetration of an overt act in a criminal attempt?

Held. No. Judgment reversed.

- ♦ Solicitation is a separate crime; therefore, more needs to be shown than mere solicitation in order to establish an overt act.

- ♦ Intent was clearly established but an overt act going to the very essence of the murder attempt is required.

Comment. In *United States v. Church*, 29 Mil. J. Rptr. 679 (Ct. Milit. Rev. 1989), Church "contracted out" the murder of his wife; the hired killer was an undercover agent, and the "murder" was staged. The court expressed its disagreement with *Davis*, and found Church's actions constituted a substantial step toward commission of the crime and established the requisite overt act amounting to more than mere preparation. Church, the court stated, did all he could do to effect the crime.

5. Impossibility

a. Negation of intent

If the actor knows that it is impossible for him to commit the crime because of some physical impossibility, then no attempt can exist because the required intent element will not be present. There must be at least an apparent ability to commit the crime (a reasonable person standing in the defendant's position must think the crime could be committed).

b. Factual and legal impossibility

The tough cases are the ones where the defendant thinks that it is possible for him to commit the crime, but for some reason unknown to him, it is factually impossible. For example, A picks B's pocket, which happens to be empty. There has been an attempt. In contrast, mistake of law is a defense when the defendant mistakenly believes that his conduct is prohibited by law.

c. Mistake regarding attendant circumstances

People v. Jaffe
78 N.E. 169 (N.Y. 1906).

Facts. Jaffe (D) made an offer to buy goods that he thought were stolen, but before he had purchased them, they had been returned to their rightful owner. The goods were no longer stolen property but D was under the impression that they were. D was convicted of attempting to receive stolen property. D appeals.

Issue. May a person be convicted of an attempt to receive stolen goods if the goods were not in fact stolen goods?

Held. No. Judgment reversed.

- ♦ D is not guilty of an attempted crime. If D had completed the crime, he would not have received stolen property. He could not know it was stolen, an essential element of the defense, because it was not in fact stolen. Belief that property is stolen does not satisfy the statutory requirement of knowledge.

Comment. Modern statutes would reach a contrary result by defining attempt so as to include the kind of mistake that D made.

d. Elimination of impossibility defense

People v. Dlugash
363 N.E.2d 1155 (N.Y. 1977).

Facts. Dlugash (D) was out drinking with Bush and Geller, the victim, with whom Bush was staying. Geller demanded that Bush pay part of the rent, and Bush threatened Geller with a shooting unless Geller "shut up." They went to Geller's apartment and Geller again demanded money. Bush shot Geller three times in the chest, one shot piercing Geller's heart. Two to five minutes later, D went to Geller's body and fired five shots into Geller's head. D was tried for murder. No expert witnesses could determine at what point Geller died, although the estimates ranged from "very rapidly" to about 10 minutes after Bush first shot him. The jury was instructed on intentional murder and attempted murder. D was convicted of murder. On appeal, the murder conviction was reversed for failure of proof beyond a reasonable doubt that Geller was still alive when D shot him. The court declined to find an attempted murder because D thought Geller was dead when he shot him. The people (P) appeal.

Issue. May a person be guilty of an attempt if completion of the crime was impossible?

Held. Yes. Judgment modified.

♦ The general rule has been that legal impossibility is a good defense to a charge of attempt but that factual impossibility is no defense. This rule has been changed by the Model Penal Code, substantially adopted in New York. The new rule eliminates the defense of impossibility in virtually all situations. It emphasizes the actor's mental frame of reference because it is that intent that actually presents the danger to society.

♦ If a person intends to commit a crime and takes action that tends to effect a commission of the crime, he is guilty. Impossibility is irrelevant if the crime could have been committed if the circumstances had been as the actor thought them to be. Here, the jury must have found that D intended to kill the victim. There is evidence to support that finding, although there was insufficient evidence that Geller was still alive. Therefore, D is guilty of attempted murder.

e. Federal law

Under federal law, one cannot commit a criminal attempt when it is legally impossible to commit the crime. In *United States v. Berrigan*, 482 F.2d 171 (3d Cir. 1973), Berrigan was convicted of sending letters out from prison by courier without permission of the warden. Unbeknownst to Berrigan, prison officials intercepted the first letter and knew of subsequent letters. Berrigan was convicted of trying to take something out of a federal prison not permitted by regulation. His conviction was reversed on the basis that because the warden knew and consented to the carrying out of letters, there was a legal impossibility of his actions being criminal. While most states and the Model Penal Code would hold otherwise based on common law theory, federal law is purely statutory. Gaps in federal statutes cannot be filled by a common law theory. Thus, in *United States v. Oviedo*, 525 F.2d 881 (5th Cir. 1976), the court reversed the defendant's conviction of attempt to distribute heroin because of insufficient proof of intent. The defendant had agreed to sell heroin to an undercover agent at an agreed place and time. The defendant appeared with what he claimed to be heroin and gave it to the agent. The defendant was subsequently arrested and prosecuted for distribution of what still appeared to be heroin. However, later testimony revealed that the powder that was transferred was a nonnarcotic, uncontrolled substance. The court held that the defendant could not be convicted of attempting to sell heroin when he in fact only transferred a nonnarcotic substance. The court further held that to obtain a conviction, it is necessary that the defendant perform objective acts that are criminal in nature. It is insufficient to show that he believed the substance to be narcotic if it was not narcotic.

Chapter VII
Group Criminality

A. Accountability for the Acts of Others

1. Introduction

Suppose X is going to kill A and Y goes along with X to watch the spectacle. Is Y guilty of the crime for standing around and watching? This section is concerned with ascertaining the extent of a person's liability for a crime that he did not commit personally but to which he has some relationship.

a. The dividing line

In the hypothetical above, Y would not be guilty of any crime. He did not aid X in any way. If aid or encouragement is the dividing line, consider the following cases:

1) Y is prepared to jump in and render assistance to X if he has trouble killing A. Does Y's presence aid X? Does it hinder A?

2) What if Y has told X that he will help him, but A does not know this?

3) What if during the fight Y yells, "Get him"?

4) What if Y yells encouragement to X, but X is deaf and cannot hear a word he says?

5) What if there is a crowd of 50 people and they are all yelling encouragement to X?

6) What if Y is standing in the crowd, knowing this will encourage a fight, but he has no intent or purpose to so encourage it (he just wants to see what happens)?

b. Common law categories

1) Principal in the first degree

This is one who actually commits the crime, or who gets an innocent third party to do it for him. For example, A may give poison to B (who does not know it is poison) to give to C. A is guilty of murder; B is not a party to the crime because she is an innocent agent.

2) Principal in the second degree

a) Definition

A principal in the second degree is one who is present when the crime is committed and who aids in its commission (for example, the driver of the getaway car).

b) Constructive presence

Presence need not be actual (that is, at the immediate scene of the crime); it may be constructive. A person is constructively present where she acts pursuant to a common design with the one who commits the criminal act and aids that person (as by keeping lookout), or is situated so as to be able to help him in committing the crime. One who conspires with another, but who is not on the scene during the crime's commission, is treated as constructively present.

c) Aiding and abetting

To be guilty as a second degree principal, the defendant must make some "substantial contribution" to the commission of the crime by aiding or encouraging its commission.

3) Accessory before the fact

a) Definition

An accessory before the fact is one who is absent at the time the crime is actually committed but who procured, incited, counseled, advised, encouraged, or commanded that the crime be committed.

b) Knowledge

Mere knowledge that a crime is going to be committed is not sufficient. There has to be some actual encouragement that it be committed.

c) Proceeds

A person can be such an accessory even though she does not share in the proceeds from the commission of the crime.

4) Accessory after the fact

a) An accessory after the fact is a person who, knowing that a felony has been committed, aided, assisted, comforted, or received the felon.

b) Mere failure to notify the police about a felony that one knows has been committed does not make a person such an accessory. There has to be some actual intent or motive to assist the felon.

5) The derivative principle

According to the derivative principle that existed at common law, a principal of the second degree or an accessory could not be convicted unless the principal in the first degree had already been convicted, since until this time there was said to be no crime in which these persons could have aided.

6) Where distinctions are made

The distinction between first and second degree principals is recognized for all crimes. But only in felonies are distinctions made between principals and accessories (all persons involved in misdemeanors are treated as principals).

7) Punishment

At common law, little distinction was made in the punishment given to the various parties to a crime. This has been changed by modern statutes, which typically differentiate, giving lesser punishment to accessories, for example, man to principals.

c. Modern rules

The common law has been changed to some degree by statute. The parties to a crime are classified as either principals or accessories.

1) Principals

All persons who participate in the commission of any crime, whether they directly commit the act, or aid, abet, advise, or encourage its commission, and whether they are present at the scene of the crime or not, are principals.

    a) Thus, there are no accessories before the fact, and no distinction is made between principals of the first degree and principals of the second degree.

    b) One may "commit a crime" (by aiding and abetting) that he is technically incapable of committing. So, for example, a husband can aid another man to rape his wife and be guilty of rape.

2) Accessories

Every person who, after a felony has been committed, conceals or aids a principal in such felony with the intent that the principal escape arrest and punishment, having knowledge that the principal has committed or been charged with such felony, is an accessory.

2. Mens Rea

Criminal liability for the acts of others is predicated on the individual's criminal intent. When the defendant did not actually perform the crime, but only assisted in some way, determination of the necessary mens rea is often difficult.

a. Intent to assist

Hicks v. United States
150 U.S. 442 (1893).

Facts. Hicks (D), a Cherokee Indian, and Colvard, a white who was friendly with the Indians and had a Cherokee wife, rode their horses together down a road and were met by Rowe, another Cherokee, who was armed. The three conversed but the witnesses could not hear or understand what was said. Twice Rowe pointed his rifle at Colvard and D laughed. Then D removed his coat and told Colvard to take off his hat and die like a man. Rowe then shot Colvard dead and D and Rowe rode off together. D testified that Rowe was in a dangerous mood and that he did not know whether Rowe would kill Colvard or D himself. D also said he rode off with Rowe at his demand and soon left him. The trial judge instructed the jury that if the intentional use of words had the effect of encouraging Rowe to shoot Colvard, D would be presumed to have intended the effect. D was convicted of murder. D appeals.

Issue. May a person be found guilty of murder when the words he intentionally uttered had the effect of encouraging the murder, but he did not intend that effect?

Held. No. Judgment reversed and case remanded for a new trial.

    ♦   The judge should have instructed the jury that the words of encouragement must have been used by D with the intention of encouraging and abetting Rowe. The effect of the words is irrelevant to D's criminal liability. If he did not intend to encourage Rowe, he may not be found guilty. The facts are not conclusive as to D's intent, so a new trial with proper instructions is necessary.

b. Intent to associate with perpetrator

State v. Gladstone
474 P.2d 274 (Wash. 1980).

Facts. The police hired Thompson as an informant and told him to buy marijuana from Gladstone (D). Thompson visited D but D did not sell him any marijuana. Instead, D told Thompson that Kent might sell him some. D showed Thompson how to get to Kent's place. Thompson bought marijuana from Kent and D was charged with aiding and abetting the sale. There was no evidence of communication between D and Kent. D was convicted of the crime charged. D appeals.

Issue. May one be guilty of aiding and abetting when he does nothing in association or connection with the principal to accomplish the crime?

Held. No. Judgment reversed.

- ◆ A Washington state statute makes a principal of one who aids and abets another in the commission of a crime. The aider and abettor need not be present at the commission of the crime, but to be guilty he must do something in association or connection with the principal.

- ◆ Here there was no such nexus between D and Kent. D's only involvement was communication that Kent might commit a criminal offense. This is not aiding and abetting.

Dissent. The jury could properly conclude that D intended that his information would encourage Kent's participation in the crime.

Comment. A couple of states have created a crime of criminal facilitation, which imposes criminal liability for providing a person the means or opportunity to commit a crime.

c. Mens rea related to final act

State v. McVay
132 A. 436 (R.I. 1926).

Facts. Three people were killed by escaping steam when a boiler aboard a steamer exploded. McVay, the captain, and his engineer (Ds) were indicted for manslaughter as principals. Kelley was indicted as an accessory before the fact. Kelley challenged the indictment on the ground that no one could be an accessory before the fact to manslaughter that arose out of criminal negligence. The issue was certified to the state supreme court.

Issue. May a defendant be indicted as being an accessory before the fact to manslaughter that arose through criminal negligence?

Held. Yes.

- ◆ The indictment charged that Kelley "feloniously and maliciously" did "aid, assist, abet, counsel, hire, command and procure" Ds to commit the manslaughter. Ds in turn were charged with manslaughter "without malice." Kelley claims that a sudden and unpremeditated crime cannot be maliciously incited ahead of time. This may be true when the actual crime involved a sudden and unpremeditated act, but not all manslaughter occurs in that manner.

- ◆ Manslaughter also includes unlawful acts that result in unintentional homicide, and gross negligence in doing lawful acts. These may be premeditated acts that a person such as Kelley could aid or abet.

- ◆ In this case, Kelley was indicted for procuring the commission of the crime before it happened. Ds need not have consciously intended to kill, but their negligence in creating excess steam may have been sufficiently gross to permit imposition of criminal liability. Ds chose this course of action, allegedly with Kelley's participation, and the jury could find

Kelley an accessory if he acted with knowledge of the possible danger to human life when he advised Ds to take the chance of the negligent acts.

d. *Mens rea* for an accomplice

Commonwealth v. Roebuck
32 A.3d 613 (Pa. 2011).

Facts. Evidence was presented that showed that the victim was lured to an apartment complex where he was ambushed, shot and killed. Roebuck (D) took part, with others, in orchestrating the events, but he did not shoot the victim. D was charged with third-degree murder based on an accomplice theory and found guilty following a bench trial. A discretionary appeal was allowed.

Issue. Is a conviction for third degree murder supportable under complicity theory where the prosecution proves the accomplice acted with the culpable mental state required of a principal actor, *i.e.*, malice?

Held. Yes. Judgment affirmed.

♦ D argues that it is a logical impossibility to adjudge a defendant guilty of third-degree murder as an accomplice. "[A]ccomplice liability attaches only where the defendant *intends* to facilitate or promote an underlying offense; third-degree murder is an *unintentional* killing committed with malice; therefore, to adjudge a criminal defendant guilty of third-degree murder as an accomplice would be to accept that the accused *intended* to aid an *unintentional* act...."

♦ The relevant statute mirrors the Model Penal Code (MPC), Section 2.06(4): "When causing a particular result is an element of an offense, an accomplice in the conduct causing such result is an accomplice in the commission of that offense, if he acts with the kind of culpability, if any, with respect to that result that is sufficient for the commission of the offense."

♦ Shared criminal intent establishes the required criminal culpability as in this case where D participated in staging an extremely dangerous altercation. It is rational to hold one who assists another in malicious conduct to account to the same degree as the principal for foreseeable consequences of the wrongful acts.

The requisite *mens* rea for an accomplice is set forth in the MPC, sect. 2.06(3),(4):

"(3) A person is an accomplice of another person in the commission of an offense if... with the purpose of promoting or facilitating the commission of the offense, he ... aids or agrees or attempts to aid such other person in planning or committing it[.]

"(4) When causing a particular result is an element of an offense, an accomplice in the conduct causing such result is an accomplice in the commission of that offense if he acts with the kind of culpability, if any, with respect to that result that is sufficient for the commission of the offense."

Commentary accompanying these sections explains that the commission of the offense as described focuses on the conduct of the accomplice, not the result. This negates any conclusion that an accomplice must always intend results essential to the completed crime.

Concurrence. D's syllogism is based on a false premise and his argument fails. An accomplice to third degree murder does not intend to aid an unintentional murder; he intends to aid a malicious act which results in a killing. If an accomplice gives a gun to the principal and tells him "'shoot that victim—I don't care if he dies or not, but shoot him,'" and the victim is shot in the leg, but dies, this is classic third degree murder. There is no proof of specific intent to kill, but there is clearly a malicious act regardless of the consequences. The same logic that permits a murder charge against the principal attaches to the accomplice as well—both committed an intentional malicious act that resulted in the death of another, and both are guilty of the murder charge that follows.

e. "Community of purpose"

People v. Russell
91 N.Y.2d 280, 639 N.E.2d 193 (N.Y. 1998).

Facts. Russell and two others (Ds) engaged in a gun battle on the mall of a housing project. During the battle, a school principal was fatally wounded by a stray bullet. Ds were all charged with second degree murder. Ballistics tests were inconclusive as to which defendant's gun fired the fatal bullet. The prosecutor theorized each of the Ds acted with the mental culpability required for commission of the crime and each intentionally aided the defendant who fired the fatal shot. Ds were convicted of second degree depraved indifference murder. Ds appeal.

Issue. Could the evidence, viewed in the light most favorable to the prosecution, lead a rational trier of fact to find, beyond a reasonable doubt, that each defendant was guilty of depraved indifference murder as charged?

Held. Yes. Judgment affirmed.

- ◆ A conviction for a depraved indifference murder requires proof that a defendant under circumstances evincing a depraved indifference to human life, recklessly engaged in conduct creating a grave risk of death to another person, and thereby caused the death of another person.

- ◆ Ds argue that because they were adversaries in a gun battle, there is no "community of purpose" required for accomplice liability. We do not agree. The fact that Ds set out to injure each other does not preclude a finding that they intentionally aided each other to engage in mutual combat that caused a person's death.

- ◆ Ds' acts made the death possible. They agreed to engage in a gun battle that placed an innocent person at grave risk and they killed him. The gun battle was not an ambush that took Ds by surprise; Ds accepted each other's challenge to engage in battle on a public mall.

f. Acts of others

People v. Luparello
231 Cal. Rptr. 832 (Cal. Ct. App. 1987).

Facts. Luparello (D) tried to locate his former lover through Martin, a friend of the former lover's current husband. D told his friends that he wanted the information at any cost. After Martin failed to provide the information sought, D's friends, without D present, lured Martin outdoors and killed him. D was charged and convicted of murder. D appeals.

Issue. Is a defendant liable for the unplanned and unintended act of co-conspirators?

Held. Yes. Judgment affirmed.

- ◆ Accomplice liability derives from the aider and abettor's intent to commit or encourage the commission of a crime. Liability is extended to reach the actual crime committed as opposed to the crime "intended" based on the policy that aiders and abettors should be responsible for the criminal harms they have naturally, probably, and foreseeably put in motion. D is guilty of any foreseeable offense committed by anyone he aids and abets.

Concurrence. I concur because of the controlling case law, but find that law to be unsound. It is illogical to assess D's degree of culpability by the mental state of the perpetrator and/or the circumstances of the crime. If the jury found that the shooter lay in wait, demonstrating malice, D would be guilty of murder in the first degree. But if the shooter was drunk and unable to form malice, D would men only be guilty of voluntary manslaughter. Such fortuity of result is irrational.

1) Insufficient evidence for a "natural and probable consequence"

In *Roy v. United States,* 652 A.2d 1098 (D.C. Ct. App. 1995), paid police informant Miller approached Roy to try to buy a handgun. When Miller returned with $400, as Roy had instructed, Roy was referred to Ross, who took him to another area and gave Roy the gun while Miller counted the money. Then Ross asked for the gun back, said he changed his mind, and robbed Miller of the $600 he had in his possession. When Miller asked why, Ross said it was revenge for Miller's earlier holdup of one of his own group. Roy was convicted as an accomplice to Ross's armed robbery. The jury was instructed that Roy could be found liable if the robbery was the natural and probable consequence of the illegal attempt to sell a handgun, even if he did not intend that Ross rob Miller. The court of appeals reversed, finding insufficient evidence to support this theory. It determined that the government wanted the conviction sustained without requiring a showing that Roy intended to take part in the robbery or in any other violent crime. Armed robbery is a felony punishable by life imprisonment; selling a handgun is a misdemeanor for which Roy has been independently convicted. The court restated its determination that "an accessory is liable for any criminal act which in the ordinary course of things was the natural and probable consequence of the crime that he advised or commanded, although such consequence may not have been intended by him." It stated the phrase "in the ordinary course of things" refers to what may reasonably take place from the planned events, not to what might conceivably happen. More important, it suggests the absence of intervening factors. It is not enough for the prosecution to show that the accomplice knew or should have known that the principal might commit the crime that the accomplice is charged with aiding and abetting.

3. Actus Reus

a. Introduction

In deciding whether particular conduct is such as would justify criminal liability, the materiality of aid or encouragement is a major factor. The "but for" test used to determine causation need not be satisfied for a determination of accessorial liability, as long as the necessary mens rea is present. The threshold of materiality of the act is not always clear, however.

b. Encouraging commission of an illegal act

Wilcox v. Jeffery
1 All E.R. 464 (1951).

Facts. Aliens were forbidden to take employment, paid or unpaid, while in the United Kingdom. Hawkins, a United States saxophone player, was invited to the United Kingdom. Wilcox (D), who owned a jazz music magazine, greeted Hawkins upon his arrival, attended a jazz concert given by Hawkins, and wrote and published an article praising the illegal concert. D was convicted of aiding and abetting Hawkins in violating the alien order. D appeals.

Issue. May a person be guilty of aiding and abetting a criminal act simply by being a paid spectator at the event and by publishing an article about it?

Held. Yes. Judgment affirmed.

♦ If D's presence had been accidental, he would probably not be guilty. But D took part in the illegal act by encouraging it. D knew the act was illegal, yet affirmatively encouraged its commission.

Comment. Similarly, in *State ex rel. Attorney General v. Tally, Judge,* 15 So. 722 (Ala. 1894), the court found the judge was an accomplice in the killing of the deceased in that he deprived the deceased of a chance of life. There, the deceased's relatives had sent him a telegram warning him that he was being sought after for the seduction of the judge's sister-in-law. The judge, however, advised the telegraph operator not to deliver the warning telegram. Ultimately, the assailants caught up with the deceased and killed him. The court concluded that one can be held criminally responsible if one renders it easier for the principal actor to accomplish the intended act, even though it would have been attained without such help.

4. Comparison of the Parties' Liability

a. Introduction

In some cases, the parties will not share the same motive for their actions. For example, the aider and abettor may be intending to assist the commission of a crime when the other does not so intend, as when the aider and abettor forces the other to act through threats. Alternatively, the principal may not be subject to conviction (*e.g.,* diplomatic immunity). The general rule, however, is that an aider and abettor may not be convicted unless a crime was actually committed.

b. Principal without intent

State v. Hayes
16 S.W. 514 (Mo. 1891).

Facts. Hayes (D) and Hill agreed to burglarize a store. Hill actually pretended to agree in order to obtain the arrest of D. The two men arrived at the store, then D boosted Hill into the store, and Hill handed a side of bacon out to D. They were then arrested. The trial court charged that if D, with felonious intent, assisted and aided Hill to enter the building, D would be guilty of burglary, even though Hill (who actually entered the building) had no criminal intent. D appealed his conviction.

Issue. Should a party who does not actually enter a building, but only assists someone into the building who has no criminal intent, be found guilty of burglary?

Held. No. Conviction reversed.

♦ Trial court erred in charge to the jury. D did not commit every overt act necessary to make up the crime. To make D responsible for the acts of Hill, they must have had a common motive or design. The motives here were dissimilar, since Hill had no intention to burglarize. The act of Hill can thus not be imputed to D.

Comment. Other courts have taken a position contrary to *Hayes. See, e.g., Valden v. State,* 768 P.2d 1102 (Alaska 1989).

B. Conspiracy

1. Definition

Conspiracy is an agreement between two or more persons to do an unlawful act or to do a lawful act in an unlawful manner. At common law, conspiracy was a misdemeanor, and if the substantive crime was actually committed, then the misdemeanor merged into the actual crime committed. Today, however, conspiracy is punishable as a separate and distinct crime. Therefore, the defendant may be prosecuted for both the conspiracy and the complete crime and the sentences added together on conviction.

2. Particular Aspects of Conspiracy

a. Relationship to the law of evidence

1) Introduction

It is difficult to understand the law of conspiracy unless one understands the law of evidence.

a) Hearsay rule

The hearsay rule requires that one testify only about those things that he has actually observed; that is, one cannot put into evidence the out-of-court statement of another to prove the truth of that statement.

b) Exceptions to hearsay rule

There are exceptions to the hearsay rule. One of these is the "admissions exception"—anything that the defendant himself has said out of court can be introduced in court to prove the truth of the fact asserted in the out-of-court statement. Also, admissions by the agent of a party will often be received against the party. For example, if a truck driver hits A, then admits to A that he was going too fast, A may testify in court about the statement and such testimony will be used against the owner of the truck and the employer of the driver (*i.e.*, the principal).

3. The Actus Reus of Conspiracy

a. The agreement itself

Interstate Circuit, Inc. v. United States
306 U.S. 208 (1939).

Facts. Interstate Circuit, Inc. and Texas Consolidated Theaters (Ds), film distributors that dominated the market for film exhibition in various cities, entered into contracts with each of eight film distributors, which, in total, controlled 75% of all first run films. The individual contracts were permissible, but the government showed that the eight distributors had an agreement with one another. The showing was made by introducing a letter from Interstate to each of the eight distributors, that showed each of the eight as addressees, and that made certain pricing demands as a condition of Interstate doing further business with the distributor. Subsequently, each distributor agreed and on that basis the trial court found that the distributors had conspired with one another. The district court restrained Ds from continuing in a combination and conspiracy condemned by the court as a violation of section 1 of the Sherman Antitrust Act. Ds appeal.

Issue. Where evidence shows that members of a group independently entered into an agreement with one party, and each of the members were aware that the other members of the group were considering the same agreement, will such evidence support a finding that the group members entered into an agreement among themselves?

Held. Yes. Judgment affirmed.

- ◆ Since the letter named as addressees the eight distributors, each distributor knew that the proposal was being considered by the others.

- ◆ Each distributor knew that group cooperation would lead to increased profits, while nonparticipation would lead to losses.

- ◆ Knowing that concerted action was being invited, each distributor participated in the plan.

- Each distributor became aware that the others had joined and, with that knowledge, they renewed the arrangement and carried it into effect for two successive years.

- An unlawful conspiracy does not require simultaneous action or agreement among the conspirators.

4. The Mens Rea of Conspiracy

a. Introduction

Conspiracy is generally held to be a specific intent crime; that is, the defendant must have the specific intent to commit the act that is a crime.

b. Is knowledge enough?

To be guilty of a conspiracy, one must have more than mere knowledge. There has to be an improper purpose or desire; *i.e.*, the defendant must in some sense promote the venture herself, make it her own, or have a stake in its outcome.

1) Provider of services

People v. Lauria

59 Cal. Rptr. 628 (Cal. Ct. App. 1967).

Facts. Lauria (D) ran a telephone answering service. Among his customers were nine or 10 prostitutes. D knew they were prostitutes, but he did not charge them extra, nor did they provide him with a major part of his business. D was charged with conspiracy to commit prostitution, but the indictment was dismissed. The People (P) appeal.

Issue. May a person be guilty of conspiracy for knowingly providing services that are used to commit misdemeanors when he has no stake in the venture?

Held. No. Judgment affirmed.

- Knowledge of another's criminal activity is not necessarily a conspiracy to further the activity. A supplier of goods and services has a variable duty to screen his customers. In *United States v. Falcone*, 311 U.S. 205 (1940), distributors of sugar, yeast, and cans were not guilty of conspiracy to produce illegal liquor. However, in *Direct Sales Co. v. United States*, 319 U.S. 703 (1943), a drug wholesaler was convicted of conspiracy with the buyer, who was supplying addicts.

- Knowledge of criminal activity must be combined with one of the following to justify a conspiracy conviction:

    A "stake in the venture," such as an inflated price for the service, so the seller has an interest in having the activity go on;

    No legitimate use for the goods or services (*e.g.*, a prostitution directory);

    An unusual volume of business not proportionate to any legitimate demand.

2) Imputing the acts of one conspirator to the others

a) Introduction

The general rule is that each conspirator is held accountable for any and all crimes that result from the furtherance of the conspiracy. It is no defense to say that the crime committed was not part of the original plan (even if it was expressly agreed that the act should not be done) if it can be said that the commission of such an act or crime was reasonably foreseeable. The courts are generally liberal in finding that acts were the natural and probable consequence of the conspiracy.

b) No direct participation necessary

Pinkerton v. United States
328 U.S. 640 (1946).

Facts. The Pinkertons (Ds), Daniel and Walter, were prosecuted for conspiracy to commit violations of the Internal Revenue Code and for substantive violations. Only Walter committed the actual violations, but both brothers were convicted of conspiracy and certain of the substantive violations. Daniel appeals.

Issue. May a conspirator be convicted of committing the offense intended by the conspiracy although he had no direct participation in the actual commission?

Held. Yes. Judgment affirmed.

♦ Once Daniel conspired with Walter, he became equally responsible with Walter for acts done in furtherance of the conspiracy. The conspiracy was continuous. There is no evidence that Daniel withdrew from the conspiracy before Walter acted. The criminal intent necessary was established by the formation of the conspiracy. Thus, Daniel was properly convicted of the substantive offenses.

Dissent (Rutledge, J.). All the government proved was that Daniel had, in the past, conspired with Walter to commit violations similar to those committed in this case. There is no evidence that Daniel conspired to commit the particular acts that Walter committed here. Daniel was even in prison when Walter committed some of the acts.

Comment. In *People v. McGee*, 399 N.E.2d 1177 (N.Y. 1979), the court expressly refused to follow the *Pinkerton* rule in state prosecutions, requiring participation in the substantive offense to support a conviction for the substantive offense.

c) Reasonably foreseeable results

State v. Bridges
628 A.2d 270 (N.J. 1993).

Facts. Bridges (D) got into a fight with Strickland at a birthday party for a 16-year-old friend. D went to get help and recruited Bing and Rolle. The three stopped at Bing's house where they picked up a gun to use to intimidate Strickland's friends while D fought with him. Instead, when they arrived at the party, D fought with a friend of Strickland while Bing and Rolle tried to keep the crowd back. After someone in the crowd hit Bing in the face, he and Rolle began firing into the air and then into the crowd. One person was shot and killed. D was convicted of conspiracy to commit aggravated assault and other crimes, including murder. For the murder conviction, D was sentenced to life and was ineligible for parole for a minimum of 30 years. D appealed, and the murder conviction was reversed. The prosecution appeals.

Issue. May a co-conspirator be held liable for the commission of substantive criminal acts that are not within the scope of the conspiracy if they are reasonably foreseeable as the necessary or natural consequences of the conspiracy?

Held. Yes. Judgment reversed.

♦ The appellate division determined that the provision of the Code of Criminal Justice that imposes criminal liability on the basis of participation in a conspiracy requires "complete congruity" between accomplice and vicarious conspirator liability. The appellate division reasoned that *Pinkerton, supra,* requires that a crime was within a co-conspirator's contemplation when he entered into the agreement. However, that view is not supported.

♦ *Pinkerton* sought to impose vicarious liability on each conspirator for the acts of the other conspirators based on an objective standard of reasonable foreseeability. Under a standard of reasonable foreseeability, that liability would be broader than that of an accomplice, where the defendant must actually foresee and intend the result of his acts.

- ◆ To address the special dangers inherent in group activity, the legislature intended to include the crime of conspiracy as a distinctive basis for vicarious criminal liability.

- ◆ Here, the killing of another was not the objective of the conspiracy, but the conspiratorial plan included bringing loaded guns to keep a large hostile crowd at bay while a friend was beaten. It could have been anticipated that a gun might be fired at the crowd.

Concurrence and dissent. Life imprisonment imposed on the basis of the negligent appraisal of a risk is not in harmony with our criminal code. If D did not intend that the person in the crowd be killed, he could not have been convicted of attempted murder, of being an accomplice to the murder, or even of conspiracy to commit the murder. There is no liability other than for the crime or crimes that were the object of the conspiracy.

d) Relation back doctrine

If a new person joins a conspiracy and has an awareness as to its general purpose and the past acts that have been committed in its furtherance, the doctrine of "relation back" applies and such a person becomes responsible for all of the acts of the conspirators up to that time.

e) Atypical application of *Pinkerton*

In *State v. Alvarez,* 755 F.2d 830 (11th Cir. 1985), after a lengthy negotiation, a drug "buy" was set up in a run-down motel in Miami. Undercover ATF agents waited with the drug dealers for another dealer to return with an amount of cocaine the agents had agreed to buy for $147,000. When the cocaine arrived, other agents converged on the motel and a shoot-out began in the room. One agent was killed and another wounded; two dealers were wounded, also. All of the dealers were convicted of conspiracy to commit and commission of several drug offenses. Alvarez and Simon, the two who had shot the agents, were also convicted of first-degree murder of a federal agent. Three dealers were convicted of second-degree murder although they played no part in the shooting. The three argued that their murder convictions were based on an unprecedented and improper extension of *Pinkerton.* The Court agreed that it may have been an unprecedented application of *Pinkerton,* but not an improper application. The Court found evidence that the jury could have concluded that murder was a reasonably foreseeable consequence of the drug conspiracy. It established the conspiracy was designed to effectuate the sale of a large quantity of cocaine, and based on the amount of drugs and money, the jury could infer that some actors would be carrying weapons and deadly force would be used, if necessary to protect the conspirators' interests. It noted this case was not a typical *Pinkerton* case, *i.e.,* the murder of the agent was not within the original scope of the conspiracy; it was the result of an unintended turn of events. The Court was mindful of the potential due process limitations on the *Pinkerton* doctrine in cases where there were attenuated relationships between the conspirator and the substantive crime. However, the Court did not agree that the three defendants were minor members of the conspiracy. One was armed and served as a lookout; one introduced the agents to Alvarez, the leader of the conspiracy, and was present when the shooting started, and the third was the motel manager and allowed the deal to take place on the premises; he also acted as a translator during the negotiations. The Court determined *Pinkerton* liability was properly imposed.

f) Admissions of one admissible against all

In *Krulewitch v. United States*, 336 U.S. 440 (1949)Krulewitch and a woman defendant allegedly conspired to persuade another woman to travel interstate (from New York to Florida) for the purpose of prostitution, and then did transport her for that purpose. Such activity is illegal under the Mann Act. After Krulewitch was arrested, the complaining witness (the prostitute) told the prosecution of an alleged conversation she had with the woman defendant. The conversation occurred after the witness had returned to New York and involved a suggestion not to implicate Krulewitch. Krulewitch was tried alone, and this conversation was admitted over objection. Krulewitch was convicted- and the conviction was affirmed on appeal. The Supreme Court reversed. In determining whether a conspirator's statements may be admitted into evidence against a co-conspirator—if the statements were not made in furtherance of the crime charged, the Court held that they could not. The testimony about the alleged conversation, the Court found, was hearsay, and not admissible unless covered by a hearsay.

An exception to the hearsay rule does apply to out-of-court statements made by one conspirator, but only if made in furtherance of the objectives of an ongoing conspiracy. The government asserted that the statement was made in furtherance of a subsidiary phase of the conspiracy; *i.e.*, to avoid detection. But the conversation took place well after the criminal act was completed. It was too far removed from the conspiracy alleged to have been made in furtherance of that conspiracy. The Court held the exception to the hearsay rule should not be extended to such statements or the hearsay rule would effectively cease to exist in conspiracy cases.

3) Hypotheticals

a) Suppose A recruits B to do a bank job saying, "Come on, do it with us. We've got C, a great safecracker." The police want B to testify against C. Such testimony is admissible, since it was said by one of the members of the conspiracy during the course of and in furtherance of the conspiracy. Conspiracy is like the partnership idea—each member of the conspiracy is said to have authorized all of the other members to do all of the acts that they do.

b) Suppose A came into the bar and said, "Boy, are we lucky. We've got C to be the safecracker." This statement is not admissible (except against A), since it was not made in furtherance of the conspiracy.

4) Imputing the acts of one conspirator to the others

a) Introduction

The general rule is that each conspirator is held accountable for any and all crimes that result from the furtherance of the conspiracy. It is no defense to say that the crime committed was not part of the original plan (even if it was expressly agreed that the act should not be done) if it can be said that the commission of such an act or crime was reasonably foreseeable. The courts are generally liberal in finding that acts were the natural and probable consequence of the conspiracy.

5. Scope of the Agreement—Single or Multiple Conspiracies

a. The "hub of the wheel" conspiracy

Kotteakos v. United States
328 U.S. 750 (1946).

Facts. There were originally 32 defendants. Brown was the key figure; he acted as a broker for the others in getting loans under the National Housing Act (charging them all a commission). Brown knew that these loans were taken for illegal purposes under the Act. None of the parties dealing through Brown knew of the others. Seven of the defendants (Ds) were convicted. The appellate court held that there were actually several conspiracies rather than one, but that there was no prejudicial error. Ds appeal.

Issue. When one person deals with others having no connection with each other, are all defendants guilty of one conspiracy?

Held. No. Judgment reversed.

- There are several conspiracies, not just one big one. By allowing the case to proceed on the theory of one conspiracy, the court improperly allowed the specific acts of unrelated conspirators to be considered against all the others.

Comments.

- The "hub of the wheel" conspiracy might be diagrammed as follows:

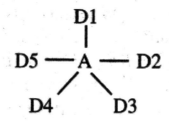

If the hub of the wheel acts alone, then there are five different conspiracies (there is no connection between the individual radii). But if the hub is a *known* source for all of the radii or the scheme depends on all radii to function, then there is one big conspiracy.

- Similarly, in *Blumenthal v. United States*, 332 U.S. 539 (1947), the Court found that only one large conspiracy in fact existed. The Court held that the two separate agreements (one between the distributor and an unidentified man and the other between the distributor and two local businessmen) were merely steps in the formation of a larger and more general conspiracy. The schemes were the same and the salesmen knew, or should have known, that they were sharing in a larger project. The Court stated that it is not necessary that one know everyone involved or exactly what part each person is playing in carrying out the common design of the conspiracy. Here, all knew of and joined in the scheme of disposing of whiskey at prices over the ceiling.

- In *Anderson v. Superior Court*, 177 P.2d 315 (Cal. 1947), Stern was performing abortions. He had several people referring women to him, the defendant being one of them. The court found one large conspiracy. The rationale: The doctor is a full-time abortionist; the defendant who brings him one woman a week knows that there have to be other suppliers also. If the doctor were an osteopath, knowledge of the others would less easily be imputed to the defendant.

- ♦ In summary, if one large conspiracy is found, one conspirator can be held liable for possibly hundreds of crimes. Also, all co-conspirators can be tried together, which makes the defense of any one defendant more difficult.

b. The "fork-chain" conspiracy

United States v. Bruno
105 F.2d 921 (2d Cir. 1939), *rev'd on other grounds*, 308 U.S. 287 (1939).

Facts. There are 88 defendants (two on trial here) being prosecuted for conspiracy to import, sell, and possess narcotics. The defendants argue that there are several separate conspiracies, not one large one. This is an appeal from a conviction for conspiracy to import, sell, and possess narcotics.

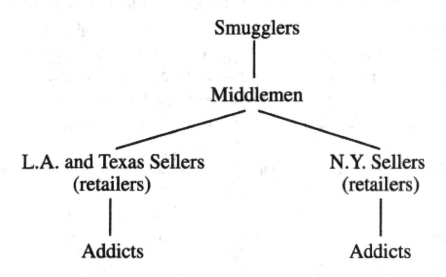

Issue. Can a single conspiracy exist even though none of the conspirators either cooperated or communicated with each other?

Held. Yes. Judgment affirmed.

- ♦ The trial court allowed the jury to find that there was one great conspiracy. The evidence showed no communication between the smugglers and the retailers, or between retailers, etc., but each part of the organization knew of the others and the success of the individual parts was dependent on the success of the whole.

Comment. This is a "fork-chain" conspiracy:

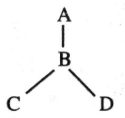

c. Beyond the scope of the agreement

United States v. McDermott
245 F.3d 133 (2d Cir. 2001).

Facts. McDermott (D) was president, CEO, and chairman of Keefe Bruyette & Woods, a New York investment bank that specialized in mergers and acquisitions. D began an extramarital affair with Kathryn Gannon, an adult film star and alleged prostitute. At the same time, unbeknownst to D, Gannon was having an affair with Pomponio. D gave Gannon stock recommendations, and Gannon passed them on to Pomponio. Together, Gannon and Pomponio earned about $170,000 in profits during the relevant period. The three were indicted for conspiracy to commit insider trading and for insider trading. The evidence centered on D's relationship with Gannon and Gannon and Pomponio's trading activities. The circumstantial evidence connecting records of 800 telephone calls between D and Gannon (as many as 29 calls in one day) with trading activities of Gannon and Pomponio served as the foundation of the government's case. Also, audiotapes of Pomponio's S.E.C. deposition, in which he poorly told lies, evaded questions, and affected incredulous reactions, undermined his defense and credibility. D was convicted of conspiracy to commit insider trading and of insider trading. D appeals.

Issue. Was the evidence sufficient to support D's conviction for a single conspiracy with Pomponio?

Held. No. Conspiracy count reversed and case is remanded.

♦ D must show that no rational trier of fact could have found the essential elements of the crime charged beyond a reasonable doubt. Measured against this high standard, we find that there was insufficient evidence on the conspiracy count.

♦ The prosecution argues that Gannon and Pomponio had a unitary purpose to commit insider trading based on D's information and that, therefore, D was part of the conspiracy even though he made no agreement to pass on information to both of them. However, in *United States v. Carpenter*, 791 F.2d 1024 (2d Cir. 1986), *aff'd*, 484 U.S. 19 (1987), the conspiracy conviction of a reporter who took part in a scheme with his friends, Felis and Brant, to misappropriate insider information and use it for personal gain was reversed to the extent that it involved trades of another person, Spratt, who was unknown to the defendant. Felis passed the information to Spratt without defendant's knowledge. We found that Felis had gone beyond the scope of the original agreement.

♦ In *Carpenter*, we outlined three hypothetical avenues of liability against the defendant. If the scope of the trading agreement had been broader, allowing for persons other than the small group, he might have been liable. He might have been liable if the Spratt trades had been part of the ramifications of the plan that could be reasonably foreseen as a necessary or natural consequence of the unlawful agreement. Finally, he might have been liable if he had at least known of the Felis-Spratt relationship.

♦ None of these avenues of liability applies in this case. Thus, D is not liable for the trades that Pomponio made. The most basic element of a conspiracy, an agreement to pass insider information to Gannon and possibly to another person, is absent from the government's case.

6. Parties

a. Introduction

There must be two or more persons to a conspiracy.

b. Two-party crimes

1) General rule

Certain crimes require an agreement *and* the active participation of at least two persons. For example, bribery requires action by the giver and the receiver of the bribe. In these situations, there can be no separate offense of conspiracy, since the agreement between the two persons is a necessary part of the substantive crime.

2) Three or more persons

Note, however, that if three persons become involved in such a crime, there can be a conspiracy.

3) Two guilty parties required

Gebardi v. United States
287 U.S. 112 (1932).

Facts. Gebardi (D) and the woman he transported across state lines to have sexual relations with were charged with a conspiracy to violate the Mann Act. Gebardi made all of the arrangements; the woman voluntarily consented to go. Ds were convicted of conspiracy to violate the Mann Act. Ds appeal.

Issue. May a woman be convicted of conspiracy to violate the Mann Act when she has not actually violated it?

Held. No. Judgment reversed.

♦ Congress intended the Mann Act to exempt the woman of the substantive crime. Therefore, the woman may not be convicted of conspiracy to violate the Act. Since she is not guilty, the man cannot be either, since it takes two persons for a conspiracy (there must be an "agreement").

Comment. The Model Penal Code would convict the man in *Gebardi, i.e.*, if one agrees with another to commit a crime, one is guilty of a conspiracy even if the other person is not. Most courts, however, follow the *Gebardi* rule.

c. Feigned acquiescence by one party

Garcia v. State
394 N.E.2d 106 (Ind. 1979).

Facts. Garcia (D) complained to Young that her husband beat her and her children, and she asked Young to find someone to kill her husband. Young contacted the police, who set up a meeting between D, Young, and a plainclothes detective. D made a down payment to the detective and provided information to help him kill her husband. D was then arrested and later convicted of conspiracy to commit murder. D appeals, claiming there was no conspiracy because the detective only feigned acquiescence in the plan.

Issue. May one commit a conspiracy with a police officer who merely feigns acquiescence to the conspiracy?

Held. Yes. Judgment affirmed.

♦ The traditional view of conspiracy is termed "bilateral" and requires that two or more persons conspire to commit a crime, each with the intent to do so. If all but one co-conspirator merely feign acquiescence, there is no conspiratorial agreement and no conviction for conspiracy is possible.

- The Model Penal Code adopts a "unilateral" approach by which a culpable party's guilt is unaffected by whether other co-conspirators are also guilty. The rationale is that the unequivocal evidence of a firm purpose to commit a crime, which is the basis of conspiratorial liability, is the same regardless of the true intentions of co-conspirators.

- Indiana makes illegal an agreement with another to commit a felony. This term does not require a meeting of the minds but rather reflects the unilateral approach.

7. RICO

a. Introduction

Title 18, U.S.C. sections 1961–1964, provides for criminal penalties and civil remedies involving Racketeer Influenced and Corrupt Organizations—hence the name RICO. The statute provides a broad definition of "racketeering activity" and prohibits any person who has profited from racketeering to use or invest such profits to acquire an interest in an interstate enterprise. Any interest acquired in violation of the statute is subject to forfeiture to the United States and violators can be punished by a fine or up to 20 years' imprisonment. Any person injured by violations of this law can sue for damages.

b. The enterprise concept of conspiracy

United States v. Elliott
571 F.2d 880 (5th Cir. 1978).

Facts. Elliott and five other defendants (Ds) were indicted under a single indictment for conspiracy to violate RICO. RICO makes it unlawful to engage in any racketeering activity that affects interstate commerce. The criminal enterprise in which Ds were alleged co-conspirators engaged in murder, numerous thefts, arson, illicit drug transactions, and obstruction of justice. Not all the Ds had contact with all the other Ds, but all had participated in some way in the criminal activities of the enterprise. At trial, the prosecutor introduced evidence of multiple conspiracies. All six Ds were convicted and now appeal.

Issue. In a trial for conspiracy to violate RICO, does proof of multiple conspiracies under an indictment alleging a single conspiracy constitute a material variance requiring reversal?

Held. No. All the convictions are affirmed but Elliott's. The evidence against Elliott was insufficient to prove that he had agreed to participate in the enterprise through a pattern of racketeering.

- A single conspiracy could not be demonstrated by applying pre-RICO conspiracy concepts to this case, but through RICO Congress intended to authorize the single prosecution of a multifaceted, diversified conspiracy through the enterprise concept.

- RICO creates a substantive offense that ties together diverse parties and crimes. Each conspirator need not participate in or have knowledge of all the crimes of the enterprise, only two or more. It is irrelevant to one conspirator what another conspirator has agreed to do because, under RICO, a defendant is charged with agreeing to participate in the enterprise through his own crimes, not with agreeing to commit each of the enterprises.

- Our society disdains mass prosecutions, but we recognize that conspiracy must be punished because it is more dangerous than individual action. When many conspire, they invite mass trial by their conduct.

Comment. Before this case, the United States Supreme Court had held that proof of multiple conspiracies under an indictment alleging a single conspiracy constituted a material variance requiring reversal. [*See* Kotteakos v. United States, *supra]* At issue was the right not to be tried en masse for the conglomeration of distinct and separate offenses committed by others. This case takes the opposite position where conspiracy to violate RICO is involved. Note the importance the Fifth Circuit places on Congress's intent to take strong action against criminal enterprises.

C. Corporate Crimes

1. Introduction

Business crimes include traditional crimes committed in the course of doing legitimate business as well as violations of criminal regulatory statutes. The latter types of business crime, including antitrust violations, environmental protection violations, etc., present policy problems because they deviate in substantial ways from traditional criminal activity and therefore require a different kind of justification. In addition, when the crime is committed by a corporation, the liability of individual agents versus that of the entity is a major issue.

2. Use of Criminal Law

a. Policy considerations

When the criminal law is used to regulate the economic conduct of business (antitrust, price controls) or to promote public welfare objectives (environmental protection, consumer safety), the result is to undermine the restraints imposed on the use of criminal law generally.

1) Specificity

A basic limitation on criminal statutes is that they must clearly describe the proscribed conduct. Many statutes have been declared void for vagueness. Yet the antitrust laws especially are notorious for not specifically defining what conduct is illegal.

2) Personal guilt

Criminal justice requires that the person to be punished be personally guilty of the illegal act. Yet criminal sanctions on corporations fall on stockholders rather than on those who commit the crimes.

3) Deserved punishment

Intent is a fundamental principle of criminal law because the stigma of criminal sanction should be reserved for those who intended the harm for which they are punished. Yet corporate punishment is far removed from those who intend the harm.

b. Deterrence

Some commentators feel that criminal sanctions may make business too timid, stifling innovation; criminal sanctions provide excessive deterrence. Others feel that criminal sanctions would have an ideal deterrent effect. However, criminal penalties have not been effective in the area of business regulation.

1) One explanation is that business regulatory violations are not commonly regarded as morally reprehensible. The spirit of the free enterprise system denies moral culpability, thereby rendering criminal sanctions unjust.

2) Generally, the cases are complex. It is difficult to prove unlawful intent, and it is difficult to carry the burden of proof necessary to gain a criminal conviction.

3) Often the law is unclear as to what constitutes unlawful conduct.

4) Law enforcement is in the hands of members of a social class who are likely to sympathize with those in business.

3. Corporate Criminal Liability

a. Introduction

Once particular business conduct has been declared illegal, the question remains as to how sanctions will be imposed, and on whom.

1) Acts for which the corporation is bound

a) When is a corporation punished as a substitute for punishment of individuals?

b) What acts of what corporate employees justify criminal penalties imposed on the corporation?

2) Vicarious liability

When may higher corporate officials be held liable for the acts of lesser ones? This question raises the possibility that corporate officials may be held liable even when they would not be held under normal legal doctrines as an accomplice.

b. Corporate liability

1) Corporate liability for employee activity

New York Central & Hudson River Railroad Co. v. United States
212 U.S. 481 (1909).

Facts. An employee of the New York Central & Hudson River Railroad Co. (D) made arrangements with a shipper whereby D would pay the shipper rebates in return for its use of D's lines. D and the employee were each convicted of violating a federal law. D appeals, contending that the law was unconstitutional.

Issue. May Congress make a corporation criminally liable for the acts of its employees?

Held. Yes. Judgment affirmed.

- ♦ D claims that the law allowing punishment of corporations actually punishes innocent stockholders without giving them an opportunity to be heard. The early common law rule did exclude corporations from criminal liability.

- ♦ The modern rule reflects the realization that what a corporation does, it can intend to do. If a corporation can lay down tracks and run railroad cars on them, it can also intend to do so. A corporation acts by its officers and agents, and must be held accountable for their acts.

- ♦ The payment of rebates inures to the benefit of D, and if only the individuals may be held liable, the law against rebates cannot be effectively enforced.

2) Corporate liability for employee acts in violation of corporate policy

United States v. Hilton Hotels Corp.
467 F.2d 1000 (9th Cir. 1972).

Facts. Hilton Hotels Corp. (D) was one of several hotels, restaurants, and hotel and restaurant supply companies that organized an association to attract conventions to their city. Members were to contribute specified amounts, and D and other hotels allegedly agreed to buy supplies only from suppliers who contributed. The agreement, if proved, constitutes a per se violation of the Sherman Act. D's purchasing agent admitted that he had been instructed not to participate in a boycott against noncontributing suppliers but that he had threatened one such supplier with a boycott because he personally disliked the supplier's agent. This threat was the evidence upon which D was convicted. D appeals, claiming that it should not be held responsible when its agent had violated express instructions not to participate in the illegal activity.

Issue. May a corporation be held criminally liable for acts of its agents, done within the scope of their employment, even though the corporation's policy and specific instructions prohibited such acts?

Held. Yes. Judgment affirmed.

- ◆ Congress has power to impose criminal liability on corporations through general principles of agency, so that the illegal acts of employees acting within the scope of their employment are imputed to the corporation. This is so even when the agent is disobeying express instructions.

- ◆ Congress may reasonably conclude that corporate exposure to criminal conviction provides an incentive to prevent illegal actions by employees. In many cases it is impossible to pinpoint particular corporate agents who acted illegally, although the participation of the corporation is evident. Even when particular agents can be identified, their conviction and punishment is ineffective as a deterrent to the corporation.

- ◆ D could not avoid liability by giving general instructions without taking appropriate steps to enforce the instructions.

3) Corporate liability for acts committed without authorization

Commonwealth v. Beneficial Finance Co.
275 N.E.2d 33 (Mass. 1971).

Facts. Two employees of Beneficial Finance (D), one a vice president, together with other companies and several of their employees, bribed members of state regulatory boards to get favorable action in setting maximum interest rates on loans. D was convicted of bribery and conspiracy to engage in bribery. D appeals, arguing that it cannot be held liable for the acts of its employees since they were not authorized by the board of directors or someone high enough in the corporate hierarchy to indicate that the acts were acts of "corporate policy."

Issue. Is the corporation liable when its agent, who has the authority to act for and on behalf of the corporation in handling its business, commits a crime while engaged in corporation business?

Held. Yes. Conviction sustained.

- ◆ The standard that must be met is that the corporation placed a person in a position where he had the power, responsibility, and authority to act for and on behalf of the corporation in handling the particular business or operation of the corporation in which he was engaged at the time the criminal act was committed, and that he had the power to decide what he would or would not do while acting for the corporation. It must also be shown that he was acting for and on behalf of the corporation in the accomplishment of that particular business or operation, and that he committed a criminal act while so acting.

- ◆ In reaching a determination on this standard, the jury may consider (i) the extent of the agent's control and authority, (ii) the extent of use of corporate funds in the crime, and (iii) a repeated pattern, if any, of criminal conduct that might show corporate toleration or ratification of the agent's acts.

- ◆ In effect, this is a respondeat superior doctrine.

4) Punishing the Corporation

United States v. Guidant LLC

708 F.Supp 2d 903 (D. Minn. 2010).

Facts. Guidant, LLC (D), developed, manufactured, and sold implantable cardioverter defibrillators (ICDs), medical devices implanted in a patient to treat abnormal heart rhythms that could result in sudden cardiac death. After learning two of its models contained defects that could cause them not to work, D fixed the defects but did not notify the Food and Drug Administration (FDA) in the time and manner required by federal law. D offered to plead guilty to two misdemeanor counts: (1) making materially false and misleading statements on reports required to be filed with the FDA, and (2) failing to promptly notify the FDA of a medical device correction. The Plea Agreement also provides that the parties recommend jointly that D be required to pay the United States a criminal fine of $253,962,251, and that D agrees to a criminal forfeiture in the amount of $42,079,675 and a special assessment of $250. There was also joint agreement not to include provisions that ordered restitution or probation. During the plea hearing, the court also heard argument from attorneys representing alleged victims. They urged the court to reject the Plea Agreement because it did not require the court to place D on probation, presumably because the alleged victims recognize that the court can, as a part of probation, order restitution. Rather than accepting the Plea Agreement, as is customary, the court took the matter under advisement.

Issue. Whether the court will accept and be bound to the specific provisions of the Plea Agreement.

Held. No.

- Manufacturers control the quality of their products and are the first to know whether a product is defective, dangerous, underperforming. It serves society's best interest if they are liable for the safety and effectiveness of their products.

- D is a repeat offender; to allow only a fine, that would be paid by its shareholders, would not hold D fully accountable and would undermine patient safety.

- We disagree with the government's position that probation would be a waste of the taxpayers' money since D would, as a condition of probation, to reimburse the government for any costs connected with the probation.

- Further, we do not agree that the corporate structure renders probation meaningless, most significantly because Boston Scientific recently entered into a $22 million settlement and corporate integrity agreement based on certain pre-acquisition actions by D. D became Guidant LLC less than two weeks before the government filed the Information in this case. Justice is not served by allowing a company to avoid probation simply by changing their corporate form.

- At the least, probation would serve the public's interest in accountability. And we believes that a period of probation would likely benefit, rather than harm, D's and Boston Scientific's public image.

- D could be ordered to perform community service to repair the harm it caused, specifically, to help build public confidence in the FDA regulation process, in medical device manufacturer's efforts at quality control, and in the cardiac healthcare industry in general. D could be ordered to contribute a certain amount of its resources to charitable programs.

c. Corporate agent liability

In the corporate context, courts have applied general principles of accomplice liability. However, when applied to corporate bureaucracy, liability may be difficult to impose on the highest officers without adopting a form of vicarious liability.

1) Basic rule

Gordon v. United States
203 F.2d 248 (10th Cir. 1953), *rev'd*, 347 U.S. 909 (1954).

Facts. Gordon (D) was a partner in an appliance selling business. Certain salespeople violated the Defense Production Act by making sales without collecting the required down payment. D and the other partners were charged individually with the violation on the theory that the knowledge of their agents could be imputed to them personally. Ds were convicted and appeal.

Issue. When an employee knowingly commits a criminal act in the course of his employment, may that knowledge be imputed to individual partners (employers) who did not actually know of that act?

Held. Yes. Judgment affirmed.

♦ The statute requires willfulness as an essential element of the crime. However, D, by being an employer, had constructive knowledge of the acts of his employees. Therefore, D was properly convicted.

Dissent. D lacked the necessary intent. An employer is not criminally liable for acts of his employees unless he directs the acts or has guilty knowledge thereof. The majority has erroneously applied principles of corporate liability to individual partners. A corporation may be deemed to have constructive knowledge of what its employees know. However, that rule exists because a corporation can only act through its agents, not because it is an employer.

Comment. The Supreme Court later reversed, essentially for the reasons given by the dissent here. [347 U.S. 909 (1954)] However, the Court has held that a partnership itself, as an entity, may be held criminally liable for the acts of its employees. [United States v. A & P Trucking Co., 358 U.S. 121 (1958)]

2) Position of authority justifying liability

United States v. Park
421 U.S. 658 (1975).

Facts. Park (D) was the chief executive officer of a national supermarket chain. One of the company's regional warehouses was infested with rodents and food stored therein was contaminated in violation of the Federal Food, Drug, and Cosmetic Act. The company pled guilty to charges of violations but D, who was also charged, pled not guilty. The evidence at trial showed that D had the responsibility of running the corporation and that he delegated the various phases of its operation to subordinates. D admitted that by virtue of his position he was responsible for the entire operation of the company, including the provision of sanitary food storage conditions. The jury was instructed that the issue was whether D, "by virtue of his position in the company, had a position of authority and responsibility in the situation out of which these charges arose." D was convicted, but the court of appeals reversed. The United States (P) petitioned for certiorari.

Issue. May a corporate officer be convicted of a criminal offense without proof of any wrongful action, as long as he was in a position of authority to prevent or to correct the violation that formed the basis for the complaint?

Held. Yes. Judgment reversed.

♦ D was convicted under a statute that does not require an awareness of some wrongdoing, but simply that the person stand in responsible relation to a public danger. The statute can extend to all who have a responsible share in the furtherance of the transaction that the statute outlaws. The question of responsibility depends on the evidence of each case and on the judgment of the jury.

♦ This type of statute imposes both a duty to seek out and remedy violations and a duty to take measures to insure that violations do not occur.

♦ A defendant may raise the defense of powerlessness to prevent or correct the violation.

Dissent. The instructions given were inadequate because they did not require a finding beyond a reasonable doubt that D engaged in wrongful conduct amounting at least to common law negligence.

3) Strict liability

United States v. MacDonald & Watson Waste Oil Co.
933 F.2d 35 (1st Cir. 1991).

Facts. MacDonald & Watson Waste Oil Co. ("MacDonald") was hired to remove solid waste. A company employee supervised removing the contaminated soil to an improper location. D'Allesandro (D), president of MacDonald, was convicted under the "responsible corporate officer" doctrine of knowingly transporting and causing the transportation of hazardous waste to an improper facility. MacDonald was also convicted. The case against D was proven by showing he had knowledge as a "responsible corporate officer," which is shown by proving that a person: (i) is a corporate officer; (ii) had direct responsibility for the alleged illegal activity; and (iii) knew or believed the alleged illegal activity occurred. D appeals.

Issue. May a district court properly adapt the "responsible corporate officer" doctrine traditionally applied to strict liability offenses, thus allowing the jury to find a defendant guilty without finding that he had actual knowledge, which is required by statute?

Held. No. Conviction reversed.

♦ The seminal cases of *United States v. Dotterweich*, 320 U.S. 277 (1943), and *United States v. Park*, 421 U.S. 658 (1975), eliminated the scienter requirement and established the "responsible corporate officer" doctrine. However, when Congress has specifically included a knowledge requirement, there is no precedent for ignoring it, especially where the offense charged is a serious felony as in the instant case.

♦ The trial court properly instructed the jury that knowledge could be inferred. However, under its instructions, the jury's belief that D lacked actual knowledge of, and had not willfully blinded himself to, the criminal transportation alleged would be insufficient for acquittal if the jury found that the responsible corporate officer knew or erroneously believed that the same type of illegal activity had occurred on another occasion.

♦ Belief of a prior illegal action does not necessarily show knowledge of a subsequent illegal action. In a crime having knowledge as an express element, a mere showing of official responsibility is not an adequate substitute for direct or circumstantial proof of knowledge.

4) Sentencing

Once a person has been convicted of a business crime, an appropriate sentence must be administered. A typical complaint is that business offenders "get off easy" when compared with other types of criminals. Others suggest that large fines replace imprisonment because fines provide more benefits to the public while serving equally well the purposes of punishment. There is no consensus on these points, however.

Chapter VIII
Exculpation

A. Introduction: The Concepts of Justification and Excuse

Justification and excuse are both defenses to criminal liability. In both, the defendant admits that he committed the act and did so with the requisite mens rea. With justification, the claim is that the defendant, although he fulfilled all of the elements of the crime, nevertheless did nothing "wrong" under the circumstances. With excuse, the defendant acknowledges that his conduct was "wrong," but asserts that he is not morally blameworthy due to the circumstances under which he committed the act.

B. Principles of Justification

1. Protection of Life and Person

Generally, a person is privileged to use such force as reasonably appears necessary to defend herself against an apparent threat of unlawful and immediate violence from another. In all cases where the defendant claims that she acted in self-defense, the following elements must be established.

a. Reasonable belief in necessity

The defendant must have believed that the force used was necessary for her own protection and this belief must have been reasonable (*i.e.*, a belief that a reasonable person in the same or similar circumstances would have formed). But, at the same time, an honest and reasonable belief is enough—the defense is still available even though it turns out that the belief was wrong and there was, in fact, no actual need to use force in self-defense.

b. Threatened harm imminent

The defendant must have reasonably believed that the threatened harm was imminent; *i.e.*, that it would be inflicted immediately if she did not act in self-defense. Thus, it is necessary to consider whether the threatening person was actually present and, if so, whether the person appeared willing and able to injure the defendant.

c. Threatened harm unlawful

The threatened harm must have been unlawful. This raises the issues of whether force can be used to resist an unlawful arrest and whether one who is the initial aggressor in an affray can claim the defense at all, an issue discussed below.

d. Reasonable force

The force that the defendant used must have been reasonable. In other words, it must have been no greater than appeared necessary under the circumstances to prevent the victim from inflicting the harm.

e. Necessity

In *United States v. Peterson, infra*, the court explained that the doctrine of self-defense is strongly grounded on the concept of necessity. Thus, before deadly force can be used there must be a threat, actual or apparent, of the use of deadly force against the defender; the threat must be unlawful and immediate; the defender must believe he is in imminent peril of death or serious bodily harm, and that his response was necessary to save himself; and these beliefs must be honestly entertained and objectively reasonable in light of the circumstances.

f. Special limits on the use of deadly force

"Deadly force" is force used with the intent to cause death or serious bodily injury or that is known by its user to create a substantial risk of death or serious bodily injury. Although there is no absolute prohibition against the use of deadly force in self-defense, there are some special limits on when it may be used.

1) Perceived threat of death or serious bodily injury

All courts agree that deadly force may be used in self-defense only if the defendant reasonably believed that the other person was about to inflict death or great bodily injury upon her and that deadly force was necessary to prevent the harm.

2) Objective standard

People v. Goetz
497 N.E.2d 41 (N.Y. 1986).

Facts. Goetz (D) entered a subway car and sat on a bench. He was approached by two black youths, one of whom stated to D, "Give me five dollars." These two youths were accompanied by two others who were also in the subway car. D pulled out a handgun and shot four shots, hitting three of the youths. He then fired another shot at the youth he had missed, severing his spinal cord. D then told the conductor who responded that the youths had tried to rob him. D fled the scene, but turned himself in about a week later. D told the police that he was carrying a gun because he had been mugged and injured three years earlier and had successfully protected himself on two prior occasions by displaying the gun to would-be assailants. D also described his deliberate intent to hurt the youths and to shoot each of them, and stated that he would have shot more times if he had had more bullets. D was charged with attempted murder, assault, and weapons possession. The prosecutor instructed the grand jury that the defense of self-defense applies only when the defendant's beliefs and reactions are those of a reasonable person, an objective standard. D was indicted, but the appellate court reversed. The People (P) appeal.

Issue. Must a claim of self-defense be evaluated based on what a reasonable person in the defendant's position would have believed?

Held. Yes. Judgment reversed.

♦ The use of force may be justified in certain circumstances, such as the defense of a person, but only to the extent the person "reasonably believes" the use of force to be necessary to defend himself from what "he reasonably believes" to be the use or imminent use of unlawful force by the aggressor. The use of deadly physical force is permitted only when the person "reasonably believes" that the aggressor is using or about to use deadly physical force, or is committing or attempting to commit a robbery or other such violent crime.

♦ In explaining the meaning of the term "reasonably believes," the prosecutor stated that the jurors should consider whether D's conduct was "that of a reasonable man in D's situation." The lower court in reversing held that the statute requires consideration of whether D's reactions and beliefs were "reasonable to him," which is a subjective standard. This is incorrect.

♦ The common law required an objective standard of reasonableness when applying self-defense, and the legislature followed this approach when they modified the Model Penal Code section on self-defense. Whereas the Model Penal Code permits self-defense when the defendant believes that the use of deadly force is necessary, the New York statute requires that the defendant "reasonably" believe.

♦ An interpretation that permits a subjective standard would fundamentally change the law; it would allow a defendant to escape responsibility simply for believing the actions taken were reasonable and necessary to prevent a perceived harm. Citizens may not be free to set their own individual standards for the justifiable use of force.

♦ Even under the objective standard, however, the individual defendant's personal knowledge and experience must be considered when assessing the reasonableness of the defendant's belief.

g. Expert testimony on battered-woman's syndrome

State v. Kelly
478 A.2d 364 (N.J. 1984).

Facts. The day after Kelly (D) got married, her husband got drunk and knocked her down. Thereafter, for seven years, he beat her frequently while drunk, threatening to kill her and cut off parts of her body if she left him. One day, they went shopping and did not have enough money to buy the week's food. D's husband told D he would give her more money the next day, but when D asked for the money he became angry and began beating her in public. D escaped, but then her husband ran toward her again with his hands raised. D took some scissors from her purse to scare him, but she stabbed him instead, killing him. At D's murder trial, she claimed self-defense and sought to call as a witness an expert on battered-woman's syndrome. The court refused to permit the expert's testimony and D was convicted of reckless manslaughter. D appeals.

Issue. Is expert testimony regarding the battered-woman's syndrome admissible to prove a claim of self-defense?

Held. Yes. Judgment reversed.

♦ The battered-woman's syndrome is increasingly accepted as an identifiable set of common characteristics shared by women who are abused physically and psychologically over time by a dominant male figure. The male figure coerces the woman to do what he wants regardless of her rights. The syndrome takes effect once the woman remains in a situation after she has been abused at least twice.

♦ The battering cycle that develops in physically abusive relationships consists of: (i) the tension-building stage, when the woman placates relatively minor abuse; (ii) the acute battering stage, in which the violence escalates; and (iii) the contrition stage, in which the male seeks forgiveness and promises to change. The cycle repeats itself over time, with the final stage giving the woman hope that the relationship will improve.

♦ The effect of the battering cycle is to give the victim low self-esteem, a feeling of guilt for a failed marriage, and acceptance of responsibility for the batterer's actions, as well as resistance to leaving the relationship for fear of the batterer's response. These effects create a special state of mind that experts are able to explain.

- ♦ D's claim of self-defense was based primarily on her own testimony about her belief that her husband was about to kill her. The expert testimony she sought to present was relevant to her belief, and would have bolstered D's credibility by showing that her experience was common to other women in similar situations; *i.e.*, that she would remain in the marriage despite her fears and the abuse she suffered. The testimony was also relevant to the reasonableness of D's belief regarding the danger she faced. These aspects of battered-woman's syndrome are not within the normal knowledge and experience of a jury.

- ♦ The offered testimony satisfies the three basic requirements for admissibility of expert testimony: (i) that the subject matter is beyond the average juror's knowledge; (ii) that the area of expertise is sufficiently developed that the testimony is reliable; and (iii) that the witness is qualified by expertise to testify.

h. No perfect self-defense

State v. Norman
378 S.E.2d 8 (N.C. 1989).

Facts. Norman (D) had been badly abused by her husband during most of their 25-year marriage. He frequently punched and kicked her, threw things at her, and burned her with cigarettes and hot coffee. He forced her into prostitution, humiliated her in public, and forced her to eat pet food from a bowl on the floor. For years he threatened to maim and kill her. This behavior continued until D shot her husband three times in the back of the head, while he slept. The day before the killing, D was beaten to the point that police were summoned. However, the police would do nothing unless D filed a complaint, which she was afraid to do. D was convicted of voluntary manslaughter and sentenced to six years in prison. D appealed to the court of appeals, which found in favor of D, holding that the trial court should have instructed the jury that it could acquit D by reason of perfect self-defense. The Government appeals.

Issue. Should the trial court have instructed the jury as to the right of perfect self-defense?

Held. No. Judgment reversed.

- ♦ In a perfect self-defense, at the time of a killing, a defendant believes it necessary to kill to save herself from imminent death or harm. That belief must be reasonable based on the circumstances as they appear, and as would create the same belief in an ordinary person.

- ♦ In an imperfect self-defense, a defendant is the initial aggressor, but does not have intent to kill or seriously injure, and the victim escalates aggression to such a point that the defendant reasonably believes she is in imminent danger of death or great bodily harm.

- ♦ The evidence here shows no danger of imminent death or bodily harm. The deceased was sleeping at the time D shot him three times in the back of his head.

Dissent. The evidence presented showed a 20-year history of beatings and dehumanizing treatment suffered by D, who believed escape was impossible. She reasonably believed that the law could neither help nor protect her. D could reasonably believe that the next potentially fatal attack was imminent, especially in view of how the husband's behavior worsened during the three days prior to the shooting.

i. No imminent danger

Commonwealth v. Sands
553 S.E.2d 733 (Va. 2001).

Facts. Thomas Sands began beating his wife (D) about two years after they were married. The beatings grew more severe over time and became a daily occurrence. D repeatedly asked for a divorce, but Thomas beat her and threatened to kill her and her family members if she left him. D asked her parents to help her have Thomas arrested for selling cocaine, marijuana, and bootleg whiskey, but shortly thereafter her parents were seriously injured in a car accident. D was afraid to take any action on her own for fear of being killed. One morning, a neighbor saw Thomas follow D out onto the back porch where he pushed her down several concrete steps and fired a gun into the ground near her. D's aunt arrived soon thereafter, but Thomas would not let D leave with her aunt. Thomas kept pacing the floor and saying, "I'll kill you and your whole family I've knocked off a few and I can knock off a few more." For the rest of the day, Thomas paced the floor, drank beer, used cocaine, physically abused D, and threatened to kill her. D called a sister-in-law, Shelton, to come to the house. After the call, Thomas beat her again, using his fists and the butt of a gun. After Shelton arrived, D told her that Thomas was the devil, that she had to get him out of the house, and that he was going to kill her. D then got a gun and shot Thomas five times while he was in bed watching television. At trial, the court ruled that there was insufficient evidence for a self-defense instruction. The appellate court reversed D's murder conviction. The prosecution appeals.

Issue. Was there sufficient evidence for a self-defense instruction?

Held. No. Judgment reversed and conviction reinstated.

- ♦ D reasonably believed that she was in danger of serious bodily harm or death, but the evidence does not show any overt act by Thomas that presented imminent danger at the time of the shooting.

j. Duty to retreat

State v. Abbott
174 A.2d 881 (N.J. 1961).

Facts. Abbott (D) shared a common driveway with the Scaranos. When the Scaranos paved their portion of the driveway, D made a doorstop to keep his garage door from swinging onto the Scarano's property. Nicholas Scarano objected and a fight ensued. Nicholas's parents came to his aid with a hatchet and a carving knife. All of the parties were wounded by the hatchet. D claimed that they were injured during a struggle for the hatchet. D was separately indicted for atrocious assault and battery. At trial, the jury acquitted D of the charges relating to the parents, but found D guilty as to Nicholas. D appeals.

Issue. Is a person who is being attacked required to retreat only if he intends to use deadly force?

Held. Yes. Conviction reversed.

- ♦ Deadly force is not justifiable when an opportunity to retreat is available. Deadly force is force used with the purpose of causing, or that the actor knows will create, a substantial risk of death or serious bodily harm.

- ♦ It is not the nature of the force defended against that raises the issue of retreat, but the nature of the force that D employed in his defense.

- ♦ If a person does not resort to deadly force, one who is assailed may hold his ground and defend himself against the attack.

- ♦ The jury should be instructed that D could have held his ground when Nicholas came at him with his fists and when the parents came at him with the instruments. The issue of retreat could arise only if D resorted to deadly force.

Comment. Contrary to the common law position, most American jurisdictions no longer require the defendant to retreat before using deadly force. However, a substantial minority of states still adhere to the common law rule, requiring retreat before resort to the use of deadly force in self-defense. Of course, there is no duty to retreat where retreat cannot be done safely, or where the attack takes place in the defendant's own home.

k. Aggressor's right to defense

Generally, a person cannot use force to defend herself if she was the initial aggressor in the situation. By beginning the altercation, she forfeits her right to assert self-defense later. However, there are some situations in which a person, although an initial aggressor, may regain her right to act in self-defense.

1) Nondeadly aggressor met with deadly force

If the victim responds to the aggressor's use of nondeadly force with deadly force, the aggressor can use whatever force appears reasonably necessary (including deadly force) to repel the attack. The rationale is that because nondeadly force cannot be met with deadly force, the victim by responding with deadly force has threatened unlawful harm.

2) Aggressor withdraws

An aggressor may regain her right to act in self-defense by withdrawing from the affray. Ordinarily, the defendant must actually notify her adversary of the desire to desist, but some jurisdictions hold that even unsuccessful efforts to do so, if reasonable, will suffice.

3) Aggressor's duty to withdraw

United States v. Peterson
483 F.2d 1222 (D.C. Cir. 1973).

Facts. Keitt and two friends drove to an alley in back of Peterson's (D's) house and started removing D's car windshield wipers. D came out, saw what was going on, and became involved in a verbal exchange. D went back into his house and came out with a pistol. In the meantime, Keitt got into his own car and was about to leave. When D reappeared, he loaded his gun and told Keitt, "If you move, I will shoot." Keitt got out of his car, took a few steps toward D, turned back to his car, and got a lug wrench. Keitt, with the wrench raised, then advanced toward D. D, who was standing just inside his backyard gate, warned Keitt not to take another step. Keitt continued to approach D, and D shot him in the face from 10 feet away, killing him. At trial, the judge instructed the jury that the use of deadly force in self-defense is not ordinarily available to one who provokes a conflict or is the aggressor in it and that mere words do not constitute provocation or aggression. D was convicted of manslaughter and appeals.

Issue. May one who is the aggressor in a confrontation use deadly force in defense of himself?

Held. No. Judgment affirmed.

♦ A claim of self-defense may not arise from a self-generated necessity to kill. One who is the aggressor in a conflict culminating in death cannot invoke the necessities of self-preservation. A claim of self-defense may arise, however, if the aggressor communicates to his adversary an intent to withdraw and then in good faith attempts to do so.

♦ Here, Keitt was about to leave when D returned with a gun. Even if Keitt was the original aggressor, he no longer was. D paused in his yard to load the gun, told Keitt not to move, walked to the rear gate, dared Keitt to come in, and threatened to kill him if he did. The jury could readily find D's challenge to be an aggression which, unless renounced, nullifies the right of homicidal self-defense.

Comment. The Model Penal Code allows self-defense against any escalation of the confrontation. If the original defender uses excessive force to respond, the original aggressor may defend against the excessive force, unless his original aggression was intended to provoke a necessity to kill in self-defense.

2. Protection of Property and Law Enforcement

a. Protection of property

The right to use force in the protection of property is much more limited than the right to use force in the protection of persons.

1) Deadly force not allowed

A person cannot use deadly force simply to defend her property against unlawful interference, even if there is no other way to prevent the threatened harm. This rule is based on the premise that the interest in security of property does not justify jeopardizing the lives of others.

2) Nondeadly force

Nondeadly force may be used to protect both real and personal property in one's possession if it reasonably appears necessary to prevent or terminate an unlawful intrusion onto or interference with that property.

a) Request to desist

But force is not reasonable unless a ***prior request*** has been made for the other to desist from interfering with the property.

b) Property in possession of another

Moreover, the traditional rules apparently require that the property defended be in the *possession* of the person using the force. Thus, there is *probably* no right to use force in defense of property in the possession of another.

c) Compare—use of force to regain or reenter property

Traditionally, one illegally dispossessed of property cannot use force to regain it or, in the case of real property, to reenter it. An exception is made, however, where action is taken immediately after the loss of the property or in "hot pursuit" of the dispossessor.

3) Use of mechanical device

People v. Ceballos
526 P.2d 241 (Cal. 1974).

Facts. Ceballos (D) lived alone in a garage and in an apartment above the garage. D had some tools stolen from his house and a few months later noticed pry marks on one of the garage doors. One of the locks had also been bent. D set up a trap gun. Two boys who decided to break in and see if there was anything to steal opened the door. The gun fired and hit one of the boys in the face. D was convicted of assault with a deadly weapon. D appeals, claiming the trap gun was justified.

Issue. May a person use a trap gun to protect property in his house while he is away?

Held. No. Judgment affirmed.

♦ The general rule imposes criminal and civil liability for setting up a deadly mechanical device that actually kills or injures another. An exception has arisen when the intrusion is such that the person, if present, could inflict the harm with his own hands. That exception should not apply to criminal cases, however, because under it liability depends on fortuitous events, and because the use of trap guns presents an unacceptable danger to children, firefighters, etc.

◆ Even if the exception applied, D would be liable. Although homicide is justifiable as a defense against a forcible and atrocious crime, the burglary by the boys here did not threaten death or serious injury to anyone since they were the only persons present. Nor can the use of deadly force be justified solely for the protection of property.

b. Law enforcement

The dangers of law enforcement present many difficult questions as to the scope of justified violence. Problems arise when citizens assist law enforcement officers, when officers effectuate arrests, and when suspects resist arrest.

1) Assistance to police

Citizens may properly assist law enforcement agencies in good faith. However, the use of force as part of such assistance could endanger others. The defense of aiding law enforcement agencies does not exonerate a citizen from all liability for his conduct. The defense essentially nullifies criminal intent. The factfinder must scrutinize the defendant's conduct to determine whether it shows a lack of criminal intent. A private citizen called upon by a police officer to assist in making an arrest, however, has the same privilege as the officer because the citizen is required by law to comply with the police officer's order.

2) Effectuating arrest

Both private citizens and police officers may use force in making an arrest, but different standards apply to the two groups.

a) Police officers

A police officer is entitled to act on reasonable appearances in using force in making an arrest. A police officer may use whatever nondeadly force reasonably appears necessary to make an arrest for a felony or misdemeanor. The right to use deadly force has traditionally been limited to situations in which the officer reasonably believes the suspect committed a felony. The modern approach is more restricted; deadly force is permitted only if the suspect has committed a dangerous felony or presents a significant risk of harm to others.

b) Traditional rule

Durham v. State
159 N.E. 145 (Ind. 1927).

Facts. Durham (D), a game warden, arrested Long for illegal fishing. Long fled to his boat to attempt an escape. D pursued Long; Long hit him with an oar. D shot Long in the arm and was prosecuted for assault and battery. D appeals his conviction.

Issue. May an arresting officer use injuring force to capture a fleeing misdemeanant?

Held. Yes. Judgment reversed.

◆ For misdemeanors, the officer may use all the force necessary to make the arrest, except that he may not use deadly force or inflict serious bodily harm on one merely fleeing arrest. However, if the person resists the officer such that the officer's life is in danger or serious bodily harm is threatened, the officer may take the person's life if necessary. Because the victim resisted arrest, D was justified in using the force he did.

c) Modern approach—use of deadly force to stop fleeing burglar not permitted

Tennessee v. Garner
471 U.S. 1 (1985).

Facts. The Tennessee fleeing felon statute authorized police officers to use deadly force to capture unarmed suspects fleeing from nonviolent felonies. One night an unarmed 15-year-old boy broke into an unoccupied house to steal money and property. Two police officers responded and yelled at the boy to stop as he fled. As the boy tried to get over a fence, the police shot and killed him. Garner (P) sued the Memphis Police Department for wrongful death. The state of Tennessee (D) intervened to defend the statute. The district court upheld the state law, but the court of appeals reversed. D appeals.

Issue. May a state authorize police officers to use deadly force to capture an unarmed suspect fleeing from a nonviolent felony?

Held. No. Judgment affirmed.

- ◆ Under state law, the reasonableness and necessity of using deadly force to capture a fleeing felon is a jury question. However, once it is determined that the officer could not have caught the felon without shooting, shooting is reasonable under the statute. The nature of the felony or the actual dangerousness of the felon is irrelevant.

- ◆ The Fourth Amendment protects against unreasonable seizures. Killing a fleeing suspect is certainly a "seizure" of the person. Under common law, killing a felon who resisted arrest was permitted, but at that time, all felonies were capital crimes. Any felon at large would be executed if caught and tried, so such outlaws were considered automatically dangerous. The use of deadly force was not permitted when the fleeing suspect's crime did not require execution.

- ◆ Tennessee's law is inconsistent with the rationale of the common law. There are now hundreds of state and federal felonies not recognized at common law, including white collar crimes and possession of contraband. To permit the use of deadly force against a suspect without regard to the risk of danger presented to the community presents an unnecessarily severe and excessive police response that violates the Fourth Amendment.

- ◆ The officers as individuals cannot be held liable because they reasonably relied on the state statute. D, however, is liable for constitutional damages even though it relied on the state statute.

Dissent (O'Connor, J., Burger, C.J., Rehnquist, J.). The reasonableness of the officer's seizure of P depends on the public interest involved and the intrusion on P's legitimate interests. The public interest in using deadly force to apprehend a fleeing burglar relates to the seriousness of the crime. Burglary is a serious and dangerous felony, and the public has a compelling interest in preventing and detecting the burglaries. Apprehension of the suspect is critical. On the other hand, while P has an obvious interest in his life, he does not have a right to flee unimpeded from the scene of a burglary. Use of deadly force as a last resort to apprehend a fleeing burglar at night is not unreasonable.

3. Residual Justification

a. General principle of justification

1) Problem

The problem is illustrated by *Regina v. Dudley and Stephens, supra*, where a ship went down and the crew on a lifeboat ate the cabin boy in order to survive. One of the most difficult problems to solve is to determine when people really do act out of necessity. If those who take others' lives out of necessity are to be exculpated, then the test for their excuse should be formulated around the conditions that existed at the time they acted and not on conditions that happened long after the act was completed.

2) General rule

Criminal acts, done out of necessity, may be excused if the accused can show that they were done to avoid otherwise unavoidable consequences to himself or others he is bound to protect, the results of which would have been irreparable; that no more was done than was absolutely necessary; and that the evil inflicted was not out of proportion to the evil that was threatened. Some courts hold that acts of "economic" necessity are not justified. Almost all courts hold that acts that result in taking another's life are never justified. For example, most courts would not excuse the defendants in the *Dudley and Stephens* case. However, had such a group taken food that did not belong to them from the ship, this would have been excused.

3) Model Penal Code

The Code formulates rules different from that of the majority of jurisdictions:

a) Conduct the actor believes to be necessary to avoid an evil to himself or another is justifiable, provided:

(1) The evil sought to be avoided by such conduct is greater than that sought to be prevented by the law defining the crime; and

(2) The law does not provide for such a situation specifically.

b) When the actor is reckless or negligent in bringing about the situation requiring a choice of evils or in appraising the necessity for his conduct, the justification afforded by this action is unavailable in a prosecution for any offense for which recklessness or negligence, as the case may be, suffices to establish culpability.

4) Necessity to escape from prison

People v. Unger
362 N.E.2d 319 (Ill. 1977).

Facts. Unger (D) was convicted of the crime of escape. D produced evidence that such escape was justified by the affirmative defense of necessity. D had been threatened with homosexual assault, was sexually assaulted, and then threatened with death by his attacker, who thought D had reported the attack. D testified that he was unable to defend himself and that he intended to turn himself in once he had obtained the legal advice of an attorney. D brings this appeal because the trial judge instructed the jury to disregard the reasons given for D's escape and failed to instruct the jury of the affirmative defense of necessity. The appellate court reversed and remanded for a new trial. The People (P) appeal.

Issue. May the defense of necessity be used by a convict who escapes prison?

Held. Yes. Judgment affirmed.

- ♦ The introduction of evidence to support the defense of necessity is sufficient to require the giving of an appropriate instruction. D was forced to choose between two admitted evils: an illegal escape or a homosexual assault and fear of reprisal. D was not compelled to escape, but the escape could be considered necessary.

- ♦ In *People v. Lovercamp*, 118 Cal. Rptr. 110 (Cal. Ct. App. 1974), the court allowed the defense of necessity in a similar context. The court set forth five conditions to the defense:

(i) Specific threat of death or serious attack in the immediate future;

(ii) No time for complaint, or a history of futile complaints to authorities;

(iii) No chance to resort to the courts;

(iv) No force or violence towards innocent persons during escape; and

(v) Immediate contact with prison officials when prisoner is safe.

- ♦ These factors are relevant to the propriety of the defense but they are not necessary. D was entitled to an appropriate instruction.

Dissent.

- ♦ The use of the necessity defense in prison escape cases must be confined within well-defined boundaries such as those in *Lovercamp*. D did not satisfy those conditions here.

- ♦ Unless the necessity defense is specifically confined, it will encourage potential escapees, disrupt prison discipline, and result in injury to prison guards, police, or private citizens.

5) Necessity defense

United States v. Schoon
971 F.2d 193 (9th Cir.1992).

Facts. Schoon (D) was one of 30 people who gained admittance to the Tucson IRS office where they chanted "Keep America's tax dollars out of El Salvador" and splashed simulated blood on counters, walls, and carpeting, obstructing office operations. They refused to disperse when so ordered by a federal police officer. At trial, D attempted to assert a necessity defense, contending they acted to avoid further bloodshed in El Salvador. The trial court precluded the necessity defense, and D was convicted of obstructing the activities of the IRS office and failing to comply with an order of a federal officer. D appeals.

Issue. May a defendant who is charged with indirect civil disobedience raise the defense of necessity?

Held. No. Convictions affirmed.

- ♦ A necessity defense must show that one: (i) was faced with a choice of evils, and chose the lesser; (ii) acted to prevent imminent harm; and (iii) reasonably anticipated a direct causal relationship between the conduct and the harm to be averted.

- ♦ The trial court held that: (i) there was no immediacy; (ii) the action taken would not abate the evil; and (iii) other legal alternatives existed.

- ♦ Direct civil disobedience involves protesting a law by breaking the law. Indirect civil disobedience involves violating a law or interfering with a government policy that is not, itself, the object of the protest. In addition to agreeing with the trial court's reasoning, we find that D engaged in indirect civil disobedience because the group was not challenging the laws under which they were charged.

- ♦ The necessity defense requires that the commission of a crime avert the occurrence of an even greater harm. For example, prisoners may escape a burning prison. But we assume in such cases that the lawmaker, if confronted with such facts, would have carved out the exception which is subsequently claimed as justified by necessity.

- ♦ Indirect civil disobedience, however, involves the breaking of a law (other than the one sought to be repealed) as symbolic and to draw attention to a cause. We rule that the necessity defense is inapplicable to acts of indirect civil disobedience because legal alternatives will never be deemed exhausted when the harm can be mitigated by congressional action.

6) Extreme necessity

Regina v. Dudley and Stephens. (*See* brief of case, *supra*)

7) Necessity defense for interrogators

Public Committee Against Torture v. State of Israel
H.C. 5100/94 (Sept. 6, 1999).

Facts. Israel (D) permits the General Security Service ("GSS") to use torture under restricted circumstances. GSS officers are instructed to weigh the severity of the attack the interrogation was intended to prevent and to look for alternate ways to prevent the danger. Officers are required to evaluate a suspect's health and "ensure that no harm comes to him." GSS contends these measures are effective and indispensable. The Public Committee (P) petitioned the court for an order prohibiting "the use of physical means."

Issues.

(i) Does GSS's general mandate to conduct interrogations encompass the authority to use physical means?

(ii) If not, in exceptional circumstances, could such an authority be based on the concept of necessity?

Held. (i) No. (ii) No. The order preventing physical means of interrogation is absolute.

♦ While an interrogation is likely to cause discomfort, in ordinary cases it must be free of torture or any degrading handling or infringement on human rights.

♦ An individual officer may out of "necessity" employ physical means when there is an imminent threat, where the danger is certain to materialize, and there is no other way to prevent it from happening. But, the State cannot authorize the use of physical means during an interrogation. If such means are deemed appropriate for D, it is for the legislature to decide.

Concurrence and dissent In "ticking time bomb" situations, a State and its agents have a right to defend its existence. The judgment should be suspended for one year, during which the GSS can use physical means in "ticking time bomb" cases and the legislature will have an opportunity to consider the issue.

8) Euthanasia

Cruzan v. Director, Missouri Department of Health
497 U.S. 261 (1989).

Facts. Nancy Cruzan suffered severe injuries in a motor vehicle accident, and as a result, was in a vegetative state. Nancy's parents (Ps) sought to have her artificial nutrition and hydration procedures halted. The state court held that Nancy had a constitutional right to refuse or direct the withdrawal of "death prolonged procedures." The state court also held that Nancy's wishes had been expressed during a conversation with a close friend. The Supreme Court of Missouri reversed, finding that Nancy's conversation with her friend was unreliable for the purpose of determining her intent. The Supreme Court granted certiorari.

Issue. Does a person in a vegetative state have a constitutional right to require the hospital to withdraw life-sustaining treatment?

Held. No. Supreme Court of Missouri is affirmed.

♦ We have long held that medical treatment requires the informed consent of a patient, thus indicating that one possesses a constitutionally protected liberty interest not to consent and to refuse treatment.

- We assume for the purposes of this case that the United States Constitution would grant a competent person the right to refuse lifesaving measures.

- But Ps argue that an incompetent person should possess the same right, ignoring the fact that an incompetent person is unable to make an informed or voluntary choice.

- It is a surrogate who must exercise Nancy's right, which Missouri permits in accordance with procedural safeguards. Missouri requires an incompetent person's wishes to be proven by clear and convincing evidence.

- Such a procedural requirement is not barred by the Constitution.

9) Assisted suicide

Washington v. Glucksberg
521 U.S. 702 (1997).

Facts. Glucksberg and several other terminally ill patients and their doctors (Ps) sued Washington (D) for a declaratory judgment that the state statute prohibiting assisted suicide was unconstitutional. The federal district court agreed, and -the circuit court affirmed. We granted certiorari.

Issue. Is the state's ban on assisted suicide a violation of a fundamental right protected by the Due Process Clause of the Constitution?

Held. No. Judgment reversed.

- Centuries of legal doctrine and practice have punished or otherwise disapproved of suicide and assisting suicide.

- While the "liberty" protection of the Due Process Clause has been applied to marriage, having children, contraception, abortion, and the right to refuse unwanted lifesaving medical treatment, we are reluctant to expand the concepts of substantive due process to assisted suicide because there are few guideposts for responsible decisionmaking in this area. Extending constitutional protection to tins interest, would to a great degree, remove the matter from public debate and legislative action.

- Ps' reliance on *Cruzan v. Director, Missouri Department of Health, supra*, is misplaced. The right in *Cruzan* was not drawn from abstract concepts of personal autonomy. There is a long tradition protecting against forced medication (battery) and the decision to refuse unwanted medical treatment. The asserted "right" to assisted suicide is not a fundamental liberty interest.

- The ban is rationally related to legitimate government interests: first, the preservation of human life; second, protecting the integrity and ethics of the medical profession; third, protecting vulnerable groups from abuse, neglect, mistakes, and social indifference; and fourth, fear that permitting assisted suicide would start the progression toward voluntary (and perhaps involuntary) euthanasia.

C. Principles of Excuse

1. Introduction

Because punishment for crime is based on the existence of a culpable mental state, some allowance must be made for situations where the mental state is affected to preclude formation of the culpable intent.

2. Duress and Coercion (Compulsion)

a. Statement of the rule

Acts done under the immediate threat of death or serious bodily injury, where there is both reasonable cause to believe and actual belief that such harm is threatened, will be excused.

b. Model Penal Code

1) It is an affirmative defense that the actor engaged in conduct because he was "coerced" to do so by the use of, or a threat to use unlawful force against his person or the person of another, which a person of reasonable firmness in his situation would have been unable to resist.

2) The defense is unavailable if the actor recklessly placed himself in the situation in which it was probable that he would be subjected to duress. It is also unavailable if he was negligent in placing himself in such a situation, whenever negligence suffices for culpability.

3) Note that under the duress sections, if A threatens to kill B unless B kills C and D, and B kills them, B may be excused. Why is B excused here and not under the section on necessity?

c. Subjective test

State v. Toscano
378 A.2d 755 (N.J. 1977).

Facts. Toscano (D), a chiropractor, was involved in a conspiracy to defraud insurance companies by staging accidents and filing fraudulent claims. D admitted that he made up a medical bill and medical reports, but claimed he did so only because of threats made by the co-conspirators. D did not receive compensation for his participation. The trial court instructed the jury that the peril allegedly faced by D was not imminent, present, and pending such that he could not seek police protection, and therefore D had no defense of duress. D was convicted. The conviction was upheld on appeal and the state supreme court granted certification to consider the issue.

Issue. In order to establish a defense of duress, must a defendant have acted in response to a threat of harm that was present, imminent, and impending?

Held. No. Judgment reversed and new trial ordered.

♦ The common law rule allowed a defense of duress but only when the alleged coercion involved a use or threat of harm that was present, imminent, and pending, inducing an apprehension of death or serious bodily harm unless the act was done. Such a threat to a close relative would suffice. Some cases vary the seriousness of the threat necessary according to the crime committed. This rule has been criticized for impairing the deterrent value of the criminal law.

♦ Some commentators have proposed a duress defense based on the subjective reaction to unlawful demands. The Model Penal Code approach allows consideration of a reasonable person's reaction to the threat faced by the defendant, allowing consideration of age, sex, etc., but not temperament. This is the best approach and is hereby adopted as the standard for a duress defense in all but murder cases.

Comment. The New Jersey Legislature subsequently adopted a statute along the lines of the Model Penal Code.

1) No "immediacy"

Consider *United States v. Fleming,* 23 C.M.R.7(1957), a court martial wherein Fleming was charged with willfully and knowingly collaborating with the enemy, while a prisoner of war, by joining with, participating in, and leading discussion groups reflecting opinions that the United Nations and the United States were illegal aggressors in the Korean conflict. Evidence showed Fleming made communist propaganda recordings, praised the enemy and attacked the war aims of the U.S. Further evidence showed what Fleming endured while a prisoner. Just before being captured, he was wounded in his back and legs; for ten days after capture he was given no food or water. He was forced to march seventy miles to the prison camp in this condition; throughout the march he was questioned and when he refused to answer, he was kicked, slapped and otherwise abused. He lost 40 pounds. There was no room at the camp for the prisoners to lie down at night, nor were they provided with clothing or shoes. They were fed two cups of millet a day. The death rate was so high the corpses were piled like wood in the freezing cold and not buried for days. Fleming resisted his captor's, Colonel Kim's demand that the prisoners write and record propaganda scripts. He was then threatened with another forced march to a camp 150 to 200 miles away. Testimony was presented that Fleming could not have survived in his weak condition. Fleming complied with Kim's demand that he lead a discussion with the prisoners about Communist propaganda subjects in order to bargain for more food and better conditions, and he did receive more food occasionally. Fleming was told that unless he signed appeals that called on President Truman to withdraw troops from North Korea, he would be sent to the "Caves," wet and muddy recesses in a hillside without heat where prisoners lived like animals. When Kim took Fleming to show him the "Caves" the first time, there were 14 American prisoners; on Fleming's last visit only one man was alive. Fleming signed. The rest of the prisoners did not. The Court of Military Appeals affirmed Fleming's conviction of dismissal and total forfeitures, held that the instruction on duress, that "one must have acted under a well grounded apprehension of immediate and impending death or of immediate serious bodily harm" was correct. The mere threat of the march was not sufficient; if Fleming had started on the march and realized he would not survive, it would have been a different situation, the Court said. The prospect of death was too remote.

2) Triable issues of fact

In *United States v. Contento-Pachon*, 723 F.2d 691 (9th Cir. 1984), Contento-Pachon, a taxicab driver in Columbia, was offered a job driving a privately owned car by one of his passengers, Jorge. When he went to meet the owner of the car the next day, Jorge asked him to swallow cocaine-filled balloons he would not do it, Jorge threatened to kill his wife and child. Upon arrival in the U.S., Contento-Pachon consented to have his stomach x-rayed and the cocaine was discovered.

At trial, evidence of duress or necessity was suppressed, and Contento-Pachon was convicted. On appeal, the court focused on the immediate threat of death or serious bodily injury and no reasonable opportunity to escape the harm elements of the duress defense. Contento-Pachon had presented evidence that showed he believed he was being watched the whole time he was smuggling. He claimed he did not have a reasonable opportunity to escape because he thought the police were corrupt and it would be too dangerous. The court found there was enough evidence that a factfinder could reasonably conclude the threat was immediate and for the issue of whether escape was reasonable. The conviction was reversed.

3) Threat not immediate

The Canadian Criminal Code, Section 17, excuses one who, reasonably believing that the threat will be carried out, commits a crime under the compulsion by threats of immediate death or bodily injury from a person who is present when the crime is being committed. In *Regina v. Ruzic, [1998] D.L.R.4th 358*, the 21-year-old defendant traveled from Yugoslavia to Toronto with two kilos of heroin; she argued duress, claiming a known killer had stabbed her and burned her arm and threatened to "do something" to her mother if she didn't carry the drug. Defendant claimed she did not report the threat because she didn't trust the police. The court refused to specify in jury instructions that the threat had to be immediate, made against the defendant herself, and made by a person present when the crime was being committed. Defendant's acquittal was upheld on appeal; the court reasoned that to convict her would be a violation of fundamental justice. Defendant's actions were involuntary because she had no realistic choice but to comply. She was morally innocent.

3. Intoxication

a. General rule

Voluntary intoxication is no defense to a crime. However, evidence of drunkenness may be introduced to show that the defendant did not have the requisite intent that is required when specific intent is an element of the crime. For example, murder in the first degree requires premeditation and deliberation; intoxication would perhaps negate this. However, where no specific intent is required (such as for involuntary manslaughter), intoxication would be no defense to the crime.

b. Analysis

1) The idea is that the individual has control over drinking; *i.e.*, he can decide whether he will drink in the first place. He knows the dangers from doing so, and therefore if he drinks he must accept the consequences.

2) If A is drunk and kills a person as a result, if A is punished, is it not for drinking that A is being punished? If this is so, and deterrence of drinking is the rationale, should not all drinkers (not just those who commit crimes) be punished? For example, if A voluntarily fires a gun into the middle of a crowd, even if he does not want to injure someone, if B is killed thereby, A may be held for murder (*i.e.*, he intended to fire the gun into the crowd, and objectively speaking the killing of a person was substantially certain to follow).

a) Proof of general intent

Intent is inferred by the results that occur. Therefore, general intent may be proved simply by showing that the prohibited result was caused by a voluntary act of the defendant.

b) Transferred intent

When a person has the required intent to commit one criminal act, he may be held responsible for results that he did not intend if he inflicts the kind of harm intended and if the injuries sustained do not require a different mens rea.

(1) Usually the intent from the first crime will only be transferred to the second where the first act was "malum in se." For example, where A attempts to hit B and unintentionally hits and injures C, A is guilty of assault on C.

(2) The transfer generally occurs only where the unintended result involves the same mens rea requirement as the intended act. Therefore, if A shoots at B, misses, and the bullet strikes an oil lamp, igniting a fire, A is not guilty of arson because arson requires that specific intent to start a fire be shown (specific intent is discussed below), and here A can only be held to have had the intent to do personal injury.

c. Culpable intent while intoxicated

Roberts v. People
19 Mich. 401 (1870).

Facts. Roberts (D) was convicted of assault with the intent to murder. D testified that he was too drunk at the time of the act to have the required intent. D appeals.

Issue. May voluntary intoxication be a legitimate defense to a crime requiring intent?

Held. Yes. Judgment reversed.

- ◆ Voluntary drunkenness will not excuse the assault part of the offense but, if sufficient, it will excuse the specific intent. If D's drunkenness was so extensive that D's mental faculties were incapable of entertaining the necessary intent, he will be excused.

- ◆ If D's drunkenness was such that he could not appreciate right and wrong, yet he still formed the necessary intent, he would be guilty. He would, in that case, be treated as having intended the obscuration of his facilities, which followed from his voluntary intoxication. He would be held to have purposely blinded his moral perceptions and set his will free from the control of reason.

- ◆ As long as D had the intent, he is guilty, even if he would not have had the intent if he had not been intoxicated. These are all questions for the jury upon retrial.

d. Specific and general intent

People v. Hood
462 P.2d 370 (Cal. 1969).

Facts. Hood (D) had been drinking before a police officer attempted to arrest him. D resisted the arrest and, using the police officer's gun, shot the police officer. D was convicted of assault with a deadly weapon and assault with intent to commit murder.

Issue. Is assault a specific intent crime to which evidence of intoxication is material?

Held. No. Convictions reversed because of conflicting jury instructions given on the effect of intoxication.

- ◆ The problem of intoxicated offenders caused courts to develop the distinction between specific and general intent crimes. A drunken criminal may be less culpable for his acts than a sober criminal, but he should not entirely escape die consequences of his conduct.

- ◆ General criminal intent is that intention to do a proscribed act. Specific intent is the intent to do some further act or achieve some additional consequence. A drunken person is usually able to form the intent to strike someone else, to commit an assault. However, he would be unlikely to be able to formulate an intent to commit a battery for the purpose of killing.

- ◆ Assault is a general intent crime, and intoxication is no defense.

Comment. The court reaffirmed that assault with a deadly weapon was a general intent crime in *People v. Rocha*, 479 P.2d 372 (Cal. 1971). A specific intent crime requires not only that the defendant do the prohibited act, but that he do it with a particular state of mind.

e. Limiting intoxication defense

In *State v. Stasio*, 396 A.2d 1129 (N.J. 1979), a New Jersey appellate court reversed a defendant's conviction of assault with intent to rob. Although the Supreme Court of New Jersey affirmed the appellate court's decision, finding that the trial court improperly ruled on admissibility of evidence of voluntary intoxication, the supreme court stated that unless one of the exceptions to the general rule applies, voluntary intoxication will not excuse criminal conduct. The court reasoned that distinguishing between specific and general intent crimes would give rise to incongruous results by irrationally allowing intoxication to excuse some crimes but not others. Some defendants would be completely acquitted because not every specific intent crime has a lesser included general intent offense. The court noted that the criminal law's primary function is to protect society from the results of behavior that endangers the public safety. However, the court acknowledged that voluntary intoxication is relevant in some criminal proceedings, such as to show the absence of premeditation and deliberation in a murder trial. The dissent asserted that a person who intentionally commits a bad act is more culpable than one who engages in the same conduct without any evil design.

f. Involuntary intoxication

Regina v. Kingston
4 All E.R. 373 (1993), *rev'd*, House of Lords, 3 All E.R. 353 (1994).

Facts. Penn lured a 15-year-old boy to his flat, drugged him, and then invited Kingston (D) to come there to sexually abuse the boy. Penn photographed and audiotaped what took place, for the purpose of blackmailing D. D was subsequently charged with indecent assault and battery, and at trial testified he sometimes drank coffee at Penn's but was not sure if he had on that evening. D's words on the audiotape indicated that he did drink coffee and asked if Penn had put something into the coffee causing D to feel sleepy. The trial court instructed the jury that if it found that D intended to commit the indecent assault, prior to being drugged, then the drug was irrelevant. The jury could acquit only if it found that because of the drug, D did not intend to commit an indecent assault. D was convicted. D appeals.

Issue. If an intentional act arises out of circumstances for which an accused bears no blame, may he be entitled to a judgment of acquittal?

Held. Yes. Conviction set aside.

♦ The pedophiliac inclinations of D are not illegal; acting upon them is. However, if D crossed the boundary between inclination and action because of a third party's clandestine act, then justice is not served by convicting the person who crossed the line.

♦ Involuntary intoxication, by alcohol or drugs, negates the mens rea.

Dissent. The drug is not alleged to have created D's desire, but rather to have enabled its release. But the reasoning is that where blame is absent, the necessary mens rea must be absent. This is not logical. These factors being used to require a judgment of acquittal would be more appropriately considered for determining D's sentence, not his guilt or innocence.

Comment. Some would argue that, contrary to the dissent's apparent belief that recognizing involuntary intoxication as an absolute defense would impact upon a vast number of prosecutions, instances of involuntary intoxication are relatively rare. The more common scenario does not involve a clandestine act by a third party. More often than not, it involves a defendant who suffered unexpected effects from a new medication or an interaction between alcohol and medication of which he had not been forewarned.

4. Mental Disorder

a. Insanity defense

An accused may be found not guilty if, at the time of the crime, he was so impaired by mental illness or retardation that he was "insane." There is a general presumption of sanity, however, so that an accused must affirmatively raise the defense. Many states require die prosecution to prove beyond a reasonable doubt that the accused was sane at the time of the offense, while others require the accused to persuade the jury of his insanity by a preponderance of the evidence. Every jurisdiction has procedures for commitment of an accused found not guilty by reason of insanity. There are several different standards for insanity applied by the various jurisdictions.

1) Insanity defense rejected

In both State v. Green, 643 S.W.2d 902 (Tenn.1982), and Yates v. State, 171 S.W.3d 215 (Tex.App.2005), the trial juries rejected the insanity defense. Green shot and killed a police officer when he was 18. A note found on the officer's body brought the police to an FBI agent who told them Green had come to the FBI building a few weeks prior to the murder and complained that he was "directed" by "voices." The agent suggested Green seek mental health assistance. He did not. He had started treatment at the age of 7 and continued for two years, having been diagnosed with paranoia. He attacked his mother with a knife when he was 12 and again underwent treatment. He was hospitalized as a teen because he heard voices and engaged in bizarre behavior. When his family's health insurance ran out, he received in-patient care, but stopped taking his medications and refused to continue treatment. He graduated from high school but was discharged from the Navy for failure to adapt to regulations. Still hearing voices, he attacked his brother with a knife, ran away from his parents' home, lived with two relatives who finally rejected him because of his strange and potentially dangerous behavior. He spurned his father's attempts to get him to return home, so his father gave him some money and bought him a new pair of shoes. Two months later, the murder took place. Green was first found incompetent to stand trial, but through intensive drug therapy in a mental facility, his ability to think coherently gradually improved and he was found competent to stand trial. All of the experts at trial agreed Green was insane at the time of the murder; the prosecution offered no expert testimony, but police officers who knew Green at the time of the murder testified he seemed "normal" to them. He was convicted of first degree murder. Yates shared a similar fate. She drowned her five children, ranging in age from seven months to seven years to save them from Satan. After having three children in three and a half years and moving with her husband to a converted bus in a trailer park, her husband responded to her complaints of being depressed and overwhelmed with a suggestion that she talk to her mother and a friend. She tried to commit suicide after giving birth again a year later. She was admitted to a psychiatric unit of a hospital for a week and continued to see a psychiatrist upon her release. A month later, her husband found her holding a knife to her throat and she was again hospitalized. She told her doctor that she had started having visions and hearing voices after the birth of her first child. The doctor said she was one of the sickest five patients he had ever seen and warned her husband that she had a high risk of another psychotic episode if she had another child. Fifteen months later, her fifth child was born. Shortly thereafter, he father died. She was depressed and hospitalized again. She was on a suicide watch and observed as catatonic and delusional. By her and her husband's request, she was discharged two weeks later. The discharging psychiatrist recommended she never be alone with her children. Her mother-in-law moved in and reported Yates was almost catatonic, did not eat, scratched her head until she created bald spots and stared into space. She was hospitalized again but discharged after ten days. When she didn't report any suicidal or psychotic thoughts to her psychiatrist during the following month, he decided to start to lessen her dosage of Haldol, a powerful antipsychotic medication. Four weeks later, she killed her children. She was found guilty of capital murder and sentenced to life in prison.

Both defendants had their convictions reversed on appeal, Green on the basis that the prosecution failed to prove insanity, as it was required to do at the time, and Yates on the basis that the only expert who testified against her defense suggested she made up the defense after watching an episode of Law & Order where a woman drowned her children and was found to be insane. There was no such episode. On retrial, Yates was found not guilty by reason of insanity. Both cases were unusual in that insanity defenses are rarely raised and even more rarely successful, and both defendants were able to offer extensive expert testimony.

b. Nature and quality of the act

M'Naghten's Case
10 Cl. & F. 200, 8 Eng. Rep. 718 (1843).

Facts. M'Naghten (D) shot Drummond by mistake. D told the arresting officers he had come to London to murder Peel, the Prime Minister, because the tories in his city followed, harassed, and persecuted him. D introduced experts that testified that he was obsessed with delusions and suffered from acute insanity. The instruction given to the jury read: "The question to be determined is whether at the time the act in question was committed, the prisoner had or had not the use of his understanding, so as to know that he was doing a wrong or wicked act. If the jurors should be of opinion that the prisoner was not sensible, at the time he committed it, that he was violating the laws both of God and man, then he would be entitled to a verdict in his favor: but if, on the contrary, they were of opinion that when he committed the act he was in a sound state of mind, men their verdict must be against him." D was found not guilty on the ground of insanity. The verdict caused great alarm. The Queen had just suffered three assassination attempts and one attacker had been acquitted on the ground of insanity. The House of Lords debated the issue and invited members of the judiciary to attend to respond to questions on the matter. Lord Chief Justice Tindal presented the responses that have become known as the M'Naghten Rule.

Issues.

(i) What are the proper questions to be submitted to the jury when a person alleged to be afflicted with insane delusions respecting one or more particular subjects or persons is charged with the commission of a crime (murder, for example) and insanity is set up as a defense?

(ii) In what terms ought the question to be left to the jury as to the prisoner's state of mind at the time when the act was committed?

Response.

(i) In all cases, jurors should be told every person is presumed to be sane until the opposite is proved to their satisfaction. To establish a defense of insanity, it must be proved that at the time of the act, the party was "laboring under such a defect of reason, from a disease of the mind, as not to know the nature and quality of the act he was doing; or, if he did know it, that he did not know he was doing what was wrong."

(ii) The jury is asked to determine not whether the accused knew the difference from right and wrong generally, but in "reference to the party's knowledge of right and wrong in respect to the very act with which he is charged. If the accused was conscious that the act was one that he ought not to do, and if the act was at the same time contrary to the law of the land, he is punishable; and the usual course therefore has been to leave the question to the jury whether the party had a sufficient degree of reason to know that he was doing an act that was wrong: and this course we think is correct, accompanied with such observations and explanations as the circumstances of each particular case may require."

c. Criticism of *M'Naghten* approach

Under *M'Naghten*, an accused must show that as a result of his mental illness he either (i) did not know the nature and quality of his act, or (ii) did not know that the act was wrong. The test assumes that a person's understanding or reasoning ability may be separated from other aspects of personality. Most psychiatrists now agree that personality is unitary and interrelated. The test limits admissible evidence to matters concerning the understanding, thereby excluding much relevant information on the accused's mental condition relevant to determining whether he should be held criminally liable.

d. Irresistible impulse approach

Some states permit the acquittal of an accused whose commission of the crime was caused by an insane impulse that controlled his will. This approach is added to *M'Naghten* as an additional grounds for a finding of not guilty.

e. *Durham* or product approach

New Hampshire formulated a test whereby an accused could be acquitted by reason of insanity upon a showing that the crime was the product of a mental illness. The approach was adopted by the Court of Appeals for the District of Columbia in *Durham v. United States*, 214 F.2d 862 (D.C. Cir. 1954), but was later abandoned in *United States v. Browner*, 471 F.2d 969 (D.C. Cir. 1972). Many authorities criticize the rule as being far too broad and vague, and it is little followed today.

f. Model Penal Code approach

The Model Penal Code permits an acquittal by reason of insanity if, because of a mental disease or defect, the accused either (i) lacked substantial capacity to appreciate the criminality of his conduct, or (ii) lacked substantial capacity to conform his conduct to the requirements of law. This test is broader than *M'Naghten*. The main criticism has been directed at the second part of the test.

1) Substantial capacity standard

Blake v. United States
407 F.2d 908 (5th Cir. 1969).

Facts. Blake (D) was tried and convicted of bank robbery. His principal defense was insanity. The evidence showed that D came from a well-to-do family, joined the Navy after two years of college, and was given a medical discharge in 1944 at age 21 after he suffered an epileptic seizure. D received shock treatments in 1945, and after other mental difficulties, entered a VA hospital for two to three months in 1946. D married and had three children. He worked for his father in construction. D developed a drinking problem. In 1948, he spent two months in a private psychiatric hospital. Between 1948 and 1954, D received out-patient care, received further shock treatments, and spent time in three institutions. D left his father's company in 1954, and from 1955 to 1960, his behavior was characterized by heavy drinking and irrational acts. He used stimulants and drugs. He received eight electroshock treatments, and was adjudged incompetent in 1956 and placed under his father's guardianship to be placed in a private institution in lieu of commitment. He was discharged from the private institution six months later. After divorce and remarriage, D was arrested for shooting his second wife. He spent time in mental hospitals and on probation. In 1963, D spent time in prison for aggravated assault. In prison, he was hospitalized several times, was treated by a psychiatrist, and complained of blackouts. D was living in a hotel at the time of the robbery, and after stopping at a bar for a few drinks, had a hotel employee drive him to the bank and wait, during rush hour, while he went in, demanded money, got it, and walked out. By this time he was on his fourth wife. There was testimony D suffered from schizophrenia, marked by psychotic episodes. D's motion for a new trial was denied. D appeals.

Issue. Was the definition of insanity given the jury for determining the issue of not guilty by reason of insanity outmoded and prejudicial?

Held. Yes. Judgment reversed.

- The court applied the standard from dictum in *Davis v. United States*, 165 U.S. 373 (1897): "The term 'insanity' as used in this defense means such a perverted and deranged condition of the mental and moral faculties as to render a person incapable of distinguishing between right and wrong, or unconscious at the time of the nature of the act he is committing, or where, though conscious of it and able to distinguish between right and wrong and know that the act is wrong, yet his will, by which I mean the governing power of his mind, has been otherwise than voluntarily so completely destroyed that his actions are not subject to it, but are beyond his control."

- Section 4.01 of the Model Penal Code is as follows:

  (1) A person is not responsible for criminal conduct if at the time of such conduct as a result of mental disease or defect he lacks substantial capacity either to appreciate the criminality [wrongfulness] of his conduct or to conform his conduct to the requirements of law.

  (2) As used in this Article, the terms "mental disease or defect" do not include an abnormality manifested only by repeated criminal or otherwise antisocial conduct.

- The facts of this case illustrate the difference in the standards. Under the absolutes of *Davis*, and read favorably to the government, the facts do not show complete mental disorientation. D could not prevail under a *Davis* charge. He might have prevailed under a substantial lack of capacity type charge.

- A substantiality type standard is called for in light of current knowledge regarding mental illness. D may be a schizophrenic or may merely have a sociopathic personality. The evidence could go either way. He may or may not have been in a psychotic episode at the time of the robbery. But, he was not unconscious, incapable of distinguishing right and wrong, nor was his will completely destroyed in the terms of *Davis* definition.

- We adopt the Model Penal Code standard but substitute the word "wrongfulness" for "criminality" in the first paragraph.

2) Involuntary drug addiction not sufficient

United States v. Lyons
731 F.2d 243, 739 F.2d 994 (5th Cir. 1984).

Facts. Lyons (D) was tried for knowingly and intentionally securing controlled narcotics by misrepresentation, fraud, deception, and subterfuge. D disclosed that he intended to rely on a defense of insanity, based on the theory that his involuntary drug addiction affected his brain both physiologically, and psychologically, so that he lacked substantial capacity to conform his conduct to the requirements of the law. The United States (P) made a motion in limine to exclude any evidence of D's drug addiction. The court granted the motion and D appealed. A panel of the court reversed, and the court agreed to rehear the case en banc.

Issue. May involuntary drug addiction alone constitute a mental disease or defect depriving an accused of substantial capacity to conform his conduct to the requirements of the law?

Held. No. Judgment reversed on other grounds.

- Evidence of narcotics addiction, without other physiological or psychological involvement, does not raise an issue of a mental defect or disease that can serve as a basis for the insanity defense. An addict has some reasoned choice when he knowingly acquires and uses drugs. It would be inconsistent to immunize narcotics addicts from criminal sanctions for obtaining drugs when mere possession and sale of narcotics is illegal.

- Drug use may produce actual physical damage to the brain itself that may constitute mental disease or defect. D should be allowed to introduce any evidence that tends to suggest such damage to the extent that it may have resulted in his lacking substantial capacity to appreciate the wrongfulness of his conduct.

- ◆ D did seek to introduce the evidence to show that he lacked substantial capacity to conform his conduct to the requirements of the law. This prong of the Model Penal Code test does not comport with current medical and scientific knowledge. Most psychiatrists now believe they cannot measure a person's capacity for self-control. The line between an irresistible impulse and an impulse not resisted is not ascertainable, and there is no objective basis for distinguishing between offenders in the two categories. Experts and jurors alike are asked to speculate about volition with no articulated standards. Thus, this prong of the test is no longer recognized.

Dissent. A guilty verdict is a moral judgment that a person is blameworthy. An acquittal by reason of insanity means a person in unable to make an effective choice regarding his behavior, and, therefore, is not blameworthy. It is difficult to understand the majority's fear that the present test invites moral mistakes. Its decision virtually insures undeserved, and therefore unjust, punishment in the name of avoiding moral mistakes.

g. Cognitively impaired offender

State v. Crenshaw
659 P.2d 488 (Wash. 1983).

Facts. Crenshaw (D) and his wife went to Canada on their honeymoon. While there, D got in a fight and was deported. D waited for his wife in Washington but she did not come until two days later. D believed she had been unfaithful. In their motel room, D beat his wife unconscious. He then went to a store, stole a knife, and returned to the motel, where he stabbed his wife 24 times. Then D went to a farm, borrowed an ax, returned to the motel, and decapitated his wife. He placed the body in a blanket and put the head in a pillowcase. D then put the body parts in his wife's car and cleaned the room of blood and fingerprints with a bucket and sponge. Before leaving, D paid his bill and visited with the manager over a beer. When he left, D drove to a secluded area, where he hid the body parts in the brush. He drove about 200 miles before picking up hitchhikers, to whom he confessed. They reported the crime to the police, who arrested D and obtained a voluntary confession. At trial, D asserted the defense of not guilty by reason of insanity, claiming that under the Moscovite religious faith that he followed, it would be improper for him not to kill his wife if she committed adultery. He also produced evidence of his history of mental problems, for which he had been hospitalized. The court instructed the jury that the defense applies only if they found that D was unable to perceive the nature and quality of the acts with which he was charged or was unable to tell right from wrong with reference to the particular acts. "Right and wrong" was defined as "knowledge of a person at the time of committing an act that he was acting contrary to the law." D was convicted. He appeals, claiming the instruction was improper.

Issue. May an accused's sanity be tested by his knowledge that his acts were legally wrong?

Held. Yes. Judgment affirmed.

- ◆ The jury instruction relayed the traditional *M'Naghten* test, except for the last paragraph that equated "legal" and "moral" wrong. In *M'Naghten's Case*, the justices opined that a person who acts under a partial insane delusion that he was revenging some supposed grievance is punishable if he knew at the time of committing the crime that he was acting contrary to law. They also stated that an accused is punishable if he was conscious that the act was one that he ought not to do, meaning it was morally wrong, and if the act was also contrary to the law, but that the accused need not have actual knowledge of the law.

- ◆ In this case, assuming that D acted under a delusion that he was revenging the supposed grievance of his wife's infidelity, it was only a partial delusion because he acted normally to the manager and others at the time of the offense. His attempts to hide his crime showed he knew that he was acting contrary to law. It was not improper to equate moral and legal wrong since D knew that his acts were illegal. Strict application of the *M'Naghten* rule is appropriate because only those who have lost contact with reality so completely that they are beyond any of the influences of the criminal law are to benefit from the insanity defense.

♦ Another approach is that society's morals, not D's morals, are the standard for judging moral wrong. Even if D thought that, pursuant to his religious beliefs, it was not morally wrong to kill his wife, there is evidence that he knew his act was morally wrong from society's viewpoint as well as illegal. Once moral wrong is equated with society's morals, moral and legal wrong are easily equated, since the law expresses collective morality.

♦ Finally, D did not prove that his alleged delusions stemmed from a mental defect, and he did not prove that he was legally insane at the time of the crime. His conduct, other than killing his wife, was rational. No one ever kills his wife in a rational way, but not every man who kills his wife is insane.

Comment. The Washington Supreme Court held that this jury instruction was improperly given in another case in which the accused stated that he knew his crime was illegal, but that he felt it was not particularly wrong in the eyes of God because his victim was "into sorcery." The court distinguished between acting pursuant to religious beliefs, as Crenshaw had allegedly done, and acting in the belief that God was directing the act; this has been labeled the "deific decree" exception to the general rule that legal and moral wrong are the same thing. *[See* State v. Cameron, 674 P.2d 650 (Wash. 1983)]

h. Meaning of "disease"

State v. Guido
191 A.2d 45 (N.J. 1963).

Facts. Guido (D) killed her husband by shooting him several times as he slept on the couch in their living room. D had wanted a divorce, but her husband had refused, despite his ongoing extramarital affair. D's husband had physically injured her on a few occasions and had constantly threatened her. D was charged with murder. Two court-appointed psychiatrists examined her, made medical findings, and concluded that she was "legally" sane when she shot her husband. D's defense counsel met with the psychiatrists and persuaded them to change their opinion regarding "legal" insanity. This fact was elicited at the trial, and in his closing argument, the prosecutor asserted that the defense had been concocted between D's attorney and the psychiatrists. D was convicted. D appeals.

Issue. Is it fraudulent for a defense attorney to change the opinion of psychiatrists as to whether the examinee suffers from a mental "disease"?

Held. No. Judgment reversed.

♦ The psychiatrists' change in opinion did not relate to their medical findings, but instead reflected a change in their understanding of what a mental "disease" is under the law. Originally, they believed that the *M'Naghten* rule required a disease that is a psychosis, and that a lesser illness would not suffice. D's attorney explained to them that an "anxiety neurosis" such as D suffered may legally qualify as a "disease."

♦ Although the *M'Naghten* rule requires a "disease of the mind," it does not define what a "disease" is, even though the difference between criminal liability and freedom from moral blame hinges on whether the person suffers from a disease. The *M'Naghten* rule focuses on the effect of disease, not on identifying a specific disease that excuses the offense. The distinction is between one who acts with moral depravity or weakness and is thus without excuse, and one who because of a disease either does not know what she is doing, or does not know the act is wrong.

- There is no clear definition of "disease," and D should not be penalized because her attorney and the witnesses were groping for an understanding of what the law requires as a "disease."

i. Automatism

Cases have arisen in which the defendant's conduct resulted from a confused or impaired mental condition that was other than insanity; *e.g.*, epileptic seizure, sleep, hypoglycemia, etc. One approach is to view the condition as legal insanity. The Model Penal Code views this as absence of a volitional act, resulting in acquittal.

j. Diminished capacity

1) Introduction

In some jurisdictions, evidence of mental illness that does not establish insanity may still be admissible to prove that the defendant did not have the specific intent necessary for the crime charged. Even if the defendant may be aware that his act was wrongful and be able to control it, the mental defect may be characterized as diminished capacity and reduce the extent of criminal liability that would otherwise apply.

2) Adoption of ALI test

United States v. Brawner
471 F.2d 969 (D.C. Cir. 1972).

Facts. Brawner (D) appealed a conviction of second degree murder and of carrying a dangerous weapon. D's defense was insanity. The D.C. Circuit had previously applied the *Durham* test, discussed *supra*.

Issue. Should the *Durham* test for insanity be followed?

Held. No. Judgment reversed.

- The *Durham* test was adopted to allow experts to testify in their own terms and not according to legal-moral terms (the right/wrong test). Also, it reflected the notion that results should be reached according to current community standards of culpability. The test has been criticized, however.

- The use of the term "product" has resulted in expert testimony having undue influence on the jury; in effect, experts giving their medical opinions have dominated the issues. This does not reflect the fact that the defense is based on legal, moral, ethical, and other bases, which are represented in the jury.

- The ALI test provides that a person is not responsible for her unlawful conduct if, at the time the conduct occurred, as a result of mental disease or defect, she lacked the capacity to appreciate the wrongfulness of her conduct, or to conform her conduct to the requirements of the law.

- A mental disease or defect includes any abnormal condition of mind that substantially affects mental or emotional processes and substantially impairs control.

- This standard allows expert testimony, but it is in language understood by all those involved with the judicial process and thus leaves the issue ultimately to the jury, where it belongs.

3) Restriction on evidence

Clark v. Arizona
126 S. Ct. 2709 (2006).

Facts. When a police officer pulled Clark (D) over for a traffic stop, D shot and killed him. D was charged with first degree murder for intentionally or knowingly killing a police officer. In a bench trial, D denied that he had the intent to shoot an officer or knowledge that he was doing so because he suffered from undisputed paranoid schizophrenia. D presented testimony describing his bizarre behavior during the year before the shooting, including his paranoid delusions that "aliens" were trying to kill him and that some of these aliens impersonated government agents. The court, citing *State* v. *Mott*, 931 P.2d 1046 (Ariz. 1997), found that D could not rely on evidence bearing on insanity to dispute the mens rea element of the charge. The judge found that D's mental illness did not distort D's perception of reality so much that he did not know that his actions were wrong. D was convicted of first degree murder and sentenced to life imprisonment. The court of appeals affirmed. The Supreme Court granted certiorari.

Issue. Is it a violation of due process to prohibit the introduction of evidence of mental illness on the issue of mens rea?

Held. No. Judgment affirmed.

♦ In *Mott*, the Supreme Court of Arizona ruled that expert testimony could be admitted for its bearing on an insanity defense, but it could not be considered on the element of mens rea.

♦ There are a few categories of evidence with a potential bearing on mens rea. First, "observation evidence" from witnesses who saw and heard D includes expert witness testimony about D's tendency to think in a certain way. It may support a professional diagnosis of mental disease and can be relevant to show what was on D's mind when he shot the officer.

♦ Second, "mental-disease evidence" is usually that of expert witnesses, professional psychologists or psychiatrists. Here, based on factual reports, professional observation, and tests, the evidence suggested that D was psychotic at the time of the shooting.

♦ Third, "capacity evidence" is usually expert opinion evidence that deals with a defendant's capacity for cognition and moral judgment and, ultimately, his capacity to form mens rea. Here, this testimony focused on the specific details of the mental condition that make the difference between sanity and insanity under the Arizona definition.

♦ *Mott* imposed no restriction on observation evidence; we interpret it to apply to mental disease evidence (*i.e.*, whether a defendant suffered from a mental disease at the time of the crime) and capacity evidence (*i.e.*, whether the disease rendered him incapable of performing or experiencing a mental process defined as necessary for sanity, such as appreciating the nature and quality of his act and knowing that it was wrong).

♦ *Mott* distinguishes mental disease evidence and capacity evidence from observation evidence, even from an expert witness, such as a description of a defendant's behavioral characteristics or his tendency to think in a certain way. This type of testimony is admissible to rebut the prosecution's evidence of mens rea. Hence, under *Mott*, only opinion testimony regarding mental disease and its effect on the cognitive or moral capacities on which sanity depends is restricted.

♦ D argues that it violates due process to restrict him from presenting evidence on an element that must be proven to convict him. Evidence tending to show that a defendant suffers from mental disease and lacks the capacity to form mens rea is relevant to rebut evidence that he did form the required mens rea at the time in question. Here, D claims a right to require the factfinder to consider testimony about his mental illness and his incapacity directly when weighing the persuasiveness of other evidence tending to show mens rea, which the prosecution has the burden to prove.

♦ However, relevant evidence can be excluded if there is good reason (*e.g.*, its probative value is outweighed by its potential to mislead the jury). In Arizona, mental disease evidence and capacity evidence is limited to its bearing on the insanity defense; it is given effect only if the defendant has the burden to convince the factfinder of insanity. We find that the reasons for so limiting the evidence satisfy the standard of fundamental fairness that due process requires.

♦ The controversial character of some categories of mental disease cautions against treating psychological classifications as predicates for excusing otherwise criminal conduct. Also, there is the potential for evidence of mental disease to mislead jurors by suggesting that a defendant with a recognized mental disease lacks cognitive, moral, volitional, or other capacity, when that is not so.

♦ In this case, the experts had conflicting opinions. They agreed that D was schizophrenic, but they disagreed as to whether his disease left him without moral or cognitive capacity. Because mental-disease evidence on mens rea can mislead easily, it is reasonable to deal with this problem by confining consideration of this kind of evidence to insanity, where the defendant may have the burden of persuasion.

♦ Capacity evidence is also problematic; it consists of judgment. A defendant's state of mind at the crucial moment can be elusive, and the tenuous character of capacity evidence can be seen in the testimony of the defense expert in this case. He testified that D lacked the capacity to appreciate the circumstances realistically and to understand the wrongfulness of what he was doing, but he admitted that no one knows exactly what was on D's mind at the time of the shooting.

♦ The law's categories setting the terms of the capacity judgment are not the same as the categories of psychology. Concepts of psychology are devised for thinking about treatment, whereas the concepts of legal sanity are devised for thinking about criminal responsibility.

♦ Not all states will decide as Arizona has. The choices of other states dealing with the risks posed by mental-disease and capacity evidence will be expressed in their choices of insanity rules. The point here is that Arizona has sensible reasons to confine such expert evidence to consideration on the insanity defense.

Dissent (Kennedy, Stevens, Ginsburg, JJ.).

♦ D's defense was that his schizophrenia made him delusional and that he had no intent to shoot an officer or knowledge that he was doing so. Acting with intent or knowledge to pull the trigger is not the same as pulling the trigger to kill someone he knew was human and a police officer.

♦ Arizona's reasons for its categorical exclusion of evidence that may disprove an element of the offense are insufficient. Arizona has rules to bar unreliable or speculative testimony and to ensure the reliability of expert testimony. Also, the difficulty of resolving a factual issue does not justify taking it away from the jury when it is crucial to the defense. The conflicting conclusions of the state and defense experts only made the evidence contested; it did not make it irrelevant or misleading. The potential to mislead jurors is far greater if they receive observation evidence without the necessary explanation from experts.

♦ Allowing mental illness evidence in deciding criminal responsibility does not compensate for its exclusion from consideration on the mens rea elements. Although there may be overlap, criminal responsibility involves an inquiry into whether the defendant knew right from wrong, not whether he had the mens rea elements of the crime. Furthermore, there is a different burden of proof for insanity than for mens rea. Arizona requires a defendant to prove insanity by clear and convincing evidence, but the prosecution must prove all elements of an offense beyond a reasonable doubt. The shift in the burden on the criminal responsibility issue cannot be applied to the question of intent or knowledge without relieving the state of its responsibility to establish this element of the offense.

♦ Arizona allows a defendant to introduce evidence of behavioral tendencies to show that he did not have the required mental state, but psychiatric testimony regarding mental illnesses is excluded. This forces a jury to decide guilt in a fictional world with unexplained behaviors but without mental illness.

5. Changing Patterns of Excuse

a. Introduction

The opinions of behavioral scientists have had some effect on court decisions. Despite the assumption that people have free will, at one point the courts began treating people as victims in need of rehabilitation, rather than as criminals in need of punishment. However, due to the perceived limitations of societal institutions to solve these problems, more recent decisions may be reverting back to those of an earlier time.

b. Drug addiction

Robinson v. California
370 U.S. 660 (1962).

Facts. Robinson (D) was prosecuted for being "addicted to the use of narcotics." The evidence showed that D had scar tissue, needle marks, and discoloration typical of frequent narcotics users. The jury was instructed that D could be convicted if they found that D was either of the "status" or had committed the "act" proscribed by the statute. D was found guilty and appeals.

Issue. May a state criminalize mere status as a narcotics addict?

Held. No. Judgment reversed.

♦ A state has broad power to regulate narcotics traffic. It can even involuntarily confine addicts for compulsory medical treatment. However, a disease is not a criminal offense. D may have been convicted under the statute without ever having used or possessed narcotics within the state and without ever having done any antisocial act there. Criminal punishment for affliction with a disease is cruel and unusual. A drug addict is a sick person, not a criminal.

Concurrence (Douglas, J.). An addict is sick and we should not allow sickness to be treated as a crime. Civil commitment would protect society just as well.

Concurrence (Harlan, J.). Drug addiction may be something other than an illness and therefore subject to criminal sanctions, but this statute allows conviction for the bare desire to do a criminal act; *e.g.*, D's compelling propensity to use narcotics.

Dissent (White, J.). The court has made it impossible for the state to deal with defendants who continually use narcotics where the state cannot prove the precise location of use.

c. Alcoholism

Powell v. Texas
392 U.S. 514 (1968).

Facts. Powell (D) was arrested and charged with being found intoxicated in a public place. He was found guilty and fined $20. On appeal, the court ruled that chronic alcoholism, from which D suffered, was not a defense to the charge and fined D $50. D appeals.

Issue. May a person be criminally liable for merely being in a public place while suffering from a disease?

Held. Yes. Judgment affirmed.

- Alcoholism presents a serious public problem. The evidence indicates that there is no known generally effective method for treating alcoholism. Use of the criminal law to incarcerate public drunks affords an opportunity to sober up. Because penal incarceration has stringent time limits, it is probably preferable to an unlimited civil commitment when no treatment is available. The uncertainty of any deterrent effect of the criminal statute does not make the statute unconstitutional.

- In *Robinson v. California, supra*, the court held that a statute making it a crime to "be addicted to the use of narcotics" inflicted cruel and unusual punishment because it punished the person's condition. The statute here materially differs because it punishes not chronic alcoholism but public drunkenness. *Robinson* requires some actus reus before criminal penalties may be inflicted. D did commit an illegal act.

Concurrence (Black, Harlan, JJ.). *Robinson* was limited to situations where no act was involved, where the mental element is not simply one part of the crime, but all of it.

Concurrence (White, J.). If it is not a crime to have an irresistible compulsion to use drugs, it should not be a crime to yield to the compulsion. Here, however, D did not have an irresistible compulsion to be in the public area. He could have taken precautions against being drunk in public.

Dissent (Fortas, Douglas, Brennan, Stewart, JJ.). The Constitution forbids infliction of criminal penalties upon a person for being in a condition he is powerless to change. D was convicted only because he was in a condition that he had no capacity to change or avoid.

d. Possession of drugs

United States v. Moore
486 F.2d 1139 (D.C. Cir. 1973).

Facts. Moore (D) was convicted of possession of heroin; he appeals the conviction. He contends that he lacked "free will" because he had a long history of drug addiction and he was psychologically and physically dependent. He argues for a distinction between prosecuting for possession and prosecuting for crimes perpetrated to get drugs (robbery, etc.).

Issue. Is evidence of one's addiction to a drug, which results in his loss of control over the use of the drug, relevant to his criminal responsibility in unlawfully possessing that drug?

Held. No Conviction sustained.

- The logic of D's argument is unsound; if applied, it would mean that it would have to be applied to all crimes perpetrated by those dependent on drugs.

- The argument that loss of self-control is a defense is unsound; all that is needed for conviction is the requisite intent to commit the crime.

Concurrence. Just because there is a defense in one area where loss of control exists (insanity) does not mean that there must be a defense in other areas where the same argument can be made (drug addiction). There are distinctions in each instance; also, exceptions to liability are based on situations where the legitimacy of the defense is ascertainable and society's interests are manageable when the exception is allowed.

Dissent. Criminal responsibility is an expression of the moral sense of the community. Our society does not exculpate all persons whose capacity is impaired; the law assumes free will and then recognizes exceptions where there is broad consensus for doing so. Such a consensus exists now for narcotics addiction, at least in the instance of the crime of possession.

Concurrence and dissent. I would allow a jury to consider addiction as a defense to charges other than possession to determine whether the defendant was under such duress or compulsion that he was unable to conform his conduct to the requirements of the law.

Chapter IX
Theft Offenses

A. Introduction

The theft offenses were developed over a period of time as the criminal law expanded to protect property as well as people. The offenses include larceny, embezzlement, extortion, and obtaining another's property by false pretenses. The underlying harm is the unpermitted acquisition of another's property.

B. The Means of Acquisition

1. Trespassory Takings

a. Larceny

1) Common law definition

Larceny is the unlawful taking and carrying away of the personal property of another with the intent to permanently deprive the owner of it.

2) Asportation

This taking or carrying away of the property of another is usually held to mean that some acquisition of control or dominion over the property is necessary.

a) Possession or control need only be slight; that is, the length of time may be short and the distance moved not far.

b) Thus, it is sufficient asportation where a thief lifts a person's wallet from his pocket but is detected and drops it before it is removed entirely. All that is required is the entire shifting of the property from the place it has occupied.

3) Trespass

Larceny is a crime involving trespass (unlawful taking) from the possession of another. Possession does not necessarily require ownership. This taking can occur by the defendant himself or through an innocent agent (person unaware of the facts—a young child, etc.); but the taking must not be by violence or force from the person of another, or the crime is robbery. In any event, if a person came into possession of property, there was no trespass (and thus no larceny).

a) Larceny by trick or device

In larceny by trick, the person receives goods from another with the latter's consent, but this consent is not valid to impart possession because it is derived by trick, fraud, or other unlawful device. This differs from the case of fraud in that the intent to take the goods exists at the time possession is obtained.

(1) Example

A convinces B to let him take B's camera "to show it to my wife," but A has the intent to steal it and does so on obtaining possession; this is larceny by trick or device.

b) Distinguished from false pretenses

Distinguishing larceny by trick or device from false pretenses, which is discussed *infra*, can be difficult.

4) Grand and petit larceny

When jurisdictions make this distinction, usually petit larceny is only a misdemeanor even though all of the elements for the crime are the same as grand larceny. The difference relates to the fair market value of the goods that are taken (value under a certain amount being petit larceny).

b. Robbery

1) Definition

At common law, robbery was the felony of taking and carrying away the personal property of another from his person or immediate presence by violence, force, or fear, with the intent to permanently deprive him thereof.

a) Robbery includes larceny (*i.e.*, has all of the same elements).

b) In addition, robbery includes the elements of a taking without consent, by force or fear.

2) Elements of robbery

a) Intent

The defendant must take with the fraudulent intent to permanently deprive the owner of his property. There cannot be robbery, even when force is used, when the defendant honestly believes the property is his, or when he takes the property intending only temporary use.

b) Property of another

The property must be the personal property of another (which only means that he has possession thereof).

c) Taking from the person or his presence

(1) There must be a taking and a carrying away. (*See* the discussion under the crime of larceny, *supra*.) If the defendant takes a person's wallet and reduces it to his possession by force, but immediately returns it, there is a robbery because he had complete control.

(2) If the property is taken from the immediate presence of the victim, it is considered as having been taken from his person. If A, by fear, causes B to open his safe and A proceeds to take the money therefrom, this is sufficient to constitute a taking from the person.

d) Taking by force or violence

The taking must not only be without the consent of the possessor, but must also be accompanied by force or violence or the threat thereof (*i.e.*, the force of fear).

(1) It is not robbery to pick another's pocket when he is unaware it is being done, nor is it robbery to grab a person's purse from her hand and run.

(2) But the use of any force to accomplish the taking (such as grabbing the wallet after struggling with the person who has discovered he is being pickpocketed, or bumping into another to divert her attention while taking her purse) amounts to robbery.

(3) Threat of violence or force that puts another person reasonably in fear of such, when it accompanies the taking, is also sufficient to satisfy this requirement. This fear need not only be fear by the victim for his own person, but may also be fear for injury to property or the person of another.

e) Consent

The taking by force must be without the consent of the owner.

3) Statutory robbery

Many states have codified robbery. A sample state statutory system follows:

a) First degree robbery

Robbery perpetrated by torture or by a person armed with a dangerous or deadly weapon is first degree robbery.

b) Second degree

All other robbery is second degree robbery.

c. Extortion

1) Common law

At common law, the crime of extortion had a very limited meaning—the obtaining of money or property from another with his consent by the use of one's color of office or official position.

2) Today

Statutes have greatly expanded the common law crime. It now includes the obtaining of money or property by any person using force or threat.

a) Compared with robbery

Obviously, extortion is very close to the crime of robbery. One difference is that the property need not be taken from the person of the victim (for example, the instance of blackmail).

b) Consent through force

Additionally, note that extortion is a taking "with consent"; but since the consent must be induced by force (or the threat of force) or fear, it is difficult to distinguish this "consent" from the "without consent" in robbery.

(1) One difference is that the range of threats that will be sufficient for extortion is greater. All of the force or threats that hold for robbery apply to extortion.

(2) In addition, the threat to accuse the victim or members of his family of a crime, or to expose some secret causing disgrace, etc., is sufficient.

d. Receiving stolen property

In most jurisdictions, it is a felony to knowingly receive stolen property. The elements of the crime are as follows:

1) Control over property

To be found guilty, the defendant must in some way actually have control over the stolen property; it is not necessary that he actually touch it or have it in his immediate possession.

2) Stolen property

The property must still have its "stolen" status when the defendant receives it. (It will lose this status if it has been recovered by the police for the owner and men is used in an undercover operation).

3) Intent

The defendant's intent on receiving the property must be fraudulent (*i.e.*, other than an intent to return the property to the rightful owner).

4) Knowledge

The defendant must have knowledge that the property has been stolen.

e. Retention after sale

Commonwealth v. Tluchak
70 A.2d 657 (Pa. Super. Ct. 1950).

Facts. The Tluchaks (Ds) contracted to sell their farm to the complainant and his wife. The agreement did not include any personal property, but it covered "buildings, plumbing, heating, lighting fixtures, screens, storm sash, blinds, awnings, shrubbery and plants." On taking possession, the complainant found that certain articles that had been on the premises at the time of the agreement were gone (commode, an unattached washstand, hay carriage, electric stove cord, 35 peach trees). Ds were prosecuted for larceny and convicted. The trial court overruled Ds' motion for a new trial and an arrest of judgment. Ds appeal.

Issue. When sellers retain possession of property that they had agreed to sell, are they guilty of larceny?

Held. No. Conviction reversed.

- ♦ Ds were in lawful possession of the goods; they did not commit larceny by converting the goods to their own use. A criminal trespass is necessary and it cannot be committed by one who has lawful possession.

Comment. The essential element of trespass was missing. Under some statutes, this result might have been different. If Ds had been charged with fraudulent conversion or larceny by bailee, they might have been guilty on the theory that a vendor retaining possession of goods he sells is a constructive bailee of the vendor.

f. Knowledge and assistance in the taking

Topolewski v. State
109 N.W. 1037 (Wis. 1906).

Facts. Topolewski (D) arranged with a man who owed him money and was an employee of a packing company to place three barrels of meat on the loading platform for D to pick up and take away as though he were a customer. The employee informed the company and it told him to feign cooperation. D took the barrels; he was prosecuted for larceny and convicted. He appeals.

Issue. Is there a trespassory taking when the owner knew the goods were going to be taken and he facilitated the taking?

Held. No. Conviction reversed.

- ◆ The element of trespass did not exist. Trespass is lacking when the company allows its property to be taken regardless of the intent of the accused. By telling its employee to place the property on the platform for a man who would come to get it, the company consented to the taking. The company aided the commission of the offense.

2. Misappropriation

a. Introduction

When there is no trespassory interference with possession because the offender has rightful possession when she forms the intent to take, the crime is not larceny. Instead, it comes within a general class called misappropriation.

b. Conversion after obtaining lawful possession

If possession is unlawfully gained and conversion only occurs afterwards, there is no larceny because there is no trespass. Thus, if a bailee or an agent of the owner has no intent to take the property at the time she receives the goods and only afterward decides to convert them to her use, there is no larceny. If, however, the bailment period has come to an end and then the bailee decides to convert the goods, there is larceny because, at the end of the period, the possession was constructively that of the owner.

1) Exception

One exception to the rule that lawful possession could not turn into larceny with subsequent conversion was the "breaking the bulk" doctrine, which held that if something was given to a carrier or bailee (*i.e.*, lawful possession) but such person broke open the package and took the goods, this violated the bailment contract, so that the goods returned to the constructive possession of the owner and any taking was a trespass. Also, if express conditions were placed in the bailment contract (or conditions existed on delivery of possession by the owner) and these conditions were broken, some courts held that this terminated the agreement, possession returned to the owner, and any subsequent taking was a trespass.

c. Custody but not possession

In some situations property may be delivered to another in such a way or under such circumstances that the person holding the goods is seen as having only "custody," not possession (possession remaining constructively in the hands of the owner).

1) Timing of intent

No matter when the intent to take the goods arises, if an employee or a servant takes the goods of her employer or master, she is guilty of trespass to possession and thus larceny. For example, if an employer gives her employee money to deposit in the bank and on the way to the bank the employee decides to take the money, there is larceny. If the owner delivers goods to an employee in a bailment capacity, the rules mentioned above for bailees will prevail.

2) Delivery by a third person

If a third person delivered goods to an employee for the master or the employer, and the employee only afterwards formed the intent to convert them, then if the goods never entered into the possession of the master there was no trespass because the servant had lawfully come into possession. However, when the servant first placed the goods where they would ordinarily go (or where instructed to put them), the courts held that the goods then came into the constructive possession of the master and any subsequent taking by the servant was larceny. For example, if the employee delivers goods for her employer and immediately puts the money received into her pocket, there is no larceny; but if the employee takes the money and first puts it in the employer's cash register and then takes it, there is larceny.

3) Bare custody

Bare custody alone can occur in many situations, such as when goods are given to a person merely to look at, or to purchase on approval.

d. Goods delivered by mistake

When a person receives goods that are delivered by mistake (for example, more change is given than intended), and if he is unaware of the mistake at the time it occurs, a subsequent taking will not be larceny; but when the person is aware of the mistake at the time it occurs, the taking of those goods is larceny.

e. Lost property

1) When a person finds property and has no reasonable means of knowing to whom it belongs, he obtains possession of these goods. A taking of these goods will not be larceny regardless of the taker's intent.

2) If, at the time of finding the goods the person knows or has reasonable means of finding out the owner and he forms the intent to take the goods on finding them, larceny will lie. But when the intent to take the goods only subsequently arises, there is no larceny.

f. Embezzlement

Embezzlement is the statutory offense involving the unlawful and fraudulent appropriation of property by a person to whom it was entrusted.

1) Compared with larceny

Embezzlement came into being to fill in certain gaps in the common law crime of larceny. For example, larceny was a crime against possession, and thus if a bailee obtained possession and only sometime thereafter formed the intent to convert the goods, there was no larceny. Embezzlement, on the other hand, is aimed at the situation where the person lawfully gains possession of the goods of another and thereafter converts it unlawfully to his own use. The rationale is that the breach of trust or confidence is being punished, not trespass to possession.

2) Elements of the crime

a) Intent

The defendant must have the specific intent to permanently appropriate the property of another to use outside the scope of the trust that placed it in his possession. It is not embezzlement where the defendant takes the property in good faith under a bona fide claim of right, even though in fact the claim of right is untenable. There is no embezzlement where the defendant receives the money pursuant to a bona fide loan.

b) Subject matter of embezzlement

This is a question of statutory interpretation. Many statutes simply state "the property of another."

c) Relationship of confidence or trust

The property must have come into the defendant's possession as a result of his fiduciary relationship with the owner. This simply means that the defendant has possession by and for another.

d) Possession

Some courts have held that because embezzlement was meant to plug gaps in the crime of larceny, embezzlement will not lie unless the defendant has possession of the goods of another, as opposed to mere custody (because in this latter case, conversion will amount to larceny).

(1) For example, if goods are delivered by the owner to his employee, there is only custody, and the employee's subsequent conversion can only be larceny.

(2) But if a third person delivers money to the employee for the master and the employee does not put it where he is instructed to but immediately converts it, he has possession and is thus guilty of embezzlement.

e) Election

Normally the prosecution will be required to elect whether it will proceed under the theory of larceny or embezzlement.

g. Distinction between larceny and embezzlement

Nolan v. State
131 A.2d 851 (Md. 1957).

Facts. Nolan (D) was the office manager of a finance company; he took money from the company out of the cash drawer at the end of the day after the drawer had been balanced. An accomplice recomputed the report of cash receipts to conceal the theft. D appealed from his conviction for embezzlement.

Issue. When a person misappropriates money paid by customers of his employer and placed in the cash drawer, is the fraudulent conversion embezzlement?

Held. No. Conviction reversed. Case remanded for possible prosecution under larceny.

♦ D is not guilty of embezzlement because the money had reached its destination and was constructively in the owner's possession.

♦ Embezzlement statutes are designed to reach offenses outside the reach of common law larceny (which is the taking of goods from the owner's possession).

Concurrence. The effect of the decision is to reestablish many of the technical differences between larceny and embezzlement. Legislation should provide that indictment of larceny should cover either offense.

h. Conversion by a bailee

Burns v. State
128 N.W. 987 (Wis. 1911).

Facts. Burns (D), a constable, having taken an insane man into custody after a chase, received from another pursuer money dropped by the insane man in his flight. D converted some of the money to his own use. The trial court instructed the jury that if the accused converted to his own use any of the insane man's money, he did so as a bailee. D appeals his conviction of larceny by bailee.

Issue. May a person become a bailee for another in the absence of a contract between the parties?

Held. Yes. Jury instructions were proper.

♦ D was a bailee; he came into lawful possession of the money of another with a duty to account for it for the other. The duty to return the property made D a bailee. A contract is not necessary. The essential mutuality may be created by operation of law as well as by contract.

♦ At common law, a bailee could not be convicted of larceny for misappropriating the bailment because he was given lawful possession of the property. Hence, there was no trespass. To overcome this immunity, the common law distinguished between a breaking into the shipment, which was larceny, and misappropriation of all the bailed property, which was not. The legislature has eliminated that distinction through the creation of the offense of larceny by a bailee.

i. Embezzlement by an agent

State v. Riggins
132 N.E.2d 519 (Ill. 1956).

Facts. Riggins (D), owner and operator of a collection service, had an oral agreement with the complainant to collect her firm's delinquent accounts. The agreement provided for D to receive a large percentage of the accounts collected and to account only when the fund was completely collected. For two years, D had complete control over the time and manner of collecting the accounts and, with the complainant's knowledge, commingled funds collected for all his clients. D collected several accounts in full without accounting to the complainant. D was convicted under a general embezzlement statute that provided for the punishment of agents and other specified persons receiving money in a fiduciary capacity and fraudulently converting it, irrespective of their interest in the funds. D appeals.

Issue. May a person be convicted of embezzlement for failing to render an account of business conducted for another?

Held. Yes, but judgment reversed for prejudicial remarks made by the trial court and case remanded for a new trial.

♦ The embezzlement statute applies to agents regardless of whether the agent has claim to a commission or an interest in the money.

♦ D acted as an agent for collecting the funds, receiving funds in a fiduciary capacity and having a duty to account, notwithstanding his interest in the funds. He received the money in a fiduciary capacity and is therefore guilty.

Dissent. D was not an agent; he was not subject to control of the customer and the customer was not liable for D's acts.

Comment. Persons having an interest in the fund they gathered for their principals were considered outside the scope of embezzlement statutes. To reach such persons, new statutes were passed enumerating specific persons, such as brokers and collection agents and making an interest in the fund no defense. D is convicted here under such a statute.

3. Fraud

Various situations arise in which a person acquires the property of another by using fraud to obtain the other's consent.

a. False pretenses

This crime is very similar to that of "larceny by trick or device," mentioned above. The difference is that the owner of the property does not intend just to pass possession but intends to pass ownership or title to the property as well. At common law, there was no crime where title was passed, so this crime was created by statute to remedy the gap in coverage. The elements of the crime are as follows:

1) Misrepresentation of a past or existing fact

There must be some pretense or misrepresentation. This may occur in the form of words or conduct. Mere failure to disclose facts is not usually sufficient.

a) Future events

A statement by the defendant as to future events, as opposed to past or existing facts, is not usually sufficient. Therefore, prediction, promises, dealer's talk, or "puffing" do not represent actionable misrepresentations.

b) Opinions

Similarly, mere expression of "opinion" or "belief is not wrong; but some courts have held that the defendant is guilty of misrepresenting his state of mind or intention (a "fact") when he expresses an intention (as to perform or do something in the future) and does not really have that intention.

2) Intent to defraud

The facts represented must in fact be false ones, and the defendant must have knowledge of this falsity and the specific intent to permanently deprive the owner of his property. The intent to just use the property is not sufficient.

3) Reliance

The misrepresentation must be such that a reasonable person would have relied on it; and, in fact, the owner of the property must have relied on it.

4) Title

The owner must intend to part with complete ownership and title to the property, not just possession. This is a fine distinction from the crime of larceny.

5) Example

If A promises (with intent to defraud) to sell and deliver goods to B that are not in existence, B pays for them in advance, and A never delivers the goods, false pretenses will lie.

b. Forgery

1) Definition

Forgery is the false making of an instrument or document (a writing) or the material altering thereof, which might apparently be of legal efficacy or the foundation of a legal liability, with the intent to defraud.

2) Elements

a) Intent to defraud

The defendant must actually have the intent to defraud another, but no one actually need be defrauded (it is enough that one might have been defrauded).

b) Apparently valid instrument

The instrument that is the subject of forgery must be a writing or document that, if genuine, would create some legal right or obligation (such as false corporate stock, theater tickets, etc.). A false painting is not the subject of forgery since it is not a writing.

(1) The false writing need only apparently create rights or obligations. In fact, it may not do so.

(2) If an instrument is created with fraudulent intent but clearly does not create any rights or obligation (*i.e.*, a $3 bill), there is no forgery.

c) Making or alteration

If an alteration is made, it must be a "material" one so that the instrument has a different effect than it should have.

3) Examples of forgery

Signing another person's name on a check or promissory note without authority to do so is forgery; it is not forgery to sign one's own name even when one is without authority to do so (but this may be false pretenses). Another example of forgery is changing the date of a will.

c. Uttering a forged instrument

Uttering a forged instrument is the passing or using of a forged instrument with the knowledge that it is false and with the intent to defraud.

1) Apparent ability to defraud

The instrument must have the apparent ability to defraud, and it must be used with the intent to defraud; however, it need not in fact defraud anyone.

2) Uttering

Some use of a forged instrument must occur; mere possession or awareness that an instrument is forged is not sufficient. To show a forged receipt to another person in order to obtain credit is a sufficient uttering.

d. Gaining property by trick

Hufstetler v. State
63 So. 2d 730 (Ala. Ct. App. 1953).

Facts. Hufstetler (D) drove up to a service station operated by the complainant. One of D's companions asked the owner to fill the car with gas; then he asked for a quart of oil; when the owner went to get it, D drove off without paying for the gas. D was convicted in a prosecution for petit larceny; he appeals.

Issue. Is an actual trespass required for a conviction of larceny when possession is secured by a trick or fraud?

Held. No. Conviction affirmed.

- ♦ D, aided and abetted by his companion, committed larceny because the owner had no intention of parting with the ownership of his property until he had received payment therefor.

- ♦ Although there was no actual trespass, the trick of D vitiated the owner's parting with his goods and the owner retained constructive possession.

Comment. At common law, the crime of larceny was committed if the owner was induced fraudulently to part only with possession; a similar parting with title and possession constitutes the crime of false pretenses. Here, the owner parted with possession only.

e. Larceny by trick

Graham v. United States
187 F.2d 87 (D.C. Cir. 1950).

Facts. Graham (D), an attorney, agreed with an immigrant who had been arrested for disorderly conduct to talk to the police so that the arrest might not impede the attainment of citizenship. D charged a $200 legal fee and represented that he needed an additional $2,000 to bribe the police. Instead, D took the $2,000 and used it for his own purposes. D was convicted of grand larceny; he appeals.

Issue. Is a person who obtains a chattel for a special purpose, intending to convert it to his own use, guilty of larceny?

Held. Yes. Conviction sustained; jury instructions were proper.

- ♦ The offense was larceny by trick because D obtained the money from another on a representation that he would perform certain services. Instead, D intended to convert the money to his own use, which he did.

- ♦ The immigrant never really parted with title to the money (title remained with him until such time as the purpose for which he gave the money to D was accomplished). He never intended that title pass to D.

Comment. Although a false promise may support larceny by trick, it would be insufficient in a prosecution for false pretenses.

f. Comprehensive theft statute

People v. Ashley
267 P.2d 271 (Cal. 1954).

Facts. Ashley (D) was the business manager of a corporation chartered for the purpose of introducing people. He obtained loans from two women by promising them certain loan security, which he did not have. He gave them notes of the corporation; the loans were not repaid, and D used the funds for his own purposes. The case was tried under a theft statute that consolidated all theft offenses; an instruction was given to the jury as to both larceny by trick and obtaining money under false pretenses. The jury was told that it would have to agree on the type of theft, if any, that was committed. The jury gave a general verdict of guilty. D appeals from denial of his motion for a new trial.

Issue. Is a general verdict of guilty under a theft statute lawful?

Held. Yes. Conviction for obtaining money under false pretenses is affirmed.

♦ The statute allows a general verdict of an "unlawful taking"; but the conviction can be sustained only if all the elements of one of the types of theft are present. The statute was meant to eliminate the technicalities that existed in the pleading and proof of these crimes at common law.

♦ The crime of obtaining property under false pretenses requires that the specific intent of D not to perform his promise be proved.

♦ There was sufficient evidence to sustain the conviction of obtaining property by false pretenses.

g. Presumption of intent to defraud

Nelson v. United States
227 F.2d 21 (D.C. Cir. 1955).

Facts. Nelson (D) owed Potomac, a wholesaler, over $1,800 for past purchases of merchandise on credit. His account was more than 30 days in arrears. D attempted to purchase more goods on credit for immediate resale, but Potomac at first refused because of D's outstanding indebtedness. D then represented himself as the owner of a Packard car for which he had paid over $4,000, but failed to mention indebtedness on the car of over $3,000. Instead, he lied to Potomac, stating that he owed only $55 more on the car. D did have $1,000 worth of equity in the car. Relying on these representations, Potomac sold D two television sets for $349 on credit. D left town without paying. The car sustained $1,000 worth of damages in an accident and was repossessed. D was convicted of obtaining goods by false pretenses. D appeals.

Issue. Can intent to injure or defraud be presumed when an unlawful act, which results in loss or injury, is proved to have been knowingly committed?

Held. Yes. Conviction affirmed.

♦ Wrongful acts intentionally committed cannot be justified on the ground of innocent intent. It is a well-settled rule that intent is presumed and inferred from the result of the action.

♦ It is irrelevant that $349 worth of merchandise was exchanged for a security interest in a car with $1,000 worth of equity. Potomac would not have sold D the goods but for his false representation.

Dissent. D was guilty of a moral wrong in misrepresenting his equity in the car. But this is not a legal wrong. D's $1,000 equity in the car is three times the amount of his debt to Potomac. A purchaser who makes a false statement in buying on credit has not defrauded the seller if he amply secures the debt.

Comment. The crime of false pretenses does not occur unless the defendant actually knows of the falsity of his statement, believes it to be false, and it is actually false. The defendant must possess the intent to defraud, but, as this case illustrates, intent may be inferred from the act itself. To require the prosecution to give direct proof of intent to defraud would be an impossible task.

4. Blackmail

a. Threat of accusation

State v. Harrington
260 A.2d 692 (Vt. 1969).

Facts. Harrington (D) was a Vermont attorney retained by Morin to obtain a divorce. D agreed to work on a contingent fee basis (marital assets were approximately $50,000). D and Morin arranged to entice Morin's husband into having sex at a motel with a woman they hired. The woman had a tape recorder and, at the appropriate time, D and his cohorts entered the room and photographed the husband and woman naked in bed. Afterwards, with Morin present, D dictated a proposed divorce settlement in which his client would receive a lump sum of $175,000 and waive her interest in the marital assets. The letter specifically promised that such a settlement would include returning any and all recordings and photographs documenting the motel incident, and a promise that the client would not divulge the incident to anyone. The letter demanded a prompt reply or Morin would commence rather embarrassing divorce proceedings. One of the photographs taken at the motel was included with the letter. D was convicted of extortion. D moves for acquittal.

Issue. Does the threat of bringing embarrassing litigation constitute extortion?

Held. Yes. Judgment affirmed.

- D argues that his letter was not a threat to accuse another of a crime, but merely to bring an embarrassing divorce proceeding in the husband's county of residence.

- In *State v. Louanis*, 65 A. 532 (Vt. 1907), the court stated that the threat of any public accusation is as much within the reason of the extortion statute as a threat of a formal complaint.

- The letter clearly makes an accusation of adultery in support of a demand for a cash settlement.

- D also argues that he was, by inference, acting merely as an attorney attempting to secure a favorable divorce for his client. But the letter's veiled threats referring to "informer fees," which his client could obtain from the IRS, certainly exceeded the limit of proper representation.

b. Intent requirement in extortion

People v. Fichtner
118 N.Y.S.2d 392, *aff'd*, 114 N.E.2d 212 (N.Y. 1952).

Facts. Fichtner (D), a store manager, and McGuiness (D), his assistant, caught a customer shoplifting. They threatened to prosecute him unless he paid $75 for goods they claimed he had taken over a long period of time. The customer signed a paper that the money was the correct amount owed, paid part, and Ds put the money in the cash register. The customer later denied that the value of the goods taken was that high. Ds were prosecuted for extortion; the trial court refused an instruction to the jury that if Ds honestly believed the customer owed the full amount, they must be acquitted. Ds were convicted and they appeal.

Issue. If Ds honestly believed that they were entitled to the amount they demanded under a threat of criminal prosecution, but they were in fact wrong, may they be convicted of extortion?

Held. Yes. Conviction sustained.

- Good faith is no defense. One of the aims of the extortion statutes was to prevent a creditor from obtaining money owed by a debtor through threats of prosecution. The validity of the debt is irrelevant. It also does not matter whether the threatened prosecution relates to a crime from which the indebtedness arose, or relates to some other crime.

Dissent If Ds acted in good faith, without malice, they had no criminal intent and are not guilty.

Comment. Other states hold differently, especially if the defendant's claim arises out of the crime that he accuses the victim of committing.

5. Consolidation

The technicality of the various theft offenses has led to some incredible results; for example, a defendant prosecuted for one offense having his conviction reversed on appeal because the elements of the offense charged were not all present (even though he did commit another theft offense for which he was not charged). Also, many of the distinctions between the offenses are more technical than real. For these and other reasons, many states have passed statutes that deal with the whole theft area as one offense.

a. Theft

In order to consolidate some of the above crimes and do away with their highly technical distinctions, the statutory crime of "theft" has been created by many jurisdictions. It includes the common law crimes of (i) larceny, (ii) embezzlement, (iii) larceny by trick or device, and (iv) false pretenses.

1) Pleading and proof

There were formerly great pleading and proof difficulties for the prosecution due to the distinction between the four above-mentioned theft crimes. It is now much easier for die prosecution to bring charges against the defendant.

2) Degrees or classifications

a) Grand theft

Grand theft applies when the money or labor, property, etc., taken is worth over a certain amount (*e.g.*, $200) or is taken from the person (and is of any value).

b) Petty theft

All other theft is petty theft.

C. The Property Subject to Theft

1. Subject Matter of Larceny

The crime of larceny is one of trespass to the possession of another's "personal" property. This personal property has modernly been held to be "anything that is capable of appropriation." At common law, the rules as to what was personal property were highly technical (this is probably due to the fact that larceny was punishable by death).

a. Household pets

Pets were not considered "property" because of their "base nature." The rule is different today.

b. Lost and abandoned goods

Lost goods could be the subject of larceny, while abandoned goods could not be.

c. Choses in action

Bills, notes, contracts, bonds, and other evidence of indebtedness were not considered property at common law. The idea was that the piece of paper had no intrinsic value. This result has been changed by modern statutes.

d. Real property

Real property could not be the subject of larceny; thus, fixtures affixed to the land, crops, trees, etc., were not subjects for larceny.

> 1) If, however, such items of real property were first severed from the land and then carried away in a distinct transaction, they became the subjects of larceny on the theory that on their severance they came into the constructive possession of the owner as personal property.

> 2) A could come onto B's land on one day and cut down his trees; if A returned on another day and carried the trees off, A could be convicted of larceny; if the cutting and carrying were consummated at one time, there was no larceny.

e. Leased property

Taking of one's own property from one who has a right to its possession (such as a lessee), or taking property that the possessor has stolen or that is illegal to possess (for example, marijuana) all constitute larceny since a trespass to possession is involved.

f. Incorporeal property

Larceny could be committed against a person's right to possess incorporeal property, such as where A taps B's gas line.

g. Anything of value

Modern statutes have extended the law of larceny to include practically everything of value that can be actually taken and carried away. Under some statutes, the crime has even been extended to real property (such as ore or minerals) and to completely intangible items (such as trade secrets).

2. Guarantee of Indebtedness

State v. Miller
233 P.2d 786 (Or. 1951).

Facts. Miller (D) induced the Hub Lumber Co. to guarantee his indebtedness to another by falsely representing that he owned a tractor free of encumbrance and by executing a chattel mortgage on the tractor as security. In order for the false pretenses statute to apply, the defendant must have obtained "any money or property whatsoever." D was convicted of the crime of false pretenses and now appeals.

Issue. Does a guaranty obtained by false representations constitute property for the purposes of the false pretenses statute?

Held. No. Conviction reversed and action dismissed.

- ◆ English law, the source of false pretenses statutes in this country, has always applied the offense of false pretenses to personal property capable of manual delivery.

- ◆ This court has recognized that property must be capable of being possessed and have title that can be transferred. A guaranty fills neither of these requirements.

- Obtaining a loan by fraud has been held to constitute the offense of false pretenses. But in the only reported cases on the subject, the victim has lost his money, unlike the present situation.

- Under some other state false pretenses statutes, D would be guilty. These statutes include the catch-all phrase "any other thing of value," along with the terms "money" and "property" in delineating what may be taken by false pretenses. While D's conduct is morally reprehensible, the legislature has not made it a crime.

Comment. The Model Penal Code defines "property" as anything of value. Oregon now defines "property" as "any article, substance, or thing of value . . . . " If decided today, this case would probably come out differently.

3. Government Records

United States v. Girard
601 F.2d 69 (2d Cir. 1969).

Facts. Lambert (D) was an agent of the Drug Enforcement Administration ("DEA") and Girard (D) was a former agent. Girard offered to secure reports from the DEA for Bond to enable Bond to determine whether any participant in his proposed illegal smuggling venture was a government agent. Bond himself became an informant, and the DEA learned that Lambert was supplying Girard with government reports. Ds were convicted of the unauthorized sale of government property and of conspiring to accomplish the sale. On appeal. Ds contend that they cannot be convicted because the statute only covers tangible property that is a "thing of value" and not the sale of information.

Issue. Is information a "thing of value" for purposes of theft?

Held. Yes. Judgment affirmed.

- Although the content of writing is intangible, it is a thing of value and thus a protectable property right. Because the Government (P) has a property interest in the records, the misuse of the property by Ds could constitute conversion.

4. Property Subject to Theft

Regina v. Stewart
50 D.L.R. 4th 1 (1988).

Facts. A union attempting to organize 600 hotel employees was unable to obtain the employees' names, addresses, and telephone numbers, which the hotel classified as confidential. Stewart (D), a self-employed consultant, was hired by someone he assumed to be acting for the union, to obtain the information. D offered a fee to a security guard to obtain the information, but the guard informed his boss, who informed the police. After a long conversation between D and the guard was recorded, D was indicted for "counseling the offense of theft." D was acquitted by a trial judge. The acquittal was reversed on appeal. D appeals.

Issue. Can the object of theft be a pure intangible?

Held. No. Acquittal restored.

- In order to be the subject of theft, anything, whether animate or inanimate, must be property in the sense that to be stolen, it must belong in some way to someone.

- While confidential information may come to be viewed as protected property in civil law, that does not automatically make it property under the criminal code.

- Because of the inherent nature of information, treating confidential information as property for purposes of the law of theft would be impractical.

Comment. The impractical aspect of declaring the employee list as property subject to theft becomes clear when one realizes that the information consisted of names, addresses, and telephone numbers. Clearly, any employee who had her telephone number listed in the telephone book would have already made such information available to the public, so no claim of confidentiality would withstand scrutiny. Presumably, this is also the precise information many individuals have printed on their personal checks and, to some degree, placed in the return address portion of every envelope they mail. However, what if *the* employee files contained other more personal and less public information such as date of birth, marital status, educational background, and criminal history checks? Would that change the court's reasoning?

5. Honest Services

Skilling v. United States
130 S. Ct. 2896 (2010).

Facts. Enron Corporation (Enron) is the seventh highest-revenue-grossing company in the U.S. Skilling (D) was Enron's CEO from February to April 2001, when he resigned. Enron's stock plummeted and the company went into bankruptcy less than four months later. Following an investigation that uncovered an elaborate conspiracy to inflate Enron's stock prices by overstating its financial health, dozens of employees who took part in the scheme were prosecuted. Ultimately, the government indicted D and two other top executives. The indictment charged that D and the others took part in a scheme to deceive investors about Enron's actual financial performance by manipulating its publicly reported financial results and making false and misleading statements. Count 1 of the indictment charged D with conspiracy to commit "honest-services" wire fraud, by depriving Enron and its shareholders of the intangible right of his honest services. He was also charged with over 25 substantive counts of securities fraud, wire fraud, making false representations to Enron's auditors, and insider trading. The indictment alleged D was enriched through salary, bonuses, grants of stocks, stock options, and other profits. D was found guilty of 19 counts, including the "honest-services" fraud conspiracy. On appeal, D's conviction was affirmed. We granted certiorari.

Issue.

(1) Is Section 1346, which proscribes fraudulent deprivations of "the intangible right of honest services," properly confined to cover only bribery and kickback schemes?

(2) Is Section 1346 unconstitutionally vague in context?

Held. (1) Yes. (2) No. Affirmed in part; vacated in part, and remanded.

- The development of an "honest services doctrine" began in the court of appeals in the 1940s where the court interpreted the mail-fraud statute's prohibition of "any scheme or artifice to defraud" to include deprivations not only of money or property, but also of intangible rights. See, *e.g., Shushan* v. *United States*, 117 F. 2d 110.

- The honest services doctrine addresses the corruption that lacks the symmetry of traditional fraud—where the victim's loss supplies the defendant's gain. Where honest services fraud is alleged, as here, while the offender profited, the betrayed party suffered no deprivation of money or property; instead, a third party, who had not been deceived, provided the enrichment. For example, if a city official awarded a contract after he accepted a bribe from a third party, but the terms of the contract were the same as any that could have been negotiated with other service providers, the betrayed party, the city, would not suffer a tangible loss. However, even if the scheme occasioned a money or property gain for the betrayed party, courts have determined that actionable harm lay in the denial of that party's right to the offender's "honest services." While most cases of this nature involve public officials, as time passed, the courts recognized that the doctrine applied to a private employee who breached his loyalty to his employer, often by accepting bribes or kickbacks. By 1982, all Courts of Appeals had embraced the honest-services theory of fraud.

♦ *McNally v. United States*, 483 U.S. 350, stopped the development of the doctrine in 1987, holding the mail-fraud statute was limited to the protection of property rights until Congress spoke more clearly. Section 1346 was enacted the next year, and Congress specified that the mail fraud and wire fraud that was prohibited included a scheme or artifice "to deprive another of the intangible right of honest services." Congress clearly intended Section 1346 to refer to and incorporate the honest services doctrine of the pre-*McNally* cases.

♦ Rather than striking the statute as impermissibly vague, it has long been our practice to consider whether the prescription if amenable to a limiting construction. While we agree with D that some of the pre-McNally cases are inconsistent, the vast majority of the cases involved offenders who violated a fiduciary duty by participating in bribery or kickback schemes. It is clear that Congress intended to reach bribes and kickbacks.

♦ Vagueness concerns arise when the statute is read to proscribe a wider range of offensive conduct. Thus, we hold that Section 1346 criminalizes only the bribe and kickback core of the pre-*McNally* case law. We reject the government's urging to include conflict of interest cases in the core applications of the honest services doctrine, because of the infrequency of such cases and the inconsistencies they produced among the circuits.

♦ While D's conviction is flawed because he did not violate the statute as we interpret it, *i.e.,* the government never alleged D solicited or accepted side payments from a third party in exchange for making misrepresentations, this determination does not necessarily require reversal of the conspiracy conviction. Whether the error was harmless can be resolved on remand, along with the question whether reversal on the conspiracy count would affect any of D's other convictions.

Concurrence. The honest services doctrine is not limited to bribes and kickbacks. The pre-*McNally* cases provide no clarity, and no settled criterion as to what constitutes a denial of the right of honest services. Further the Court fails to address the most basic determination: "the character of the 'fiduciary capacity' to which the bribery and kickback restriction applies."

D. Mens Rea

1. Introduction

Specific intent is required for larceny. The taking had to be done with the specific intent to fraudulently and permanently deprive the possessor of his goods.

a. Bona fide claim to possession

A taking by A where A has a bona fide claim of right to possession is not larceny, even where A is actually wrong in his claim.

b. Intent to take and abandon

The intent to take property and then to abandon it without returning it to its owner is sufficient.

c. Intent to take and use

If the taker intends to just take and use the property and then to return it to the owner, this is not larceny. For example, there is no larceny when a person takes a car for a "joy ride" and then returns it.

d. "Continuing trespass" doctrine

At some point in time, the felonious intent must accompany the trespass to possession. However, it is not always required that there shall be such intent at the time the property was first taken. As long as the taking constitutes a trespass (albeit innocent or in good faith), the trespass "continues" as long as the defendant holds the goods, and if at any time thereafter he forms the intent to steal them, there is then the concurrence of trespass and felonious intent, which constitutes the crime of larceny. For example, the defendant takes the goods of another in the honest, but mistaken, belief that he owns them (innocent trespass). Later he discovers that he does not, but decides to appropriate them anyway. He is guilty of larceny.

2. Permanent Taking

People v. Brown
38 P. 518 (Cal. 1894).

Facts. Brown (D), age 17, entered the house of a boy with whom he had had an argument, and took a bicycle, intending to return it later. Before he could return it, he was arrested. D was convicted of burglary after a jury instruction that indicated that all that need be shown was an intent to deprive the owner of possession temporarily. D appeals.

Issue. Is an intent to deprive the owner of his rightful possession temporarily sufficient to support a theft conviction?

Held. No. Conviction reversed.

- ♦ The jury instruction was incorrect. A felonious taking requires that the taking be with the intent to deprive the owner of possession permanently.

Comment. If the taker abandons the property or recklessly exposes it to loss, he may have had the intent to permanently deprive.

3. Taking with Intent to Repay

Regina v. Feely
2 W.L.R. 201 (1973).

Facts. Feely (D), branch manager of a bookmaking firm, received a memo from die head office that borrowing from the till was not permitted; nevertheless, he borrowed £30. A few days later he was transferred; his successor found the shortage. D offered the explanation that he had taken the money because he was short of cash but that the employer owed him £70, that he intended to repay the money, and that it could be taken out of the amount owed him. The evidence showed that the employer did owe him this amount. D was convicted of theft. He appealed. At the trial, the jury instruction had been that D was guilty if he intended to take the money; it made no difference that he intended to repay.

Issue. May an intent to repay property taken negate the necessary intent?

Held. Yes. Conviction reversed.

- ♦ The Theft Act defines theft as taking with the intent to permanently deprive the owner of the property.

- ♦ The issue is whether D, when he took the money, intended a dishonest act (*i.e.*, not to return it). The trial judge should not have made the determination that the taking was dishonest and given the jury only the question of whether D intended to take the money. The jury should be allowed to determine whether the taking was dishonest.

4. Use of Force

People v. Reid
508 N.E.2d 661 (N.Y. 1987).

Facts. In separate incidents, Reid (D) and Riddles (D) were trying to recover money owed to them by certain individuals. In the course of so doing, Ds used weapons. Ds were each convicted of armed robbery. Ds appeal.

Issue. Does a person's good-faith claim of right negate the intent to commit robbery if the person uses force to recover money owed to him?

Held. No. Judgment affirmed.

♦ A good-faith claim of right may negate larcenous intent in theft offenses and constitutes a defense to a charge of larceny. Robbery is the use or threat of use of physical force in the course of committing a larceny. Ds claim that therefore the claim of right defense should apply to robbery, and that Ds could at most be charged with assault or unlawful possession of a weapon.

♦ Some jurisdictions have followed the approach advocated by Ds. The approach may be appropriate when the defendant was trying to recover a specific item owned by the defendant, especially since an element of the offense is taking property "from an owner thereof."

♦ In these cases, Ds were trying to recover money that did not actually belong to Ds, even though the victims purportedly owed Ds money. To permit the defense would be inconsistent with the public policy of discouraging self-help. The claim of right defense does not even apply to all forms of larceny, such as extortion, which reflects the public policy against use of force or coercion.

Chapter X

Discretion

A. The Decision to Charge

1. Prosecutorial Discretion

In our criminal justice system, if there is probable cause to believe that a suspect has committed an offense, the prosecutor has broad discretion in deciding whether to file charges. The prosecutor may also determine what charges to bring and when to bring them. The American Bar Association recommends that prosecutors consider the following mitigating factors: (i) reasonable doubt of guilt; (ii) minimum harm of offense; (iii) excessive punishment relative to offense: (iv) improper motives of party complaining; (v) reluctance of victim to testify; (vi) cooperation of accused in the arrest of others; and (vii) likelihood of prosecution in another jurisdiction. Courts have repeatedly held that prosecutors have wide latitude in deciding whether to file charges and that their decisions are not subject to direct judicial review unless there is a glaring abuse of discretion.

2. Prosecution Not Compelled

Inmates of Attica Correctional Facility v. Rockefeller
477 F.2d 375 (2d Cir. 1973).

Facts. Inmates of New York's Attica Correctional Facility and others (Ps) brought a mandamus action requiring state officials and the United States Attorney to investigate and prosecute persons who had allegedly violated certain federal and state criminal statutes in connection with their treatment of inmates during and after an inmate uprising, which resulted in the killing of 32 inmates and the wounding of many others. Ps claimed that some of the state police, troopers, and correction officers intentionally killed inmates without provocation during the recovery of the prison and assaulted and beat inmates after the prison was retaken. Ps also claimed that medical assistance was denied to more than 400 inmates. The governor of New York and other officials (Ds) filed a motion to dismiss, and the federal district court granted Ds' motion. Ps appeal.

Issue. Should the judiciary compel the investigation and prosecution of the defendants?

Held. No. Judgment affirmed.

♦ Unlike the plaintiff in *Linda R. S. v. Richard D., supra,* Ps in this case claim that some of them suffered direct physical injury from the state officers and that those crimes will continue if the officers are not prosecuted. Ps' complaint may also allege a sufficient threat of selective and discriminatory prosecution because 37 inmates have been indicted for crimes relating to the riot, and no indictment has been filed against any of the state officials. However, the issue of standing need not be decided because the relief Ps seek cannot be granted.

- Although Ps request that the United States Attorney be compelled to investigate and prosecute state officers, federal mandamus is available only to compel an officer or employee of the United States to perform a duty owed to the plaintiff. Federal courts have uniformly refrained from overturning, at the request of a private person, federal prosecutors' discretionary decisions not to prosecute persons regarding whom a complaint of criminal conduct is made. This is primarily because of the separation of powers doctrine.

- Furthermore, a prosecutor's decision to prosecute or not to prosecute is not readily amenable to judicial supervision. In the normal case of review of executive acts of discretion, the administrative record is open, public, and reviewable. On the other hand, the decision not to prosecute may be based on the insufficiency of the available evidence, in which event the secrecy of the prosecutor's file may serve to protect the accused's reputation from damage based on insufficient, improper, or malicious charges. Otherwise, anyone could file a complaint containing allegations in general terms of unlawful failure to prosecute and could gain access to the prosecutor's file and the grand jury's minutes.

- Also, it is unclear what the judiciary's role of supervision should be, at what point the prosecutor would be entitled to stop further investigation as unlikely to be productive, and what priority the prosecutor would be required to give to cases in which investigation or prosecution was directed by the court.

- As to the state defendants, Ps have not indicated any statutory language that even arguably creates a mandatory duty on the state officials to bring such prosecutions. In fact, New York law gives its prosecutors discretion to decide whether or not to prosecute in a given case, and this is not subject to review in the state courts.

3. Selective Prosecution

United States v. Armstrong
517 U.S. 456 (1996).

Facts. Armstrong and other black men (Ds) were indicted on charges of conspiring to possess with intent to distribute more than 50 grams of crack cocaine and on charges of federal firearms offenses. Informants had purchased crack from Ds and witnessed Ds carrying firearms. A search of the hotel room where the transactions had taken place resulted in the finding of more crack and a loaded gun. Ds filed a motion for discovery or dismissal of the indictment, alleging that they had been selectively prosecuted because they were black. Ds offered an affidavit by a "Paralegal Specialist," employed by the office of the federal public defender, with an accompanying "study," to the effect that in every one of the 24 drug cases closed by the office during the prior year, the defendant was black. The district court granted the motion for discovery and ordered the government to provide a list of cases involving cocaine and firearms, which showed the race of the defendants, and to explain its criteria for deciding to prosecute those defendants. The government moved for reconsideration of the court's order and submitted affidavits and other evidence showing why it had decided to prosecute Ds and why Ds' study did not support Ds' claim. One affidavit explained that there were more than 100 grams of cocaine base involved, over twice the threshold necessary for a 10-year mandatory minimum sentence, and that the overall evidence in the case was extremely strong. The motion for reconsideration was denied. But the government indicated that it would not comply with the court's order, and the case was dismissed. The court of appeals affirmed. The Supreme Court granted certiorari to determine the appropriate standard for discovery for a selective-prosecution claim.

Issue. To be entitled to discovery on a claim that a defendant was singled out for prosecution on the basis of his race, must the defendant make a threshold showing that similarly situated defendants of other races could have been prosecuted but were not?

Held. Yes. Judgment reversed.

- The standard for proving the necessary elements of a selective-prosecution claim is a demanding one. Similarly, the showing necessary to obtain discovery should itself be a significant barrier to the litigation of insubstantial claims.

- The Attorney General and United States attorneys are presumed to properly discharge their official duties. For a selective-prosecution claim, a claimant must show that the federal prosecutorial policy had a discriminatory effect and was motivated by a discriminatory purpose. To establish a discriminatory effect in a race case, the claimant must show that similarly situated persons of a different race were not prosecuted.

- If discovery is ordered, it will divert prosecutors' resources and may disclose prosecutorial strategy. Thus, the standard for discovery in aid of a selective-prosecution claim is rigorous. The majority of courts of appeal require the defendant to produce some evidence that similarly situated defendants of other races could have been prosecuted but were not.

- Here, the court of appeals presumed that people of all races commit all types of crimes, but it cited no authority for that premise. The premise is contradicted by the latest statistics of the United States Sentencing Commission, which show that more than 90% of the persons sentenced in 1994 for crack cocaine trafficking were black and 93.4% of convicted LSD dealers were white.

- The court of appeals also expressed concern that defendants faced evidentiary obstacles. If the claim is well-founded, however, it should not be that difficult to prove that persons of different races were being treated differently. Ds could have investigated whether similarly situated persons of other races were prosecuted by the state of California and were known to federal law officers but were not prosecuted in federal court. What Ds must show balances the government's interest in vigorous prosecution and Ds' interest in avoiding selective prosecution.

- Here, Ds' study did not constitute "evidence"; it failed to identify persons who were not black and could have been prosecuted. Also, Ds' affidavits recounted hearsay and reported personal conclusions based on anecdotal evidence.

Dissent (Stevens, J.). There are extremely high penalties for the possession and distribution of crack cocaine, and sentences for crack offenders average three to eight times longer than sentences for comparable powder offenders. Also, terms of imprisonment for drug offenses tend to be substantially lower in state systems than in the federal system, especially in the case of crack offenses. The severe sentences for crack crimes and the racial pattern of enforcement give rise to a special concern about the fairness of charging practices for these offenses. The district court judge acted well within her discretion in finding the evidence before her significant and requiring some explanation from the government.

B. Plea Bargaining

1. Introduction

A guilty plea is essentially a waiver by the defendant of his right to trial and of his chance for an acquittal. It must be an unequivocal and knowledgeable admission of all elements of the offense charged. Anything less than that, or any qualified or ambiguous plea, will not be construed as a guilty plea.

a. Voluntariness

A plea of guilty is presumed to be voluntary, because no conviction based upon a guilty plea can stand unless the record of the proceedings establishes that the defendant voluntarily and intelligently waived his three basic constitutional rights, *i.e.*, trial by jury, confrontation of his accusers, and privilege against self-incrimination.

b. Understanding

In most jurisdictions, the guilty plea is not deemed to have been made understandingly unless the accused comprehended (i) the meaning of the charge, (ii) what acts amount to being guilty, and (iii) the direct (as opposed to collateral) consequences of pleading guilty thereto—particularly the range of sentence that may be imposed. It is not clear whether there must be an affirmative showing that the defendant "understood" the nature of the charges, etc., but there must at least be some basis for inferring that the nature of the charge was explained sufficiently for the defendant to know what he was admitting. *[See* Henderson v. Morgan, 426 U.S. 637 (1976)]

c. Representation by counsel

The defendant should always be represented by counsel in the bargaining process to protect his interests. The defendant's statements might be admissible evidence against him.

2. Plea Withdrawal

A guilty plea that was not voluntarily and understandably made may be withdrawn at any time. Failure to allow withdrawal of such a plea constitutes a denial of the federal constitutional requirement of due process of law.

3. Justifications for Plea Bargaining

Advocates contend that plea bargains are necessary to reduce the caseload to a number that the courts can handle. Without this device, our system of criminal enforcement would break down (too many cases to try).

4. Concerns About Plea Bargaining

Critics maintain that the guilty plea, all other things being equal, should not result in a lesser punishment. But the fact remains that courts do give lighter sentences to defendants who plead guilty. Plea bargaining is widely practiced and accepted, and an effort is now made to protect the rights of those who do so plead. A defendant may plead guilty or, with the consent of the court, nolo contendere. The court may refuse to accept a plea of guilty, and must not accept the plea without first determining that the plea is made voluntarily with understanding of the nature of the charge. [Fed. R. Crim. P. 11]

5. Guilty Plea to Avoid the Possibility of Death Penalty

Brady v. United States
397 U.S. 742 (1970).

Facts. Brady (D) was charged with kidnapping and faced a maximum penalty of death if the jury so recommended. Represented by competent counsel, D first chose to plead not guilty. When D learned that his co-defendant had confessed, would plead guilty, and would be available to testify against D, D changed his plea to guilty. The judge questioned him twice as to the voluntariness of his plea. D was sentenced to 50 years in prison, later reduced to 30. D sought postconviction relief, asserting that his plea had not been voluntary because of the possibility of receiving the death penalty if his case had gone before a jury. The district court denied relief, and the court of appeals affirmed. The Supreme Court granted certiorari.

Issue. Does pleading guilty because of fear of the death penalty make that plea involuntary?

Held. No. Judgment affirmed.

♦ A waiver of a constitutional right must be a voluntary, knowing, and intelligent act done with sufficient awareness of the circumstances and the likely consequences. The government may encourage a guilty plea, but it may not produce a plea by actual or threatened physical harm or by mental coercion overbearing the defendant's will. Nothing like this is claimed here, and there is no evidence that D was so gripped by fear of the death penalty that he could not, with the help of counsel, rationally weigh the advantages of going to trial against the advantages of pleading guilty.

♦ D claims that a guilty plea is coerced and invalid if it is motivated by the fear of a possibly higher penalty if a conviction is obtained through trial. However, a defendant's unwillingness to plead guilty unless there is the possibility or certainty that the plea will result in a lesser sentence does not make the plea invalid under the Fifth Amendment.

♦ Guilty pleas offer advantages to both the defendant and the government. For a defendant who sees little chance of acquittal, his exposure is reduced, the correctional processes can start without delay, and the practical burdens of a trial are eliminated. The government can more effectively attain the objectives of punishment and conserve judicial and prosecutorial resources. These advantages may explain why over three-fourths of criminal convictions in the United States rest on guilty pleas.

♦ We cannot hold that it is unconstitutional for a state to extend a benefit to a defendant who, in turn, extends a benefit to the state and shows by his plea that he is willing to admit his crime and enter the correctional system with an attitude that offers hope for rehabilitation in a shorter period of time.

♦ In *Bram v. United States*, 168 U.S. 532 (1897), we held that, to be admissible, a confession must not be extracted by any threats or violence and must not be obtained by any direct or implied promises, however slight, or by improper influence. But unlike the present case, *Bram* dealt with a confession given by a defendant in custody, alone and unrepresented by counsel. In those circumstances, even a mild promise of leniency was deemed sufficient to bar the confession because defendants at such times are too vulnerable to inducement.

♦ A guilty plea must be entered by one fully aware of the direct consequences, including the actual value of any commitments made to him by the court, prosecutor, or his own counsel. A plea is not invalid just because it is made to avoid the possibility of the death penalty.

6. Threat of More Severe Charges

Bordenkircher v. Hayes
434 U.S. 357 (1978).

Facts. Hayes (D) was indicted on a charge of uttering a forged instrument in the amount of $88.30, an offense punishable by a prison term of two to 10 years. When D and his attorney met with the prosecutor to discuss a plea agreement, the prosecutor offered to recommend a five-year prison sentence if D pled guilty. He added that if D did not plead, he would seek an indictment under the state Habitual Criminal Act ("Act"), which would subject D to a mandatory life sentence because of two prior felony convictions. D did not plead guilty, was indicted under the Act, was found guilty, and was sentenced to life in prison. The state court of appeals affirmed. D petitioned for a federal writ of habeas corpus, but the writ was denied. The federal court of appeals reversed, finding that the prosecutor's actions violated the principles that protect defendants from the vindictive exercise of a prosecutor's discretion. The Supreme Court granted certiorari.

Issue. Is the Due Process Clause of the Fourteenth Amendment violated when a state prosecutor carries out a threat made during plea negotiations to reindict the accused on more serious charges if he does not plead guilty to the offense with which he was originally charged?

Held. No. Judgment reversed.

- ◆ We have held that vindictiveness against a defendant for having successfully attacked his first conviction must not play a role in the sentence the defendant receives after a new trial. But there is no such punishment in plea bargaining as long as a defendant is free to accept or reject the prosecution's offer.

- ◆ Plea bargaining provides a mutuality of advantage to defendants and prosecutors. Although confronting a defendant with a more severe punishment may discourage him from exercising his right to trial, that is an inevitable and permissible aspect of any system that encourages plea negotiations. By encouraging plea negotiations, this court has accepted as constitutionally legitimate the reality that the prosecutor's interest is to persuade the defendant to forgo his right to plead not guilty.

- ◆ If a prosecutor has probable cause to believe that the defendant committed an offense defined by statute, the decision to prosecute or not to prosecute and what charge to bring before a grand jury generally rests entirely in his discretion as long as the selection of the charge is not based on race, religion, or other arbitrary classification.

Dissent (Blackmun, Brennan, Marshall, JJ.). Vindictiveness is present in this case. The prosecutor admitted that the only reason for the new indictment was to discourage D from exercising his right to a trial. If a prosecutor brought the greater charge initially, and bargained afterward, the accused would have to bargain against a greater charge, would face the likelihood of increased bail, and would run the risk that the court would be less inclined to accept a bargained plea. Still, it is much better to hold the prosecution to the charge it was originally content to bring.

Dissent (Powell, J.). The prosecutor initially chose to forgo prosecution under the Act, making a reasonable, responsible judgment not to subject D to a mandatory life sentence when his only new offense was the uttering of an $88 forged check. It may be inferred that the prosecutor himself deemed it unreasonable and not in the public interest to put D in jeopardy of a sentence of life imprisonment. Implementation of a strategy calculated solely to deter the exercise of constitutional rights is not a constitutionally permissible exercise of discretion.

C. Sentencing

1. Control of Discretion

Traditionally, sentencing judges had broad discretion to impose sentences within the ranges established by statute. This led to arbitrary results, with different judges imposing disparate sentences for similar offenses. In response, the federal government and nearly all of the states have established mandatory minimum penalties. Many of the states have adopted mandatory minimum sentences for repeat offenders. The federal government and many states have also adopted sentencing guidelines that must be followed by judges. Variations from a specified range must be justified by finding certain facts specified in the statutes.

2. Constitutional Limitation on Sentencing Procedure

Because of the importance of the sentencing procedure, constitutional protections have been recognized to assure due process. Statutory control of the sentencing process is also subject to constitutional limitations.

3. Discretionary Sentencing

Williams v. New York
337 U.S. 241 (1949).

Facts. A jury found Williams (D) guilty of murder in the first degree and recommended life imprisonment. D had committed the murder while engaged in a burglary. Instead of life in prison, the trial judge imposed the death sentence. When explaining why he felt the death sentence should be imposed, the judge discussed the evidence upon which the jury had convicted D, and he stated that the evidence had been considered in light of additional information obtained through the court's probation department and other sources. The judge said that the presentence investigation revealed many material facts about D's background that were relevant to the question of punishment but could not properly have been brought before the jury when considering the question of guilt. He spoke of 30 other burglaries in the vicinity where the murder had been committed. Although D had not been convicted of these burglaries, the judge had been informed that D had confessed to some and had been identified as the perpetrator of others. The judge also said that the probation report indicated that D possessed "a morbid sexuality" and that D was a "menace to society." D did not challenge the accuracy of the judge's statements, nor did he ask the judge to disregard any of them or give him a chance to refute them by cross-examination or otherwise. However, D appealed, arguing violation of the Due Process Clause because the trial court had considered information supplied by witnesses whom D had not confronted and cross-examined. The court of appeals affirmed. D appeals.

Issue. May a judge in a sentencing proceeding consider evidence not presented at trial that is also not made subject to confrontation by the defendant?

Held. Yes. Judgment affirmed.

- New York judges have broad discretion in sentencing. New York procedural policy encourages judges to consider a convicted person's past, habits, health, conduct, and mental and moral propensities, even though such information was obtained outside the courtroom from persons whom a defendant was not permitted to confront or cross-examine.

- Due process requires that no person be tried and convicted of an offense unless he is given reasonable notice of the charges against him and is afforded an opportunity to examine adverse witnesses. Historically, sentencing judges were not limited by the same constraints.

- There are practical reasons for the different evidentiary rules applied to determining guilt and imposing punishment. Under the rules of evidence applied to the determination of guilt, the evidence must be strictly relevant to the offense charged. One reason for this is to prevent a jury concerned solely with the issue of guilt of a particular offense from being influenced by evidence that the defendant had habitually engaged in other misconduct. However, a sentencing judge is not confined to the narrow issue of guilt. It is essential that he possess the fullest information possible concerning a defendant. Concepts individualizing punishment make this even more necessary.

- New York statutes emphasize the philosophy that the punishment should fit not only the crime, but the offender. For example, individualizing sentences makes sharp distinctions between first and repeat offenders. Retribution is no longer the main objective of the criminal law; reformation and rehabilitation have become important goals. Generally, the increase in discretion in imposing punishments has been motivated by the belief that information about the lives and personalities of offenders may lead to less severe punishment, and offenders may be restored to society sooner.

- Most of the information relied upon by judges to guide them in the imposition of sentences, such as the information from probation workers' reports, would be unavailable if information were restricted to that given in open court by witnesses subject to cross-examination. The Due Process Clause does not require that the evidential procedure of sentencing be governed by the same rules as the trial itself.

Dissent (Murphy, J.). I agree with the use of probation reports, but in a capital case where the jury has recommended life in prison, I do not believe that due process requirements were obeyed where the report could not have been admitted at trial and where D did not examine it.

4. Mandatory Misnomer

In *United States v. Vasquez,* 2010 WL 1257359 (E.D.N.Y.) the sentencing judge, Judge Gleason, asked the prosecutor to reconsider applying a mandatory sentence of five years. The prosecutor could have charged Vasquez with a standard drug trafficking charge, with a maximum sentence of 20 years. Instead, he included him in a conspiracy charge with his brother and three others and cited a sentence-enhancing provision that carries a maximum of life in prison. He refused to comply with the Judge's request. This refusal, Judge Gleason stated in his Statement of Reason for Sentencing, ended the matter, rendering irrelevant all the other factors that should have been considered to arrive at a just sentence. The difficult childhood, the lifelong struggle with mental illness, the circumstances that precipitated his minor role in his brother's drug business, *i.e.,* to support an addiction, not to become a "narcotics entrepreneur," the fact that he tried to cooperate but did not have enough involvement in the drug trade to provide any assistance, the effect his imprisonment will have on the 3 and 8 year old children he is raising, the fact that he has been a good father, and the fact that his prior convictions all arose out of his ex-wife's refusal to allow him to see their three children, all of these fell by the wayside. Judge Gleason said had he been allowed to do justice for the defendant and the community, the sentence would have been a 24-month prison term, followed by a five-year period of supervision with conditions including both other forms of punishment (home detention and community service) and efforts to assist Vasquez with the mental health, substance abuse, and anger management problems that have plagued him, in some respects for his entire life. If he failed to comply, he would have gone back to jail. "The mandatory minimum sentence in this case supplanted any effort to do justice, leaving in its place the heavy wooden club that was explicitly meant only for mid-level managers of drug operations. The absence of fit between the crude method of punishment and the particular set of circumstances before me was conspicuous; when I imposed sentence on the weak and sobbing Vasquez on March 5, everyone present, including the prosecutor, could feel the injustice." Judge Gleason's words say it all: "In sum, though I am obligated by law to provide a statement of "reasons" for each sentence I impose, in this case there was but one: I was forced by a law that should not have been invoked to impose a five-year prison term."

5. Unfair Application of Sentencing Guidelines

United States v. Deegan
605 F.3d 625 (8th Cir. 2010).

Facts. After giving birth to a baby boy in her home, Deegan (D), fed, cleaned and dressed the baby, placed him in a basket and left the house, intentionally leaving the baby without food or a caregiver for two weeks. Upon her return, D placed the baby's remains in a suitcase and placed that in a ditch, where it was discovered. Pursuant to a plea agreement, D pled guilty to second-degree murder and was advised that the sentencing guidelines provided for an advisory sentence of eight to ten years' imprisonment for second-degree murder. Before imposing this sentence, the court advised D that it was considering a more stringent sentence because D's conduct "was unusually heinous, cruel, and brutal," but stated that it would await review of the presentence investigation report ("PSR"), psychological evaluations, and a review of relevant case law before making a final decision on sentencing. D argued for leniency based on what she described as her "psychological and emotional condition" at the time of the offense, her history as a victim of abuse, and the fact that she acted impulsively, among other reasons. D submitted a report by Dr. Resnick, an expert in "neonaticide," a term coined by Resnick to describe the killing of an infant within the first twenty-four hours following birth. The report addressed what Resnick viewed as an "extraordinary number of mitigating circumstances," and expressed the opinion that a prison sentence was not necessary to deter other women from committing neonaticide. It concluded that D suffered from an extensive history of abuse throughout her childhood and as an adult, suffered from major depression and dissociation at the time of the homicide, acted impulsively in leaving her baby alone, presented a very low risk of reoffending, and did not merit a lengthy prison sentence, especially because other women convicted in state court of committing similar offenses were usually sentenced to no more than three years in prison. The court explained that it understood D's life had not been easy, that she had suffered physical and sexual abuse, and that under the circumstances, a sentence under the 2007 guidelines in effect at the time of sentencing, *i.e.,* 19.5 to 24.5 years, would not be fair, but it could not ignore the loss of an innocent life. D was sentenced to 10 years in prison, the bottom of the advisory guidelines range. D appeals.

Issue. Is the sentence of 121 months' imprisonment unreasonable because the advisory guideline for second-degree murder is not based on empirical data and national experience, and because the sentence imposed is greater than necessary to comply with the statutory purposes of sentencing set forth in 18 U.S.C. Section 3553(a)(2)?

Held. No. Judgment affirmed.

♦ Where a sentence is within the advisory guideline range, as here, we accord it the presumption of reasonableness. Here, there was evidence of aggravation and mitigation. The court could reasonably view the offense as unusually heinous, cruel and brutal and deserving of harsh punishment. D presented evidence of her troubled history, and we share the dissent's condemnation of violence against American tribal women.

♦ The court did not abuse its discretion. It was entitled to "consider the need for the sentence imposed to 'reflect the seriousness of the offense, to promote respect for the law, and to provide just punishment for the offense'"

♦ We do not agree with the dissent's argument that the disparity between D's sentence and the sentence that may have been imposed had D been prosecuted in state court should have been taken into consideration. The statute addresses only disparities among federal defendants, not federal/state disparities.

Dissent. D was subject to horrible physical and sexual abuse by her father, by his buddies, by her four children's father, Mr. Hale. She was forced to protect her six younger siblings. Her crime was unlike the usual second-degree murder killings and it is only because it occurred on an Indian reservation that it became one of federal jurisdiction. Consideration of disparity was denied because D lives on a reservation in North Dakota rather than in the state of North Dakota. The PSR fails to mention this and omits much of the abuse D suffered. Neonaticide also falls outside the guidelines for second-degree murder. The guidelines do not ordinarily consider such matters as family ties, but Section 3553(a) permits such consideration. However, D's plea that her children needed her were ignored by the prosecutor, who stated it was D's choice that "caused all of this." What about Mr. Hale's abuse and his failure to support the children he fathered, and what about society's failure to aid D in her suffering?

Table of Cases